T0339701

QUALITY OF LIFE,
BALANCE OF POWER
AND NUCLEAR WEAPONS

QUALITY OF LIFE, BALANCE OF POWER AND NUCLEAR WEAPONS

A Statistical Yearbook for Statesmen and Citizens

2009

ALEXANDER V. AVAKOV

Algora Publishing
New York

Library of Congress Cataloging-in-Publication Data —

Avakov, Aleksandr V. (Aleksandr Vladimirovich), 1954-
    Quality of life, balance of power and nuclear weapons: a statistical yearbook for
statesmen and citizens / Alexander V. Avakov.
        p. cm.
    Includes bibliographical references and index.
    ISBN 978-0-87586-675-8 (soft : alk. paper) — ISBN 978-0-87586-676-5 (hard cover:
alk. paper) — ISBN 978-0-87586-677-2 (ebook: alk. paper) 1. Economic indicators. 2.
Social indicators. 3. Quality of life—Statistics. 4. Armed Forces—Appropriations and
expenditures—Statistics.. 5. Nuclear weapons—Statistics. 6. Health status indicators. I.
Title.

    HC59.3.A83 2008
    306.09'0511021—dc22
                                    2008003446

Printed in the United States

TABLE OF CONTENTS

INTRODUCTION

This statistical annual presents fundamental data in three sections: (1) Quality of Life, (2) Balance of Powers, (3) Developed Market Economies since 1960.

The advantage of this yearbook is that it contains data that is generally not available elsewhere. Sections 1 and 2 give statistics for 231 countries. By comparison, the World Bank and Encyclopedia Britannica provide statistical data for a maximum of about 160 countries. The actual number of countries in World Bank statistical tables is even smaller. The CIA World Factbook gives data for about 230 countries, but that data is limited in scope and is imprecise. Other statistical publications are even less satisfactory. I managed to increase the number of countries tallied by writing proprietary software utilizing statistical regressions and selecting data which, first of all, is important and, second, is relatively reliable, offering high correlation coefficients for these regressions.

Section 1 concentrates on data that reflect the quality of life. First, I focused on major economic and demographic indicators. In addition to data about the quality of life as measured strictly in economic terms, I sought to produce a methodologically rigorous estimate of a human rights index. The latter measures civil and political rights as well as socioeconomic rights. I also computed an integrated economico-political quality-of-life index.

In Section 2, the book deals with major indicators of the balance of power. In addition to data about each country's economic power, military personnel and military expenditures, it includes data about nuclear delivery systems and provides the number of nuclear warheads of all nuclear powers. This is based on information from reputable sources. Among others, it includes estimates of the Israeli nuclear arsenal which usually do not appear in the press. I also give a rough account of countries possessing, pursuing or capable of acquiring other weapons of mass destruction. Chances are that if the American public were more familiar with these statistics, some Middle East foreign policy failures might have been avoided.

It should also be underscored that many official estimates, for example estimates of Russian military expenditures distributed by US and British intelligence communities, are methodologically flawed. Such estimates claim to give a picture of

1

the military expenditures of the countries of the world at market exchange rates; at the same time, they apparently cite Russian military expense figures at purchasing power parity, thus inflating these numbers in comparison to those of other countries. Such deceptive practices of the Anglo-American intelligence services are counterbalanced by presenting two different tables, showing military expenditures estimates both at market exchange rates and at purchasing power parities. Members of the US Congress and others who care about the foundations of power politics in the nuclear age will find facts that speak for themselves in this section.

In Section 3, I give data on the hot topic of health care. It seems that public health expenditures as a share of total health expenditures has a stronger correlation with the comparative level (and the rates of improvement) of the main health care indicators than the absolute level (measured as a percent of GDP) of total health expenditures. It is also worth noting that, as the data demonstrates, the US has the lowest public health expenditure of developed market economies and is increasingly lagging behind other countries by main health care indicators. The proposed introduction of national health insurance in the US would probably mean some sort of tax increase. I therefore also try to shed light on modern ideological debates about the share of taxation in GDP and its influence on rates of growth. Surprisingly enough, the empirical data for the developed market economies does not seem to support the popular idea that low taxes are strongly correlated with higher rates of growth; depending on how the data is analyzed, the correlations are either low or even the reverse of what is commonly believed.

SOURCES

Sources are shown in the form: xx‹Source›, where xx is a year and ‹Source› is one of the following:

WB	The World Bank (1)
E	Encyclopedia Britannica
CIA	Central Intelligence Agency
CALC(CIA)	Calculated using Central Intelligence Agency data
UN	United Nations Development Programme
USAID	U.S. Agency for International Development
FH	Freedom House
IISS	International Institute for Strategic Studies
SIPRI	Stockholm International Peace Research Institute
BULL	Bulletin of the Atomic Scientists
UCS	Union of Concerned Scientists
WIKI	Wikipedia
REG	Regression
EST	Estimate
PRIN1(EQL)	Principal Component 1, Economic Quality-of-Life Indicators
PRIN1(PQL)	Principal Component 1, Political Quality-of-Life Indicators
PRIN1(EPQL)	Principal Component 1, Economico-Political Quality-of-Life Indicators
POP*GPC	Population multiplied by GDP Per Capita at Market Exchange Rates

*POP*GPCPPP*	Population multiplied by GDP Per Capita at Purchasing Power Parities
*(GDP*MILGDP+ MILAID)*	GDP at Market Exchange Rates multiplied by Percent of Military Expenditures as Share of GDP plus Foreign Military Aid
*(GDPPPP*MILGDP+ MILAID)*	GDP at Purchasing Power Parities multiplied by Percent of Military Expenditures as Share of GDP plus Foreign Military Aid

REGIONS

AFR	Africa
CPA	Centrally Planned Asia
DME	Developed Market Economies
EEU	Eastern Europe
LAM	Latin America
MEA	Middle East
SAS	South Asia
SEA	South-East Asia and Pacific
USR	Former U.S.S.R.

ABBREVIATIONS

OBS	Number of Countries Observed
GPC	Gross National Income (at Market Exchange Rates, in USD) Per Capita
INFMRT	Infant Mortality
LIFEXP	Life Expectancy
GPCPPP	Gross Domestic Product at Purchasing Power Parities Per Capita
EQLX	Economic Quality-of-Life Index
SCINTX	Societal Integration Index
CPRX	Civil and Political Rights Index
HDX	Human Development Index
GINI	Gini Coefficient of Income Inequality
PQLX	Political Quality-of-Life Index
EPQLX	Economico-Political Quality-of-Life Index
POP	Population
GDPPPP	Gross Domestic Product at Purchasing Power Parities
GDP	Gross National Income at Market Exchange Rates
ARMY	Armed Forces Personnel
MILGDP	Military Expenditures as Share of GDP
MILAID	Foreign Military Aid
MILXPP	Military Expenditures at Purchasing Power Parities plus Foreign Military Aid
MILEXP	Military Expenditures at Market Exchange Rates plus Foreign Military Aid
GPCxx	Gross National Income Per Capita at Market Exchange Rates, Year xx

GRPCMER	Growth Rates of GNI Per Capita at Market Exchange Rates
GPCPPPxx	Gross Domestic Product Per Capita at Purchasing Power Parities, Year xx
GRPCPPP	Growth Rates of GDP Per Capita at Purchasing Power Parities
INFMRTxx	Infant Mortality, Year xx
DRIM	Decrease Rates of Infant Mortality
LIFEXPxx	Life Expectancy, Year xx
GRLE	Growth Rates of Life Expectancy
HLTGDP	Total Health Expenditures as Percent of GDP
PUBHLT	Public Health Expenditures as Percent of Total Health Expenditures
TAXGDPxx	Taxes as Share of GDP, Year xx
GRTX	Growth Rates of Taxes as Share of GDP

1. QUALITY OF LIFE

TABLE 1.1 – GROSS NATIONAL INCOME AT MARKET EXCHANGE RATES PER CAPITA, 2006					
OBS	REGION	COUNTRY	GPC	RANK	SOURCE
1	DME	Liechtenstein	82,826	1.0	06(E)
2	DME	Bermuda	78,538	2.0	05(E)
3	DME	Luxembourg	71,240	3.0	05(E)
4	DME	Norway	68,440	4.0	06(WB)
5	MEA	Qatar	66,060	5.0	06(E)
6	DME	Jersey	66,000	6.0	05(E)
7	DME	Switzerland	58,050	7.0	06(WB)
8	DME	Denmark	52,110	8.0	06(WB)
9	DME	Iceland	49,960	9.0	06(WB)
10	LAM	Cayman Islands	47,744	10.0	05(E)
11	DME	Guernsey	45,370	11.0	05(E)
12	DME	Andorra	44,962	12.0	06(E)
13	DME	Ireland	44,830	13.0	06(WB)
14	DME	United States	44,710	14.0	06(WB)
15	DME	Sweden	43,530	15.0	06(WB)
16	DME	Netherlands	43,050	16.0	06(WB)
17	DME	Finland	41,360	17.0	06(WB)
18	MEA	UAE	41,082	18.0	06(E)
19	DME	San Marino	41,044	19.0	06(E)
20	DME	United Kingdom	40,560	20.0	06(WB)
21	MEA	Kuwait	40,114	21.0	06(E)
22	DME	Austria	39,750	22.0	06(WB)
23	DME	Japan	38,630	23.0	06(WB)
24	DME	Belgium	38,460	24.0	06(WB)
25	DME	Germany	36,810	25.0	06(WB)
26	DME	Canada	36,650	26.0	06(WB)
27	DME	France	36,560	27.0	06(WB)
28	DME	Australia	35,860	28.0	06(WB)
29	DME	Monaco	35,725	29.0	06(E)
30	DME	Isle of Man	33,960	30.0	05(E)
31	LAM	Virgin Islands, Brit.	33,142	31.0	(REG)
32	DME	Gibraltar	32,819	32.0	(REG)
33	DME	Italy	31,990	33.0	06(WB)
34	SEA	Macao	31,207	34.0	06(E)
35	DME	Faeroe Islands	30,680	35.0	03(E)
36	SEA	Hong Kong	29,040	36.0	06(WB)
37	SEA	Singapore	28,730	37.0	06(WB)
38	DME	Greenland	27,991	38.0	06(E)
39	DME	Spain	27,530	39.0	06(E)
40	DME	Greece	27,390	40.0	06(WB)

OBS	REGION	COUNTRY	GPC	RANK	SOURCE

TABLE 1.1 – GROSS NATIONAL INCOME
AT MARKET EXCHANGE RATES PER CAPITA, 2006

OBS	REGION	COUNTRY	GPC	RANK	SOURCE
41	LAM	Virgin Islands, US	27,300	41.0	06(E)
42	SEA	Brunei	26,930	42.0	06(WB)
43	DME	New Zealand	26,750	43.0	06(WB)
44	MEA	Cyprus	23,270	44.0	06(WB)
45	SEA	French Polynesia	21,766	45.0	06(E)
46	LAM	Aruba	21,625	46.0	06(E)
47	SEA	Guam	21,120	47.0	02(E)
48	MEA	Bahrain	20,609	48.0	06(E)
49	DME	Israel	20,410	49.0	06(E)
50	LAM	Guadeloupe	20,040	50.0	05(E)
51	SEA	New Caledonia	19,935	51.0	06(E)
52	DME	Falkland Islands	19,306	52.0	(REG)
53	AFR	Reunion	19,130	53.0	05(E)
54	EEU	Slovenia	18,660	54.0	06(WB)
55	LAM	Bahamas	18,570	55.0	06(E)
56	DME	Portugal	17,850	56.0	06(WB)
57	LAM	Neth. Antilles	17,691	57.0	06(E)
58	SEA	Korea, South	17,690	58.0	06(WB)
59	SEA	Taiwan	16,630	59.0	05(E)
60	DME	Malta	15,310	60.0	06(WB)
61	LAM	Martinique	14,730	61.0	03(E)
62	LAM	Puerto Rico	14,720	62.0	06(E)
63	MEA	Saudi Arabia	13,980	63.0	06(WB)
64	SEA	Northern Mariana Is.	13,350	64.0	05(E)
65	EEU	Czechia	12,790	65.0	06(WB)
66	LAM	Trinidad & Tobago	12,500	66.0	06(WB)
67	USR	Estonia	11,400	67.0	06(WB)
68	LAM	Barbados	11,291	68.0	06(E)
69	MEA	Oman	11,275	69.0	06(E)
70	LAM	Antigua & Barbuda	11,050	70.0	06(WB)
71	EEU	Hungary	10,870	71.0	06(WB)
72	EEU	Slovakia	9,610	72.0	06(WB)
73	EEU	Croatia	9,310	73.0	06(WB)
74	LAM	St. Kitts & Nevis	9,110	74.0	06(E)
75	LAM	Guiana, French	9,040	75.5	03(E)
76	SEA	Samoa, American	9,040	75.5	02(E)
77	AFR	Seychelles	8,870	77.0	06(WB)
78	AFR	Equatorial Guinea	8,510	78.0	06(WB)
79	EEU	Poland	8,210	79.0	06(WB)
80	USR	Latvia	8,100	80.0	06(WB)
81	SEA	Palau	7,990	81.0	06(WB)
82	USR	Lithuania	7,930	82.0	06(WB)
83	SEA	Nauru	7,840	83.0	06(E)
84	LAM	Mexico	7,830	84.0	06(WB)
85	SEA	Turks & Caicos Is.	7,305	85.0	(REG)
86	MEA	Libya	7,290	86.0	06(WB)
87	LAM	Chile	6,810	87.0	06(WB)
88	LAM	Venezuela	6,070	88.0	06(WB)

TABLE 1.1 – GROSS NATIONAL INCOME
AT MARKET EXCHANGE RATES PER CAPITA, 2006

OBS	REGION	COUNTRY	GPC	RANK	SOURCE
89	USR	Russia	5,770	89.0	06(WB)
90	SEA	Malaysia	5,620	90.0	06(WB)
91	MEA	Lebanon	5,580	91.0	06(WB)
92	AFR	Botswana	5,570	92.0	06(WB)
93	SEA	Cook Islands	5,450	93.0	(REG)
94	AFR	Mauritius	5,430	94.0	06(WB)
95	MEA	Turkey	5,400	95.0	06(WB)
96	AFR	South Africa	5,390	96.0	06(WB)
97	AFR	Gabon	5,360	97.0	06(WB)
98	LAM	St. Lucia	5,349	98.0	06(E)
99	LAM	Uruguay	5,310	99.0	06(WB)
100	LAM	Anguilla	5,226	100.0	(REG)
101	LAM	Argentina	5,150	101.0	06(WB)
102	LAM	Panama	5,000	102.0	06(WB)
103	LAM	Costa Rica	4,980	103.0	06(WB)
104	EEU	Romania	4,830	104.0	06(WB)
105	LAM	Brazil	4,710	105.0	06(WB)
106	LAM	Grenada	4,650	106.0	05(WB)
107	LAM	Cuba	4,571	107.0	06(E)
108	LAM	Suriname	4,210	108.0	06(WB)
109	LAM	Dominica	4,160	109.0	05(WB)
110	EEU	Montenegro	4,130	110.0	06(WB)
111	EEU	Serbia	4,030	111.0	06(WB)
112	EEU	Bulgaria	3,990	112.0	06(WB)
113	DME	St. Pierre & Miquelon	3,925	113.0	(REG)
114	USR	Kazakhstan	3,870	114.0	06(WB)
115	LAM	Belize	3,740	115.0	06(WB)
116	SEA	Fiji	3,720	116.0	06(WB)
117	LAM	Jamaica	3,560	117.0	06(WB)
118	LAM	St. Vincent	3,537	118.0	06(E)
119	USR	Belarus	3,470	119.0	06(WB)
120	EEU	Bosnia	3,230	120.0	06(WB)
121	AFR	Namibia	3,210	121.0	06(WB)
122	LAM	Colombia	3,120	122.0	06(WB)
123	SEA	Niue	3,102	123.0	(REG)
124	EEU	Macedonia	3,070	124.0	06(WB)
125	SEA	Thailand	3,050	125.0	06(WB)
126	MEA	Algeria	3,030	126.0	06(WB)
127	SAS	Maldives	3,010	127.0	06(WB)
128	SEA	Marshall Islands	2,980	128.5	06(WB)
129	LAM	Peru	2,980	128.5	06(WB)
130	MEA	Tunisia	2,970	130.0	06(WB)
131	EEU	Albania	2,930	131.5	06(WB)
132	MEA	Iran	2,930	131.5	06(WB)
133	LAM	Dominican Rep.	2,910	133.5	06(WB)
134	LAM	Ecuador	2,910	133.5	06(WB)
135	AFR	Mayotte	2,780	135.0	02(E)
136	LAM	El Salvador	2,680	136.0	06(WB)

TABLE 1.1 – GROSS NATIONAL INCOME AT MARKET EXCHANGE RATES PER CAPITA, 2006					
OBS	REGION	COUNTRY	GPC	RANK	SOURCE
137	MEA	Jordan	2,650	137.0	06(WB)
138	LAM	Guatemala	2,590	138.0	06(WB)
139	SEA	Tuvalu	2,441	139.0	06(E)
140	AFR	Swaziland	2,400	140.0	06(WB)
141	SEA	Micronesia	2,390	141.0	06(WB)
142	SEA	Samoa, Western	2,270	142.0	06(WB)
143	SEA	Tonga	2,250	143.0	06(WB)
144	MEA	Morocco	2,160	144.0	06(WB)
145	AFR	Cape Verde	2,130	145.0	06(WB)
146	CPA	China	2,000	146.0	06(WB)
147	AFR	Angola	1,970	147.0	06(WB)
148	USR	Ukraine	1,940	148.0	06(WB)
149	USR	Armenia	1,920	149.0	06(WB)
150	USR	Azerbaijan	1,840	150.0	06(WB)
151	SEA	Wallis & Futuna	1,827	151.0	(REG)
152	MEA	Iraq	1,700	152.0	06(E)
153	SEA	Vanuatu	1,690	153.0	06(WB)
154	LAM	Montserrat	1,590	154.0	(REG)
155	USR	Georgia	1,580	155.0	06(WB)
156	MEA	Syria	1,560	156.0	06(WB)
157	SAS	Bhutan	1,430	157.0	06(WB)
158	SEA	Indonesia	1,420	158.0	06(WB)
159	LAM	Paraguay	1,410	159.0	06(WB)
160	MEA	Gaza Strip	1,400	160.5	06(E)
161	MEA	West Bank	1,400	160.5	06(E)
162	SEA	Philippines	1,390	162.0	06(WB)
163	MEA	Egypt	1,360	163.0	06(WB)
164	SAS	Sri Lanka	1,310	164.0	06(WB)
165	LAM	Honduras	1,270	165.0	06(WB)
166	SEA	Kiribati	1,240	166.0	06(WB)
167	USR	Turkmenistan	1,234	167.0	06(E)
168	LAM	Guyana	1,150	168.0	06(WB)
169	CPA	Korea, North	1,108	169.0	06(E)
170	LAM	Bolivia	1,100	170.0	06(WB)
171	AFR	St. Helena	1,082	171.0	(REG)
172	USR	Moldova	1,080	172.0	06(WB)
173	AFR	Djibouti	1,060	173.0	06(WB)
174	AFR	Congo, Rep.	1,050	174.0	05(WB)
175	CPA	Mongolia	1,000	175.0	06(WB)
176	AFR	Cameroon	990	176.0	06(WB)
177	AFR	Lesotho	980	177.0	06(WB)
178	LAM	Nicaragua	930	178.0	06(WB)
179	AFR	Ivory Coast	880	179.0	06(WB)
180	SEA	East Timor	840	180.0	06(WB)
181	SAS	India	820	181.0	06(WB)
182	SAS	Pakistan	800	183.0	06(WB)
183	AFR	San Tome & Principe	800	183.0	06(WB)
184	AFR	Sudan	800	183.0	06(WB)

TABLE 1.1 – GROSS NATIONAL INCOME
AT MARKET EXCHANGE RATES PER CAPITA, 2006

OBS	REGION	COUNTRY	GPC	RANK	SOURCE
185	AFR	Mauritania	760	186.0	06(WB)
186	AFR	Senegal	760	186.0	06(WB)
187	MEA	Yemen	760	186.0	06(WB)
188	SEA	Papua New Guinea	740	188.0	06(WB)
189	CPA	Vietnam	700	189.0	06(WB)
190	SEA	Solomon Islands	690	190.0	06(WB)
191	AFR	Comoros	660	191.0	06(WB)
192	AFR	Zambia	630	192.0	06(WB)
193	AFR	Nigeria	620	193.0	06(WB)
194	USR	Uzbekistan	610	194.0	06(WB)
195	AFR	Kenya	580	195.0	06(WB)
196	AFR	Benin	530	196.0	06(WB)
197	AFR	Ghana	510	197.0	06(WB)
198	USR	Kyrgyzstan	500	198.5	06(WB)
199	CPA	Laos	500	198.5	06(WB)
200	CPA	Cambodia	490	200.0	06(WB)
201	AFR	Mali	460	201.0	06(WB)
202	SAS	Bangladesh	450	202.5	06(WB)
203	AFR	Chad	450	202.5	06(WB)
204	AFR	Burkina Faso	440	204.0	06(WB)
205	LAM	Haiti	430	205.0	06(WB)
206	AFR	Guinea	400	206.0	06(WB)
207	USR	Tajikistan	390	207.0	06(WB)
208	AFR	CAR	350	209.0	06(WB)
209	AFR	Tanzania	350	209.0	06(WB)
210	AFR	Togo	350	209.0	06(WB)
211	SEA	Tokelau	344	211.0	(REG)
212	SAS	Nepal	320	212.0	06(WB)
213	SAS	Afghanistan	319	213.0	06(E)
214	AFR	Mozambique	310	214.0	06(WB)
215	AFR	Uganda	300	215.5	06(WB)
216	AFR	Western Sahara	300	215.5	91(E)
217	AFR	Gambia	290	217.0	06(WB)
218	CPA	Burma	280	218.5	06(E)
219	AFR	Madagascar	280	218.5	06(WB)
220	AFR	Somalia	274	220.0	06(E)
221	AFR	Niger	270	221.0	06(WB)
222	AFR	Rwanda	250	222.0	06(WB)
223	AFR	Sierra Leone	240	223.0	06(WB)
224	AFR	Malawi	230	224.0	06(WB)
225	AFR	Eritrea	190	225.5	06(WB)
226	AFR	GuineaBissau	190	225.5	06(WB)
227	AFR	Ethiopia	170	227.0	06(WB)
228	AFR	Zimbabwe	131	228.0	06(E)
229	AFR	Congo, Dem. Rep.	130	229.5	06(WB)
230	AFR	Liberia	130	229.5	06(WB)
231	AFR	Burundi	100	231.0	06(WB)

TABLE 1.2 – INFANT MORTALITY, RATE PER 1,000 LIVE BIRTHS, 2006					
OBS	REGION	COUNTRY	INFMRT	RANK	SOURCE
1	DME	Iceland	2.22	1.0	06(WB)
2	SEA	Singapore	2.31	2.0	06(WB)
3	DME	Liechtenstein	2.54	3.0	06(WB)
4	DME	Andorra	2.60	4.0	06(WB)
5	DME	Japan	2.62	5.0	06(WB)
6	DME	Finland	2.89	6.0	06(WB)
7	DME	San Marino	2.92	7.0	06(WB)
8	DME	Sweden	2.94	8.0	06(WB)
9	SEA	Hong Kong	2.95	9.0	06(CIA)
10	DME	Norway	3.02	10.0	06(WB)
11	EEU	Slovenia	3.17	11.0	06(WB)
12	EEU	Czechia	3.24	12.0	06(WB)
13	MEA	Cyprus	3.32	13.0	06(WB)
14	DME	Monaco	3.34	14.0	06(WB)
15	DME	Portugal	3.39	15.0	06(WB)
16	DME	Italy	3.52	16.0	06(WB)
17	DME	Belgium	3.55	17.0	06(WB)
18	DME	France	3.58	18.0	06(WB)
19	DME	Greece	3.62	19.0	06(WB)
20	DME	Luxembourg	3.63	20.5	06(WB)
21	DME	Spain	3.63	20.5	06(WB)
22	DME	Germany	3.73	22.0	06(WB)
23	DME	Austria	3.90	23.0	06(WB)
24	DME	Denmark	3.99	24.0	06(WB)
25	DME	Switzerland	4.14	25.0	06(WB)
26	DME	Israel	4.17	26.0	06(WB)
27	DME	Netherlands	4.24	27.0	06(WB)
28	DME	Ireland	4.29	28.0	06(WB)
29	SEA	Macao	4.35	29.0	06(CIA)
30	SEA	Korea, South	4.52	30.0	06(WB)
31	DME	Guernsey	4.65	31.0	06(CIA)
32	DME	Australia	4.72	32.0	06(WB)
33	DME	Canada	4.87	33.5	06(WB)
34	DME	United Kingdom	4.87	33.5	06(WB)
35	LAM	Cuba	5.02	35.0	06(WB)
36	DME	Gibraltar	5.06	36.0	06(CIA)
37	DME	Malta	5.10	37.0	06(WB)
38	USR	Estonia	5.14	38.0	06(WB)
39	DME	Jersey	5.16	39.0	06(CIA)
40	DME	New Zealand	5.18	40.0	06(WB)
41	EEU	Croatia	5.50	41.0	06(WB)
42	LAM	Aruba	5.79	42.0	06(CIA)
43	DME	Isle of Man	5.82	43.0	06(CIA)
44	EEU	Poland	6.01	44.0	06(WB)
45	EEU	Hungary	6.04	45.0	06(WB)
46	DME	Faeroe Islands	6.12	46.0	06(CIA)

OBS	REGION	COUNTRY	INFMRT	RANK	SOURCE
		TABLE 1.2 – INFANT MORTALITY, RATE PER 1,000 LIVE BIRTHS, 2006			
47	SEA	Taiwan	6.29	47.0	06(CIA)
48	DME	United States	6.45	48.0	06(WB)
49	USR	Lithuania	6.63	49.0	06(WB)
50	AFR	Reunion	6.80	50.5	05(E)
51	EEU	Slovakia	6.80	50.5	06(WB)
52	SEA	Guam	6.81	52.0	06(CIA)
53	LAM	Martinique	6.95	53.0	06(CIA)
54	SEA	Northern Mariana Is.	6.98	54.0	06(CIA)
55	SEA	Thailand	7.15	55.0	06(WB)
56	DME	Falkland Islands	7.18	56.0	(REG)
57	LAM	Montserrat	7.19	57.0	06(CIA)
58	EEU	Serbia	7.32	58.0	06(WB)
59	DME	St. Pierre & Miquelon	7.38	59.0	06(CIA)
60	MEA	UAE	7.55	60.0	06(WB)
61	SEA	New Caledonia	7.57	61.0	06(CIA)
62	USR	Latvia	7.74	62.0	06(WB)
63	LAM	Virgin Islands, US	7.86	63.0	06(CIA)
64	SEA	Brunei	8.00	64.5	06(WB)
65	LAM	Cayman Islands	8.00	64.5	06(CIA)
66	LAM	Chile	8.14	66.0	06(WB)
67	SEA	French Polynesia	8.29	67.0	06(CIA)
68	DME	Bermuda	8.30	68.0	06(CIA)
69	LAM	Guadeloupe	8.60	69.0	05(E)
70	EEU	Montenegro	8.64	70.0	06(WB)
71	SEA	Samoa, American	9.07	71.0	06(CIA)
72	LAM	Puerto Rico	9.14	72.0	06(CIA)
73	MEA	Bahrain	9.16	73.0	06(WB)
74	MEA	Kuwait	9.47	74.0	06(WB)
75	MEA	Oman	9.60	75.0	06(WB)
76	LAM	Neth. Antilles	9.76	76.0	06(CIA)
77	SEA	Nauru	9.78	77.0	06(CIA)
78	SEA	Malaysia	9.80	78.0	06(WB)
79	SEA	Palau	9.95	79.0	06(WB)
80	LAM	Antigua & Barbuda	10.00	80.0	06(WB)
81	LAM	Costa Rica	10.70	81.0	06(WB)
82	LAM	Barbados	10.80	82.0	06(WB)
83	LAM	Uruguay	10.90	83.0	06(WB)
84	SAS	Sri Lanka	11.18	84.0	06(WB)
85	EEU	Bulgaria	11.59	85.0	06(WB)
86	USR	Belarus	11.75	86.0	06(WB)
87	LAM	Guiana, French	11.76	87.0	06(CIA)
88	AFR	Seychelles	11.80	88.0	06(WB)
89	MEA	Syria	12.10	89.0	06(WB)
90	LAM	St. Lucia	12.18	90.0	06(WB)
91	LAM	Bahamas	12.60	91.5	06(WB)
92	AFR	Mauritius	12.60	91.5	06(WB)
93	EEU	Bosnia	12.80	93.0	06(WB)

OBS	REGION	COUNTRY	INFMRT	RANK	SOURCE
		TABLE 1.2 – INFANT MORTALITY,			
		RATE PER 1,000 LIVE BIRTHS, 2006			
94	LAM	Dominica	13.03	94.0	06(WB)
95	USR	Russia	13.70	95.0	06(WB)
96	LAM	Argentina	14.14	96.0	06(WB)
97	LAM	Belize	14.45	97.0	06(WB)
98	EEU	Macedonia	14.60	98.5	06(WB)
99	CPA	Vietnam	14.60	98.5	06(WB)
100	EEU	Albania	14.80	100.0	06(WB)
101	SEA	Turks & Caicos Is.	15.18	101.0	06(CIA)
102	DME	Greenland	15.40	102.0	06(CIA)
103	SEA	Fiji	15.65	103.0	06(WB)
104	EEU	Romania	15.69	104.0	06(WB)
105	LAM	Grenada	16.20	105.0	06(WB)
106	USR	Moldova	16.35	106.0	06(WB)
107	LAM	Colombia	16.65	107.0	06(WB)
108	LAM	Virgin Islands, Brit.	16.72	108.0	06(CIA)
109	LAM	St. Kitts & Nevis	16.80	109.0	06(WB)
110	MEA	Libya	17.00	110.0	06(WB)
111	LAM	St. Vincent	17.09	111.0	06(WB)
112	LAM	Venezuela	17.65	112.0	06(WB)
113	MEA	Qatar	17.80	113.0	06(WB)
114	LAM	Panama	18.20	114.0	06(WB)
115	AFR	St. Helena	18.34	115.0	06(CIA)
116	LAM	Brazil	18.60	116.0	06(WB)
117	MEA	Tunisia	19.00	117.0	06(WB)
118	SEA	Niue	19.10	118.0	94(CIA)
119	MEA	West Bank	19.15	119.0	06(CIA)
120	LAM	Paraguay	19.40	120.0	06(WB)
121	SEA	Tuvalu	19.47	121.0	06(CIA)
122	SEA	Tonga	19.58	122.0	06(WB)
123	USR	Ukraine	19.75	123.0	06(WB)
124	CPA	China	20.05	124.0	06(WB)
125	LAM	Anguilla	20.32	125.0	06(CIA)
126	MEA	Saudi Arabia	20.60	126.0·	06(WB)
127	SEA	Wallis & Futuna	20.93	127.0	98(CIA)
128	LAM	Ecuador	21.00	128.0	06(WB)
129	LAM	Peru	21.20	129.0	06(WB)
130	USR	Armenia	21.35	130.0	06(WB)
131	MEA	Jordan	21.40	131.0	06(WB)
132	LAM	El Salvador	21.80	132.0	06(WB)
133	MEA	Gaza Strip	22.40	133.0	06(CIA)
134	LAM	Honduras	22.55	134.0	06(WB)
135	SEA	Samoa, Western	23.24	135.0	06(WB)
136	MEA	Turkey	23.70	136.0	06(WB)
137	SEA	Philippines	24.00	137.0	06(WB)
138	LAM	Dominican Rep.	24.60	138.0	06(WB)
139	SEA	Cook Islands	24.70	139.0	00(CIA)
140	AFR	Cape Verde	25.00	140.0	06(WB)

		TABLE 1.2 – INFANT MORTALITY, RATE PER 1,000 LIVE BIRTHS, 2006			
OBS	*REGION*	*COUNTRY*	*INFMRT*	*RANK*	*SOURCE*
141	LAM	Jamaica	25.80	141.5	06(WB)
142	USR	Kazakhstan	25.80	141.5	06(WB)
143	MEA	Lebanon	26.20	143.0	06(WB)
144	SAS	Maldives	26.30	144.0	06(WB)
145	SEA	Indonesia	26.40	145.0	06(WB)
146	USR	Georgia	28.25	146.0	06(WB)
147	MEA	Egypt	28.90	147.0	06(WB)
148	LAM	Mexico	29.10	148.0	06(WB)
149	LAM	Nicaragua	29.20	149.5	06(WB)
150	LAM	Suriname	29.20	149.5	06(WB)
151	SEA	Vanuatu	29.54	151.0	06(WB)
152	MEA	Iran	30.00	152.0	06(WB)
153	LAM	Guatemala	30.60	153.0	06(WB)
154	LAM	Trinidad & Tobago	32.75	154.0	06(WB)
155	SEA	Micronesia	33.05	155.0	06(WB)
156	MEA	Algeria	33.40	156.0	06(WB)
157	CPA	Mongolia	34.20	157.5	06(WB)
158	MEA	Morocco	34.20	157.5	06(WB)
159	USR	Kyrgyzstan	35.55	159.0	06(WB)
160	USR	Uzbekistan	37.50	160.0	06(WB)
161	SEA	Tokelau	38.00	161.0	01(CIA)
162	CPA	Korea, North	42.00	162.0	06(WB)
163	AFR	Namibia	45.20	163.0	06(WB)
164	USR	Turkmenistan	45.25	164.0	06(WB)
165	LAM	Guyana	46.00	165.0	06(WB)
166	SAS	Nepal	46.10	166.0	06(WB)
167	SEA	East Timor	46.75	167.0	06(WB)
168	SEA	Kiribati	47.20	168.0	06(WB)
169	AFR	Eritrea	47.80	169.0	06(WB)
170	MEA	Iraq	48.64	170.0	06(CIA)
171	LAM	Bolivia	49.80	171.0	06(WB)
172	SEA	Marshall Islands	50.20	172.0	06(WB)
173	AFR	Comoros	51.20	173.0	06(WB)
174	SAS	Bangladesh	51.60	174.0	06(WB)
175	SEA	Papua New Guinea	54.40	175.0	06(WB)
176	SEA	Solomon Islands	54.90	176.0	06(WB)
177	AFR	South Africa	56.00	177.0	06(WB)
178	USR	Tajikistan	56.40	178.0	06(WB)
179	SAS	India	57.40	179.0	06(WB)
180	CPA	Laos	59.00	180.0	06(WB)
181	AFR	Senegal	59.90	181.0	06(WB)
182	AFR	Gabon	60.00	182.5	06(WB)
183	LAM	Haiti	60.00	182.5	06(WB)
184	AFR	Mayotte	60.76	184.0	06(CIA)
185	AFR	Sudan	61.40	185.0	06(WB)
186	SAS	Bhutan	62.60	186.0	06(WB)
187	AFR	San Tome & Principe	62.65	187.0	06(WB)

		TABLE 1.2 – INFANT MORTALITY, RATE PER 1,000 LIVE BIRTHS, 2006			
OBS	REGION	COUNTRY	INFMRT	RANK	SOURCE
188	CPA	Cambodia	64.75	188.0	06(WB)
189	AFR	Zimbabwe	67.90	189.0	06(WB)
190	AFR	Togo	69.15	190.0	06(WB)
191	AFR	Madagascar	72.00	191.0	06(WB)
192	USR	Azerbaijan	73.40	192.0	06(WB)
193	AFR	Tanzania	73.60	193.0	06(WB)
194	CPA	Burma	74.40	194.0	06(WB)
195	MEA	Yemen	75.00	195.0	06(WB)
196	AFR	Western Sahara	75.70	196.0	05(E)
197	AFR	Ghana	75.95	197.0	06(WB)
198	AFR	Malawi	76.10	198.0	06(WB)
199	AFR	Ethiopia	77.45	199.0	06(WB)
200	AFR	Mauritania	77.80	201.0	06(WB)
201	SAS	Pakistan	77.80	201.0	06(WB)
202	AFR	Uganda	77.80	201.0	06(WB)
203	AFR	Kenya	79.40	203.0	06(WB)
204	AFR	Congo, Rep.	79.45	204.0	06(WB)
205	AFR	Gambia	84.00	205.0	06(WB)
206	AFR	Djibouti	86.20	206.0	06(WB)
207	AFR	Cameroon	86.80	207.0	06(WB)
208	AFR	Benin	87.80	208.0	06(WB)
209	AFR	Botswana	89.60	210.0	06(WB)
210	AFR	Ivory Coast	89.60	210.0	06(WB)
211	AFR	Somalia	89.60	210.0	06(WB)
212	AFR	Mozambique	95.60	212.0	06(WB)
213	AFR	Rwanda	97.55	213.0	06(WB)
214	AFR	Guinea	98.05	214.0	06(WB)
215	AFR	Nigeria	98.60	215.0	06(WB)
216	AFR	Zambia	102.00	216.0	06(WB)
217	AFR	Lesotho	102.30	217.0	06(WB)
218	AFR	Burundi	108.80	218.0	06(WB)
219	AFR	Swaziland	112.40	219.0	06(WB)
220	AFR	CAR	114.50	220.0	06(WB)
221	AFR	Mali	119.20	221.0	06(WB)
222	AFR	GuineaBissau	119.25	222.0	06(WB)
223	AFR	Burkina Faso	121.60	223.0	06(WB)
224	AFR	Equatorial Guinea	123.60	224.0	06(WB)
225	AFR	Chad	124.25	225.0	06(WB)
226	AFR	Congo, Dem. Rep.	129.00	226.0	06(WB)
227	AFR	Niger	148.20	227.0	06(WB)
228	AFR	Angola	154.00	228.0	06(WB)
229	AFR	Liberia	157.00	229.0	06(WB)
230	AFR	Sierra Leone	159.20	230.0	06(WB)
231	SAS	Afghanistan	160.23	231.0	06(CIA)

	TABLE 1.3 – EXPECTATION OF LIFE AT BIRTH, AVERAGE OF MALE AND FEMALE LIFE EXPECTANCY, 2006				
OBS	REGION	COUNTRY	LIFEXP	RANK	SOURCE
1	DME	Andorra	83.510	1	06(CIA)
2	DME	Japan	82.322	2	06(WB)
3	DME	San Marino	82.186	3	06(WB)
4	SEA	Hong Kong	81.629	4	06(WB)
5	DME	Switzerland	81.515	5	06(WB)
6	DME	Iceland	81.171	6	06(WB)
7	DME	Italy	81.081	7	06(WB)
8	DME	Australia	80.999	8	06(WB)
9	DME	Spain	80.801	9	06(WB)
10	DME	Sweden	80.768	10	06(WB)
11	DME	France	80.555	11	06(WB)
12	SEA	Macao	80.468	12	06(WB)
13	DME	Guernsey	80.420	13	06(CIA)
14	DME	Canada	80.356	14	06(WB)
15	DME	Norway	80.335	15	06(WB)
16	LAM	Cayman Islands	80.070	16	06(CIA)
17	DME	Israel	80.021	17	06(WB)
18	DME	New Zealand	79.930	18	06(WB)
19	SEA	Singapore	79.854	19	06(WB)
20	DME	Austria	79.837	20	06(WB)
21	DME	Gibraltar	79.800	21	06(CIA)
22	DME	Netherlands	79.698	22	06(WB)
23	DME	Monaco	79.690	23	06(CIA)
24	DME	Liechtenstein	79.680	24	06(CIA)
25	DME	Belgium	79.480	25	06(WB)
26	DME	Greece	79.415	26	06(WB)
27	DME	Ireland	79.393	27	06(WB)
28	DME	Jersey	79.380	28	06(CIA)
29	DME	Faeroe Islands	79.350	29	06(CIA)
30	MEA	UAE	79.319	30	06(WB)
31	MEA	Cyprus	79.293	31	06(WB)
32	LAM	Aruba	79.280	32	06(CIA)
33	DME	Finland	79.229	33	06(WB)
34	LAM	Martinique	79.180	34	06(CIA)
35	DME	Luxembourg	79.176	35	06(WB)
36	DME	United Kingdom	79.137	36	06(WB)
37	DME	Germany	79.132	37	06(WB)
38	LAM	Montserrat	78.850	38	06(CIA)
39	LAM	Virgin Islands, US	78.751	39	06(WB)
40	LAM	Costa Rica	78.656	40	06(WB)
41	DME	St. Pierre & Miquelon	78.610	41	06(CIA)
42	DME	Bermuda	78.577	42	06(WB)
43	DME	Malta	78.549	43	06(WB)
44	SEA	Korea, South	78.499	44	06(WB)
45	DME	Isle of Man	78.490	45	06(CIA)
46	LAM	Puerto Rico	78.416	46	06(WB)

OBS	REGION	COUNTRY	LIFEXP	RANK	SOURCE
		TABLE 1.3 – EXPECTATION OF LIFE AT BIRTH, AVERAGE OF MALE AND FEMALE LIFE EXPECTANCY, 2006			
47	DME	Portugal	78.385	47	06(WB)
48	LAM	Chile	78.294	48	06(WB)
49	DME	Denmark	78.100	49	06(WB)
50	LAM	Cuba	78.036	50	06(WB)
51	LAM	Guadeloupe	77.950	51	05(E)
52	AFR	St. Helena	77.930	52	06(CIA)
53	DME	United States	77.849	53	06(WB)
54	EEU	Slovenia	77.668	54	06(WB)
55	MEA	Kuwait	77.661	55	06(WB)
56	SEA	Taiwan	77.430	56	06(CIA)
57	LAM	Anguilla	77.280	57	06(CIA)
58	LAM	Guiana, French	77.270	58	06(CIA)
59	SEA	Brunei	77.133	59	06(WB)
60	LAM	Barbados	76.772	60	06(WB)
61	LAM	Virgin Islands, Brit.	76.680	61	06(CIA)
62	EEU	Czechia	76.484	62	06(WB)
63	DME	Falkland Islands	76.428	63	(REG)
64	EEU	Albania	76.338	64	06(WB)
65	AFR	Reunion	76.200	65	06(E)
66	SEA	Northern Mariana Is.	76.090	66	06(CIA)
67	SEA	Samoa, American	76.050	67	06(CIA)
68	EEU	Croatia	75.817	68	06(WB)
69	LAM	Uruguay	75.730	69	06(WB)
70	MEA	Bahrain	75.656	70	06(WB)
71	MEA	Oman	75.505	71	06(WB)
72	MEA	Qatar	75.496	72	06(WB)
73	LAM	Panama	75.402	73	06(WB)
74	SEA	Guam	75.361	74	06(WB)
75	SEA	New Caledonia	75.329	75	06(WB)
76	EEU	Poland	75.144	76	06(WB)
77	LAM	Argentina	75.027	77	06(WB)
78	SAS	Sri Lanka	74.967	78	06(WB)
79	LAM	Neth. Antilles	74.916	79	06(WB)
80	LAM	Dominica	74.870	80	06(CIA)
81	LAM	Ecuador	74.834	81	06(WB)
82	SEA	Turks & Caicos Is.	74.730	82	06(CIA)
83	EEU	Bosnia	74.573	83	06(WB)
84	LAM	Mexico	74.471	84	06(WB)
85	EEU	Montenegro	74.420	85	06(WB)
86	LAM	Venezuela	74.401	86	06(WB)
87	LAM	St. Lucia	74.387	87	06(WB)
88	EEU	Slovakia	74.205	88	06(WB)
89	SEA	Malaysia	74.048	89	06(WB)
90	EEU	Macedonia	73.990	90	06(WB)
91	MEA	Libya	73.980	91	06(WB)
92	SEA	French Polynesia	73.970	92	06(WB)
93	MEA	Syria	73.896	93	06(WB)

TABLE 1.3 – EXPECTATION OF LIFE AT BIRTH, AVERAGE OF MALE AND FEMALE LIFE EXPECTANCY, 2006

OBS	REGION	COUNTRY	LIFEXP	RANK	SOURCE
94	SEA	Wallis & Futuna	73.820	94	98(CIA)
95	MEA	Tunisia	73.623	95	06(WB)
96	MEA	West Bank	73.270	96	06(CIA)
97	AFR	Mauritius	73.170	97	06(WB)
98	EEU	Hungary	73.089	98	06(WB)
99	SEA	Tonga	73.030	99	06(WB)
100	LAM	Bahamas	72.913	100	06(WB)
101	EEU	Serbia	72.775	101	06(WB)
102	EEU	Bulgaria	72.612	102	06(WB)
103	LAM	Colombia	72.595	103	06(WB)
104	MEA	Saudi Arabia	72.585	104	06(WB)
105	USR	Estonia	72.572	105	06(WB)
106	LAM	Nicaragua	72.477	106	06(WB)
107	LAM	St. Kitts & Nevis	72.400	107	06(CIA)
108	USR	Azerbaijan	72.332	108	06(WB)
109	AFR	Seychelles	72.217	109	06(WB)
110	MEA	Jordan	72.205	110	06(WB)
111	EEU	Romania	72.184	111	06(WB)
112	LAM	Antigua & Barbuda	72.160	112	06(CIA)
113	LAM	Brazil	72.084	113	06(WB)
114	LAM	Dominican Rep.	72.027	114	06(WB)
115	CPA	China	72.001	115	06(WB)
116	MEA	Algeria	71.988	116	06(WB)
117	MEA	Gaza Strip	71.970	117	06(CIA)
118	LAM	Belize	71.897	118	06(WB)
119	MEA	Lebanon	71.779	119	06(WB)
120	LAM	Paraguay	71.651	120	06(WB)
121	USR	Armenia	71.596	121	06(WB)
122	LAM	El Salvador	71.541	122	06(WB)
123	MEA	Turkey	71.490	123	06(WB)
124	SEA	Philippines	71.388	124	06(WB)
125	LAM	St. Vincent	71.381	125	06(WB)
126	SEA	Samoa, Western	71.335	126	06(WB)
127	SEA	Cook Islands	71.140	127	00(CIA)
128	LAM	Jamaica	71.125	128	06(WB)
129	LAM	Peru	71.117	129	06(WB)
130	USR	Lithuania	71.042	130	06(WB)
131	MEA	Egypt	71.014	131	06(WB)
132	AFR	Cape Verde	71.000	132	06(WB)
133	USR	Latvia	70.861	133	06(WB)
134	CPA	Vietnam	70.847	134	06(WB)
135	USR	Georgia	70.725	135	06(WB)
136	MEA	Morocco	70.699	136	06(WB)
137	MEA	Iran	70.652	137	06(WB)
138	SEA	Palau	70.420	138	06(CIA)
139	SEA	Marshall Islands	70.310	139	06(CIA)
140	SEA	Thailand	70.240	140	06(WB)

OBS	REGION	COUNTRY	LIFEXP	RANK	SOURCE
		TABLE 1.3 – EXPECTATION OF LIFE AT BIRTH, AVERAGE OF MALE AND FEMALE LIFE EXPECTANCY, 2006			
141	LAM	Suriname	69.992	141	06(WB)
142	DME	Greenland	69.940	142	06(CIA)
143	LAM	Guatemala	69.914	143	06(WB)
144	LAM	Honduras	69.891	144	06(WB)
145	SEA	Vanuatu	69.811	145	06(WB)
146	LAM	Trinidad & Tobago	69.577	146	06(WB)
147	MEA	Iraq	69.010	147	06(CIA)
148	SEA	Tokelau	69.000	148	05(CIA)
149	SEA	Fiji	68.590	149	06(WB)
150	USR	Belarus	68.589	150	06(WB)
151	USR	Moldova	68.528	151	06(WB)
152	SEA	Tuvalu	68.320	152	06(CIA)
153	SEA	Micronesia	68.313	153	06(WB)
154	SEA	Indonesia	68.160	154	06(WB)
155	USR	Ukraine	68.042	155	06(WB)
156	SAS	Maldives	67.920	156	06(WB)
157	USR	Kyrgyzstan	67.695	157	06(WB)
158	USR	Uzbekistan	67.497	158	06(WB)
159	CPA	Mongolia	67.169	159	06(WB)
160	CPA	Korea, North	66.969	160	06(WB)
161	USR	Tajikistan	66.513	161	06(WB)
162	LAM	Guyana	66.281	162	06(WB)
163	USR	Kazakhstan	66.161	163	06(WB)
164	USR	Russia	65.556	164	06(WB)
165	SAS	Bhutan	65.265	165	06(WB)
166	SAS	Pakistan	65.210	166	06(WB)
167	AFR	San Tome & Principe	65.201	167	06(WB)
168	LAM	Bolivia	65.179	168	06(WB)
169	LAM	Grenada	64.870	169	06(CIA)
170	SEA	Niue	64.750	170	94(CIA)
171	SAS	India	64.473	171	06(WB)
172	CPA	Laos	63.864	172	06(WB)
173	AFR	Mauritania	63.745	173	06(WB)
174	SAS	Bangladesh	63.657	174	06(WB)
175	SEA	Solomon Islands	63.332	175	05(WB)
176	AFR	Comoros	63.240	176	06(WB)
177	SAS	Nepal	63.225	177	06(WB)
178	SEA	Nauru	63.080	178	06(CIA)
179	USR	Turkmenistan	63.014	179	06(WB)
180	AFR	Senegal	62.756	180	06(WB)
181	MEA	Yemen	62.209	181	06(WB)
182	SEA	Kiribati	62.080	182	06(CIA)
183	AFR	Mayotte	61.760	183	06(CIA)
184	CPA	Burma	61.648	184	06(WB)
185	LAM	Haiti	60.323	185	06(WB)
186	AFR	Ghana	59.695	186	06(WB)
187	AFR	Gambia	59.148	187	06(WB)

TABLE 1.3 – EXPECTATION OF LIFE AT BIRTH, AVERAGE OF MALE AND FEMALE LIFE EXPECTANCY, 2006

OBS	REGION	COUNTRY	LIFEXP	RANK	SOURCE
188	AFR	Madagascar	58.989	188	06(WB)
189	CPA	Cambodia	58.934	189	06(WB)
190	AFR	Togo	58.199	190	06(WB)
191	AFR	Sudan	58.106	191	06(WB)
192	SEA	Papua New Guinea	57.321	192	06(WB)
193	AFR	Eritrea	57.315	193	06(WB)
194	SEA	East Timor	57.164	194	06(WB)
195	AFR	Gabon	56.736	195	06(WB)
196	AFR	Niger	56.419	196	06(WB)
197	AFR	Benin	56.200	197	06(WB)
198	AFR	Guinea	55.516	198	06(WB)
199	AFR	Congo, Rep.	54.789	199	06(WB)
200	AFR	Djibouti	54.475	200	06(WB)
201	AFR	Mali	53.785	201	06(WB)
202	AFR	Kenya	53.444	202	06(WB)
203	AFR	Namibia	52.499	203	06(WB)
204	AFR	Ethiopia	52.479	204	06(WB)
205	AFR	Tanzania	51.892	205	06(WB)
206	AFR	Burkina Faso	51.871	206	06(WB)
207	AFR	Equatorial Guinea	51.100	207	06(WB)
208	AFR	Uganda	50.743	208	06(WB)
209	AFR	South Africa	50.707	209	06(WB)
210	AFR	Chad	50.598	210	06(WB)
211	AFR	Cameroon	50.281	211	06(WB)
212	AFR	Western Sahara	50.000	212	05(E)
213	AFR	Botswana	49.780	213	06(WB)
214	AFR	Burundi	49.049	214	06(WB)
215	AFR	Ivory Coast	48.081	215	06(WB)
216	AFR	Somalia	47.690	216	06(WB)
217	AFR	Malawi	47.614	217	06(WB)
218	AFR	Nigeria	46.783	218	06(WB)
219	AFR	GuineaBissau	46.188	219	06(WB)
220	AFR	Congo, Dem. Rep.	46.120	220	06(WB)
221	AFR	Rwanda	45.593	221	06(WB)
222	AFR	Liberia	45.270	222	06(WB)
223	AFR	CAR	44.383	223	06(WB)
224	SAS	Afghanistan	43.340	224	06(CIA)
225	AFR	Lesotho	42.930	225	06(WB)
226	AFR	Zimbabwe	42.687	226	06(WB)
227	AFR	Mozambique	42.455	227	06(WB)
228	AFR	Angola	42.359	228	06(WB)
229	AFR	Sierra Leone	42.237	229	06(WB)
230	AFR	Zambia	41.674	230	06(WB)
231	AFR	Swaziland	40.766	231	06(WB)

OBS	REGION	COUNTRY	GPCPPP	RANK	SOURCE
— TABLE 1.4 – GROSS DOMESTIC PRODUCT AT PURCHASING POWER PARITIES PER CAPITA, 2006						
1	DME	Luxembourg	75,611	1.0	06(WB)
2	DME	Liechtenstein	70,631	2.0	(REG)
3	DME	Bermuda	69,900	3.0	04(CIA)
4	MEA	Qatar	59,493	4.0	(REG)
5	DME	Jersey	57,000	5.0	05(CIA)
6	DME	Norway	50,078	6.0	06(WB)
7	SEA	Brunei	49,898	7.0	06(WB)
8	MEA	UAE	49,700	8.0	06(CIA)
9	SEA	Singapore	44,708	9.0	06(WB)
10	DME	Guernsey	44,600	10.0	05(CIA)
11	DME	United States	43,968	11.0	06(WB)
12	SEA	Macao	43,949	12.0	06(WB)
13	LAM	Cayman Islands	43,800	13.0	04(CIA)
14	MEA	Kuwait	43,551	14.0	05(WB)
15	DME	Ireland	40,268	15.0	06(WB)
16	SEA	Hong Kong	39,062	16.0	06(WB)
17	DME	Andorra	39,000	17.0	05(E)
18	LAM	Virgin Islands, Brit.	38,500	18.0	04(CIA)
19	DME	Gibraltar	38,200	19.0	05(CIA)
20	DME	Switzerland	37,194	20.0	06(WB)
21	DME	Iceland	36,923	21.0	06(WB)
22	DME	Canada	36,713	22.0	06(WB)
23	DME	Netherlands	36,560	23.0	06(WB)
24	DME	Austria	36,049	24.0	06(WB)
25	DME	Denmark	35,692	25.0	06(WB)
26	DME	Australia	35,547	26.0	06(WB)
27	DME	Isle of Man	35,000	27.0	05(CIA)
28	DME	Sweden	34,193	28.0	06(WB)
29	DME	San Marino	34,100	29.0	04(CIA)
30	DME	Belgium	33,543	30.0	06(WB)
31	MEA	Bahrain	33,451	31.0	05(WB)
32	DME	United Kingdom	33,087	32.0	06(WB)
33	DME	Finland	33,022	33.0	06(WB)
34	DME	Germany	32,322	34.0	06(WB)
35	DME	France	31,992	35.0	06(WB)
36	DME	Japan	31,947	36.0	06(WB)
37	DME	Greece	31,382	37.0	06(WB)
38	DME	Faeroe Islands	31,000	38.0	03(E)
39	DME	Monaco	30,000	39.0	06(CIA)
40	DME	Italy	29,053	40.0	06(WB)
41	SEA	Taiwan	29,000	41.0	06(CIA)
42	DME	Spain	28,420	42.0	06(E)
43	AFR	Equatorial Guinea	27,161	43.0	06(WB)
44	MEA	Cyprus	25,882	44.0	06(WB)
45	DME	New Zealand	25,517	45.0	06(WB)
46	DME	Israel	25,470	46.0	05(E)

TABLE 1.4 – GROSS DOMESTIC PRODUCT AT PURCHASING POWER PARITIES PER CAPITA, 2006

OBS	REGION	COUNTRY	GPCPPP	RANK	SOURCE
47	DME	Falkland Islands	25,000	47.0	02(CIA)
48	EEU	Slovenia	24,356	48.0	06(WB)
49	LAM	Guadeloupe	24,065	49.0	(REG)
50	AFR	Reunion	23,232	50.0	(REG)
51	SEA	Korea, South	22,988	51.0	06(WB)
52	LAM	Aruba	22,500	52.0	05(E)
53	MEA	Saudi Arabia	22,296	53.0	06(WB)
54	EEU	Czechia	22,118	54.0	06(WB)
55	DME	Malta	21,720	55.0	06(WB)
56	LAM	Bahamas	21,500	56.0	05(E)
57	DME	Portugal	20,784	57.0	06(WB)
58	MEA	Oman	20,350	58.0	05(WB)
59	DME	Greenland	20,000	59.0	01(CIA)
60	LAM	Puerto Rico	19,300	60.0	06(E)
61	USR	Estonia	18,969	61.0	06(WB)
62	EEU	Hungary	18,277	62.0	06(WB)
63	EEU	Slovakia	17,730	63.0	06(WB)
64	LAM	Trinidad & Tobago	17,717	64.0	06(WB)
65	SEA	French Polynesia	17,500	65.0	06(E)
66	LAM	Antigua & Barbuda	16,578	66.0	06(WB)
67	LAM	Neth. Antilles	16,000	67.0	04(CIA)
68	USR	Lithuania	15,738	68.0	06(WB)
69	USR	Latvia	15,350	69.0	06(WB)
70	AFR	Seychelles	15,211	70.0	06(WB)
71	SEA	Guam	15,000	71.5	05(CIA)
72	SEA	New Caledonia	15,000	71.5	05(E)
73	EEU	Poland	14,836	73.0	06(WB)
74	LAM	Virgin Islands, US	14,500	74.0	04(CIA)
75	LAM	Martinique	14,400	75.0	03(CIA)
76	EEU	Croatia	14,309	76.0	06(WB)
77	SEA	Palau	14,209	77.0	06(WB)
78	AFR	Gabon	14,208	78.0	06(WB)
79	USR	Russia	13,116	79.0	06(WB)
80	LAM	Chile	13,030	80.0	06(WB)
81	LAM	St. Kitts & Nevis	12,680	81.0	06(E)
82	SEA	Malaysia	12,536	82.0	06(WB)
83	AFR	Botswana	12,508	83.0	06(WB)
84	SEA	Northern Mariana Is.	12,500	84.0	00(CIA)
85	LAM	Barbados	12,240	85.0	06(E)
86	LAM	Mexico	12,177	86.0	06(WB)
87	LAM	Argentina	11,985	87.0	06(WB)
88	MEA	Libya	11,622	88.0	06(WB)
89	SEA	Turks & Caicos Is.	11,500	89.0	02(CIA)
90	LAM	Venezuela	11,060	90.0	06(WB)
91	AFR	Mauritius	10,571	91.0	06(WB)
92	EEU	Romania	10,431	92.0	06(WB)
93	EEU	Bulgaria	10,274	93.0	06(WB)

TABLE I.4 – GROSS DOMESTIC PRODUCT AT PURCHASING POWER PARITIES PER CAPITA, 2006

OBS	REGION	COUNTRY	GPCPPP	RANK	SOURCE
94	LAM	Uruguay	10,203	94.0	06(WB)
95	LAM	St. Lucia	9,992	95.0	06(WB)
96	MEA	Iran	9,906	96.0	06(WB)
97	USR	Kazakhstan	9,832	97.0	06(WB)
98	MEA	Lebanon	9,741	98.0	06(WB)
99	USR	Belarus	9,732	99.0	06(WB)
100	LAM	Costa Rica	9,564	100.0	06(WB)
101	EEU	Serbia	9,434	101.0	06(WB)
102	LAM	Grenada	9,415	102.0	06(WB)
103	LAM	Panama	9,255	103.0	06(WB)
104	LAM	Dominica	9,236	104.0	06(WB)
105	SEA	Cook Islands	9,100	105.0	05(CIA)
106	AFR	South Africa	9,087	106.0	06(WB)
107	EEU	Montenegro	9,034	107.0	06(WB)
108	LAM	Brazil	8,949	108.0	06(WB)
109	LAM	Anguilla	8,800	109.0	04(CIA)
110	USR	Turkmenistan	8,500	110.0	06(E)
111	MEA	Turkey	8,417	111.0	06(WB)
112	LAM	Guiana, French	8,300	112.0	03(CIA)
113	LAM	Suriname	7,894	113.0	06(WB)
114	EEU	Macedonia	7,850	114.0	06(WB)
115	LAM	Belize	7,846	115.0	06(WB)
116	SEA	Thailand	7,599	116.0	06(WB)
117	LAM	Jamaica	7,567	117.0	06(WB)
118	LAM	Ecuador	7,145	118.0	06(WB)
119	LAM	Peru	7,092	119.0	06(WB)
120	DME	St. Pierre & Miquelon	7,000	120.5	01(CIA)
121	LAM	St. Vincent	7,000	120.5	06(E)
122	MEA	Tunisia	6,859	122.0	06(WB)
123	EEU	Bosnia	6,488	123.0	06(WB)
124	SEA	Marshall Islands	6,429	124.0	06(WB)
125	LAM	Colombia	6,378	125.0	06(WB)
126	MEA	Algeria	6,347	126.0	06(WB)
127	USR	Azerbaijan	6,280	127.0	06(WB)
128	USR	Ukraine	6,212	128.0	06(WB)
129	EEU	Albania	5,886	129.0	06(WB)
130	LAM	Dominican Rep.	5,866	130.0	06(WB)
131	SEA	Niue	5,800	131.5	03(CIA)
132	SEA	Samoa, American	5,800	131.5	05(CIA)
133	LAM	El Salvador	5,765	133.0	06(WB)
134	SEA	Micronesia	5,665	134.0	06(WB)
135	SEA	Tonga	5,405	135.0	05(WB)
136	LAM	Guatemala	5,175	136.0	06(WB)
137	SEA	Samoa, Western	5,148	137.0	06(WB)
138	SAS	Maldives	5,008	138.0	06(WB)
139	SEA	Nauru	5,000	139.0	05(CIA)
140	MEA	Egypt	4,953	140.0	06(WB)

TABLE 1.4 – GROSS DOMESTIC PRODUCT AT PURCHASING POWER PARITIES PER CAPITA, 2006

OBS	REGION	COUNTRY	GPCPPP	RANK	SOURCE
141	AFR	Mayotte	4,900	141.0	05(CIA)
142	USR	Armenia	4,879	142.0	06(WB)
143	AFR	Namibia	4,819	143.0	06(WB)
144	AFR	Swaziland	4,671	144.0	06(WB)
145	CPA	China	4,644	145.0	06(WB)
146	MEA	Jordan	4,628	146.0	06(WB)
147	SEA	Fiji	4,548	147.0	06(WB)
148	AFR	Angola	4,434	148.0	06(WB)
149	MEA	Syria	4,225	149.0	06(WB)
150	LAM	Paraguay	4,034	150.0	06(WB)
151	SAS	Bhutan	4,010	151.5	06(WB)
152	USR	Georgia	4,010	151.5	06(WB)
153	LAM	Bolivia	3,937	153.0	06(WB)
154	MEA	Morocco	3,915	154.0	06(WB)
155	LAM	Cuba	3,900	155.0	06(CIA)
156	SEA	Wallis & Futuna	3,800	156.0	04(CIA)
157	SEA	Vanuatu	3,768	157.0	06(WB)
158	SAS	Sri Lanka	3,747	158.0	06(WB)
159	SEA	Kiribati	3,688	159.0	06(WB)
160	LAM	Guyana	3,547	160.0	06(WB)
161	LAM	Honduras	3,543	161.0	06(WB)
162	AFR	Congo, Rep.	3,487	162.0	06(WB)
163	SEA	Indonesia	3,454	163.0	06(WB)
164	LAM	Montserrat	3,400	164.0	02(CIA)
165	MEA	Gaza Strip	3,195	165.5	(REG)
166	MEA	West Bank	3,195	165.5	(REG)
167	SEA	Philippines	3,153	167.0	06(WB)
168	MEA	Iraq	2,900	168.0	06(CIA)
169	CPA	Mongolia	2,887	169.0	06(WB)
170	LAM	Nicaragua	2,789	170.0	06(WB)
171	AFR	Cape Verde	2,697	171.0	06(WB)
172	AFR	St. Helena	2,500	172.0	98(CIA)
173	SAS	India	2,469	173.0	06(WB)
174	USR	Moldova	2,377	174.0	06(WB)
175	CPA	Vietnam	2,363	175.0	06(WB)
176	SAS	Pakistan	2,361	176.0	06(WB)
177	MEA	Yemen	2,264	177.0	06(WB)
178	USR	Uzbekistan	2,192	178.0	06(WB)
179	SEA	East Timor	2,141	179.0	06(WB)
180	AFR	Cameroon	2,089	180.0	06(WB)
181	AFR	Zimbabwe	2,000	181.0	06(CIA)
182	CPA	Laos	1,980	182.0	06(WB)
183	AFR	Djibouti	1,966	183.0	06(WB)
184	AFR	Sudan	1,931	184.0	06(WB)
185	AFR	Mauritania	1,890	185.0	06(WB)
186	SEA	Solomon Islands	1,839	186.0	06(WB)
187	SEA	Papua New Guinea	1,817	187.0	06(WB)

OBS	REGION	COUNTRY	GPCPPP	RANK	SOURCE
188	USR	Kyrgyzstan	1,813	188.0	06(WB)
189	CPA	Korea, North	1,800	189.0	06(CIA)
190	AFR	Ivory Coast	1,650	190.0	06(WB)
191	CPA	Cambodia	1,619	191.0	06(WB)
192	AFR	Nigeria	1,611	192.0	06(WB)
193	USR	Tajikistan	1,610	193.0	06(WB)
194	SEA	Tuvalu	1,600	194.0	02(CIA)
195	AFR	Senegal	1,585	195.0	06(WB)
196	AFR	San Tome & Principe	1,522	196.0	06(WB)
197	AFR	Chad	1,478	197.0	06(WB)
198	AFR	Kenya	1,467	198.0	06(WB)
199	AFR	Lesotho	1,440	199.0	06(WB)
200	AFR	Benin	1,263	200.0	06(WB)
201	AFR	Zambia	1,259	201.0	06(WB)
202	AFR	Ghana	1,245	202.0	06(WB)
203	LAM	Haiti	1,224	203.0	06(WB)
204	SAS	Bangladesh	1,155	204.0	06(WB)
205	AFR	Guinea	1,149	205.0	06(WB)
206	AFR	Comoros	1,144	206.0	06(WB)
207	AFR	Burkina Faso	1,130	207.5	06(WB)
208	AFR	Gambia	1,130	207.5	06(WB)
209	AFR	Mali	1,058	209.0	06(WB)
210	SEA	Tokelau	1,000	210.0	93(CIA)
211	SAS	Nepal	999	211.0	06(WB)
212	AFR	Tanzania	995	212.0	06(WB)
213	AFR	Western Sahara	993	213.0	(REG)
214	AFR	Uganda	893	214.0	06(WB)
215	AFR	Madagascar	878	215.0	06(WB)
216	CPA	Burma	838	216.0	05(WB)
217	SAS	Afghanistan	800	217.0	04(CIA)
218	AFR	Togo	776	218.0	06(WB)
219	AFR	Mozambique	739	219.0	06(WB)
220	AFR	Rwanda	738	220.0	06(WB)
221	AFR	Malawi	700	221.0	06(WB)
222	AFR	CAR	690	222.0	06(WB)
223	AFR	Eritrea	682	223.0	06(WB)
224	AFR	Ethiopia	636	224.0	06(WB)
225	AFR	Sierra Leone	630	225.0	06(WB)
226	AFR	Niger	629	226.0	06(WB)
227	AFR	Somalia	600	227.0	06(CIA)
228	AFR	GuineaBissau	478	228.0	06(WB)
229	AFR	Liberia	334	229.0	06(WB)
230	AFR	Burundi	333	230.0	06(WB)
231	AFR	Congo, Dem. Rep.	281	231.0	06(WB)

TABLE 1.4 – GROSS DOMESTIC PRODUCT AT PURCHASING POWER PARITIES PER CAPITA, 2006

TABLE 1.5 – ECONOMIC QUALITY-OF-LIFE INDEX, PRINCIPAL COMPONENT 1
OF THE ECONOMIC QUALITY-OF-LIFE INDICATORS, 2006

OBS	REGION	COUNTRY	EQLX	RANK	SOURCE
1	DME	Andorra	1.88840	1	PRIN1(EQL)
2	DME	Liechtenstein	1.75694	2	PRIN1(EQL)
3	DME	Iceland	1.68348	3	PRIN1(EQL)
4	DME	Japan	1.67993	4	PRIN1(EQL)
5	DME	San Marino	1.66405	5	PRIN1(EQL)
6	DME	Norway	1.66123	6	PRIN1(EQL)
7	DME	Luxembourg	1.63394	7	PRIN1(EQL)
8	DME	Switzerland	1.59419	8	PRIN1(EQL)
9	SEA	Hong Kong	1.58225	9	PRIN1(EQL)
10	DME	Sweden	1.55024	10	PRIN1(EQL)
11	SEA	Singapore	1.53012	11	PRIN1(EQL)
12	DME	Jersey	1.49627	12	PRIN1(EQL)
13	DME	Guernsey	1.47960	13	PRIN1(EQL)
14	DME	Italy	1.45144	14	PRIN1(EQL)
15	DME	France	1.44822	15	PRIN1(EQL)
16	DME	Finland	1.43638	16	PRIN1(EQL)
17	DME	Australia	1.43631	17	PRIN1(EQL)
18	SEA	Macao	1.43614	18	PRIN1(EQL)
19	DME	Austria	1.41664	19	PRIN1(EQL)
20	DME	Bermuda	1.40945	20	PRIN1(EQL)
21	DME	Ireland	1.40821	21	PRIN1(EQL)
22	DME	Netherlands	1.40398	22	PRIN1(EQL)
23	DME	Belgium	1.39595	23	PRIN1(EQL)
24	DME	Spain	1.39447	24	PRIN1(EQL)
25	DME	Canada	1.39144	25	PRIN1(EQL)
26	DME	Monaco	1.38891	26	PRIN1(EQL)
27	DME	Denmark	1.35200	27	PRIN1(EQL)
28	DME	Germany	1.34924	28	PRIN1(EQL)
29	DME	Gibraltar	1.33577	29	PRIN1(EQL)
30	LAM	Cayman Islands	1.33518	30	PRIN1(EQL)
31	DME	Greece	1.32032	31	PRIN1(EQL)
32	DME	United Kingdom	1.30831	32	PRIN1(EQL)
33	MEA	UAE	1.30243	33	PRIN1(EQL)
34	MEA	Cyprus	1.26816	34	PRIN1(EQL)
35	DME	United States	1.24665	35	PRIN1(EQL)
36	DME	Israel	1.23780	36	PRIN1(EQL)
37	DME	New Zealand	1.22513	37	PRIN1(EQL)
38	DME	Isle of Man	1.21412	38	PRIN1(EQL)
39	DME	Faeroe Islands	1.21118	39	PRIN1(EQL)
40	EEU	Slovenia	1.14351	40	PRIN1(EQL)
41	MEA	Kuwait	1.12998	41	PRIN1(EQL)
42	DME	Portugal	1.12580	42	PRIN1(EQL)
43	SEA	Brunei	1.10792	43	PRIN1(EQL)
44	LAM	Aruba	1.09973	44	PRIN1(EQL)
45	SEA	Korea, South	1.08471	45	PRIN1(EQL)
46	MEA	Qatar	1.03165	46	PRIN1(EQL)

	TABLE 1.5 – ECONOMIC QUALITY-OF-LIFE INDEX, PRINCIPAL COMPONENT 1 OF THE ECONOMIC QUALITY-OF-LIFE INDICATORS, 2006				
OBS	REGION	COUNTRY	EQLX	RANK	SOURCE
47	DME	Malta	1.02537	47	PRIN1(EQL)
48	EEU	Czechia	1.00466	48	PRIN1(EQL)
49	SEA	Taiwan	0.99146	49	PRIN1(EQL)
50	LAM	Virgin Islands, US	0.94719	50	PRIN1(EQL)
51	LAM	Guadeloupe	0.93710	51	PRIN1(EQL)
52	DME	Falkland Islands	0.90919	52	PRIN1(EQL)
53	LAM	Martinique	0.90105	53	PRIN1(EQL)
54	LAM	Virgin Islands, Brit.	0.89858	54	PRIN1(EQL)
55	AFR	Reunion	0.89577	55	PRIN1(EQL)
56	MEA	Bahrain	0.89023	56	PRIN1(EQL)
57	LAM	Puerto Rico	0.85406	57	PRIN1(EQL)
58	SEA	Guam	0.78886	58	PRIN1(EQL)
59	SEA	New Caledonia	0.75416	59	PRIN1(EQL)
60	SEA	French Polynesia	0.72832	60	PRIN1(EQL)
61	EEU	Croatia	0.71696	61	PRIN1(EQL)
62	USR	Estonia	0.70598	62	PRIN1(EQL)
63	SEA	Northern Mariana Is.	0.70325	63	PRIN1(EQL)
64	MEA	Oman	0.67776	64	PRIN1(EQL)
65	LAM	Neth. Antilles	0.67408	65	PRIN1(EQL)
66	LAM	Chile	0.67298	66	PRIN1(EQL)
67	EEU	Hungary	0.67035	67	PRIN1(EQL)
68	EEU	Poland	0.65741	68	PRIN1(EQL)
69	EEU	Slovakia	0.65531	69	PRIN1(EQL)
70	LAM	Bahamas	0.61320	70	PRIN1(EQL)
71	LAM	Barbados	0.60162	71	PRIN1(EQL)
72	DME	Greenland	0.53120	72	PRIN1(EQL)
73	LAM	Costa Rica	0.51779	73	PRIN1(EQL)
74	LAM	Antigua & Barbuda	0.50823	74	PRIN1(EQL)
75	USR	Lithuania	0.50695	75	PRIN1(EQL)
76	DME	St. Pierre & Miquelon	0.50001	76	PRIN1(EQL)
77	LAM	Guiana, French	0.49134	77	PRIN1(EQL)
78	USR	Latvia	0.46462	78	PRIN1(EQL)
79	LAM	Cuba	0.46433	79	PRIN1(EQL)
80	MEA	Saudi Arabia	0.45222	80	PRIN1(EQL)
81	SEA	Samoa, American	0.42486	81	PRIN1(EQL)
82	AFR	Seychelles	0.41979	82	PRIN1(EQL)
83	SEA	Malaysia	0.41099	83	PRIN1(EQL)
84	LAM	Uruguay	0.39917	84	PRIN1(EQL)
85	SEA	Palau	0.37703	85	PRIN1(EQL)
86	SEA	Turks & Caicos Is.	0.35906	86	PRIN1(EQL)
87	LAM	Argentina	0.33948	87	PRIN1(EQL)
88	EEU	Montenegro	0.33833	88	PRIN1(EQL)
89	EEU	Serbia	0.32570	89	PRIN1(EQL)
90	LAM	St. Lucia	0.31948	90	PRIN1(EQL)
91	LAM	St. Kitts & Nevis	0.31175	91	PRIN1(EQL)
92	MEA	Libya	0.30795	92	PRIN1(EQL)

OBS	REGION	COUNTRY	EQLX	RANK	SOURCE
		TABLE 1.5 – ECONOMIC QUALITY-OF-LIFE INDEX, PRINCIPAL COMPONENT 1 OF THE ECONOMIC QUALITY-OF-LIFE INDICATORS, 2006			
93	LAM	Anguilla	0.29118	93	PRIN1(EQL)
94	AFR	Mauritius	0.28375	94	PRIN1(EQL)
95	LAM	Venezuela	0.27523	95	PRIN1(EQL)
96	LAM	Dominica	0.26603	96	PRIN1(EQL)
97	LAM	Panama	0.23913	97	PRIN1(EQL)
98	LAM	Montserrat	0.23073	98	PRIN1(EQL)
99	EEU	Bulgaria	0.23056	99	PRIN1(EQL)
100	LAM	Mexico	0.22255	100	PRIN1(EQL)
101	LAM	Trinidad & Tobago	0.19629	101	PRIN1(EQL)
102	EEU	Romania	0.18103	102	PRIN1(EQL)
103	SEA	Thailand	0.16949	103	PRIN1(EQL)
104	EEU	Albania	0.14910	104	PRIN1(EQL)
105	EEU	Bosnia	0.14790	105	PRIN1(EQL)
106	EEU	Macedonia	0.12727	106	PRIN1(EQL)
107	USR	Russia	0.12051	107	PRIN1(EQL)
108	LAM	Brazil	0.10402	108	PRIN1(EQL)
109	LAM	Belize	0.09340	109	PRIN1(EQL)
110	USR	Belarus	0.08344	110	PRIN1(EQL)
111	MEA	Lebanon	0.06009	111	PRIN1(EQL)
112	LAM	Ecuador	0.04668	112	PRIN1(EQL)
113	MEA	Turkey	0.04001	113	PRIN1(EQL)
114	SEA	Cook Islands	0.03766	114	PRIN1(EQL)
115	MEA	Tunisia	0.02169	115	PRIN1(EQL)
116	LAM	Colombia	0.01172	116	PRIN1(EQL)
117	LAM	St. Vincent	0.00786	117	PRIN1(EQL)
118	SEA	Nauru	0.00323	118	PRIN1(EQL)
119	LAM	Grenada	-0.03310	119	PRIN1(EQL)
120	SAS	Sri Lanka	-0.05993	120	PRIN1(EQL)
121	MEA	Syria	-0.06489	121	PRIN1(EQL)
122	LAM	Peru	-0.07371	122	PRIN1(EQL)
123	LAM	Jamaica	-0.07739	123	PRIN1(EQL)
124	SEA	Tonga	-0.09681	124	PRIN1(EQL)
125	LAM	Suriname	-0.10177	125	PRIN1(EQL)
126	MEA	Iran	-0.10179	126	PRIN1(EQL)
127	LAM	Dominican Rep.	-0.12334	127	PRIN1(EQL)
128	SEA	Fiji	-0.12477	128	PRIN1(EQL)
129	LAM	El Salvador	-0.12650	129	PRIN1(EQL)
130	USR	Kazakhstan	-0.13349	130	PRIN1(EQL)
131	MEA	Jordan	-0.14853	131	PRIN1(EQL)
132	AFR	St. Helena	-0.15658	132	PRIN1(EQL)
133	MEA	Algeria	-0.17250	133	PRIN1(EQL)
134	CPA	China	-0.18357	134	PRIN1(EQL)
135	SEA	Wallis & Futuna	-0.18980	135	PRIN1(EQL)
136	SEA	Samoa, Western	-0.19626	136	PRIN1(EQL)
137	USR	Armenia	-0.20653	137	PRIN1(EQL)
138	USR	Ukraine	-0.23159	138	PRIN1(EQL)
139	SEA	Niue	-0.23513	139	PRIN1(EQL)

TABLE 1.5 – ECONOMIC QUALITY-OF-LIFE INDEX, PRINCIPAL COMPONENT 1 OF THE ECONOMIC QUALITY-OF-LIFE INDICATORS, 2006

OBS	REGION	COUNTRY	EQLX	RANK	SOURCE
140	MEA	West Bank	-0.26499	140	PRIN1(EQL)
141	LAM	Paraguay	-0.27012	141	PRIN1(EQL)
142	SAS	Maldives	-0.27419	142	PRIN1(EQL)
143	LAM	Guatemala	-0.27663	143	PRIN1(EQL)
144	SEA	Marshall Islands	-0.31390	144	PRIN1(EQL)
145	SEA	Micronesia	-0.32902	145	PRIN1(EQL)
146	MEA	Gaza Strip	-0.34185	146	PRIN1(EQL)
147	MEA	Egypt	-0.34437	147	PRIN1(EQL)
148	AFR	Cape Verde	-0.36299	148	PRIN1(EQL)
149	MEA	Morocco	-0.36603	149	PRIN1(EQL)
150	USR	Georgia	-0.36605	150	PRIN1(EQL)
151	AFR	Gabon	-0.36812	151	PRIN1(EQL)
152	SEA	Philippines	-0.37862	152	PRIN1(EQL)
153	LAM	Honduras	-0.39627	153	PRIN1(EQL)
154	SEA	Vanuatu	-0.40278	154	PRIN1(EQL)
155	AFR	Equatorial Guinea	-0.40628	155	PRIN1(EQL)
156	USR	Azerbaijan	-0.42409	156	PRIN1(EQL)
157	CPA	Vietnam	-0.44646	157	PRIN1(EQL)
158	SEA	Tuvalu	-0.45881	158	PRIN1(EQL)
159	USR	Moldova	-0.46292	159	PRIN1(EQL)
160	SEA	Indonesia	-0.46321	160	PRIN1(EQL)
161	LAM	Nicaragua	-0.47944	161	PRIN1(EQL)
162	AFR	South Africa	-0.52222	162	PRIN1(EQL)
163	USR	Turkmenistan	-0.53574	163	PRIN1(EQL)
164	AFR	Botswana	-0.57181	164	PRIN1(EQL)
165	MEA	Iraq	-0.58970	165	PRIN1(EQL)
166	AFR	Mayotte	-0.60871	166	PRIN1(EQL)
167	CPA	Mongolia	-0.63734	167	PRIN1(EQL)
168	AFR	Namibia	-0.66042	168	PRIN1(EQL)
169	LAM	Guyana	-0.66144	169	PRIN1(EQL)
170	LAM	Bolivia	-0.68887	170	PRIN1(EQL)
171	SAS	Bhutan	-0.69444	171	PRIN1(EQL)
172	SEA	Kiribati	-0.73007	172	PRIN1(EQL)
173	CPA	Korea, North	-0.76807	173	PRIN1(EQL)
174	USR	Uzbekistan	-0.78481	174	PRIN1(EQL)
175	USR	Kyrgyzstan	-0.83771	175	PRIN1(EQL)
176	SAS	India	-0.87632	176	PRIN1(EQL)
177	SAS	Pakistan	-0.94426	177	PRIN1(EQL)
178	SEA	Solomon Islands	-0.97488	178	PRIN1(EQL)
179	SEA	East Timor	-0.97937	179	PRIN1(EQL)
180	AFR	San Tome & Principe	-0.98320	180	PRIN1(EQL)
181	SEA	Tokelau	-1.00094	181	PRIN1(EQL)
182	AFR	Congo, Rep.	-1.00164	182	PRIN1(EQL)
183	MEA	Yemen	-1.01005	183	PRIN1(EQL)
184	CPA	Laos	-1.01736	184	PRIN1(EQL)
185	AFR	Senegal	-1.02031	185	PRIN1(EQL)
186	AFR	Mauritania	-1.02632	186	PRIN1(EQL)

TABLE 1.5 – ECONOMIC QUALITY-OF-LIFE INDEX, PRINCIPAL COMPONENT 1
OF THE ECONOMIC QUALITY-OF-LIFE INDICATORS, 2006

OBS	REGION	COUNTRY	EQLX	RANK	SOURCE
187	USR	Tajikistan	-1.03367	187	PRIN1(EQL)
188	AFR	Swaziland	-1.05192	188	PRIN1(EQL)
189	AFR	Sudan	-1.05628	189	PRIN1(EQL)
190	AFR	Comoros	-1.06332	190	PRIN1(EQL)
191	SEA	Papua New Guinea	-1.06500	191	PRIN1(EQL)
192	SAS	Bangladesh	-1.11589	192	PRIN1(EQL)
193	AFR	Djibouti	-1.13873	193	PRIN1(EQL)
194	AFR	Angola	-1.15050	194	PRIN1(EQL)
195	CPA	Cambodia	-1.16867	195	PRIN1(EQL)
196	SAS	Nepal	-1.18140	196	PRIN1(EQL)
197	AFR	Cameroon	-1.19277	197	PRIN1(EQL)
198	LAM	Haiti	-1.20561	198	PRIN1(EQL)
199	AFR	Ghana	-1.23972	199	PRIN1(EQL)
200	AFR	Kenya	-1.28819	200	PRIN1(EQL)
201	AFR	Ivory Coast	-1.29210	201	PRIN1(EQL)
202	AFR	Benin	-1.31767	202	PRIN1(EQL)
203	CPA	Burma	-1.37663	203	PRIN1(EQL)
204	AFR	Gambia	-1.38060	204	PRIN1(EQL)
205	AFR	Lesotho	-1.38807	205	PRIN1(EQL)
206	AFR	Nigeria	-1.38890	206	PRIN1(EQL)
207	AFR	Togo	-1.39682	207	PRIN1(EQL)
208	AFR	Madagascar	-1.40414	208	PRIN1(EQL)
209	AFR	Guinea	-1.41643	209	PRIN1(EQL)
210	AFR	Eritrea	-1.44815	210	PRIN1(EQL)
211	AFR	Tanzania	-1.44907	211	PRIN1(EQL)
212	AFR	Chad	-1.46592	212	PRIN1(EQL)
213	AFR	Mali	-1.47962	213	PRIN1(EQL)
214	AFR	Zambia	-1.49687	214	PRIN1(EQL)
215	AFR	Burkina Faso	-1.50285	215	PRIN1(EQL)
216	AFR	Western Sahara	-1.50370	216	PRIN1(EQL)
217	AFR	Uganda	-1.52233	217	PRIN1(EQL)
218	AFR	Zimbabwe	-1.54862	218	PRIN1(EQL)
219	AFR	Malawi	-1.64514	219	PRIN1(EQL)
220	AFR	Ethiopia	-1.65784	220	PRIN1(EQL)
221	AFR	Niger	-1.68211	221	PRIN1(EQL)
222	AFR	Somalia	-1.68518	222	PRIN1(EQL)
223	AFR	Mozambique	-1.69395	223	PRIN1(EQL)
224	AFR	Rwanda	-1.70054	224	PRIN1(EQL)
225	AFR	CAR	-1.71042	225	PRIN1(EQL)
226	SAS	Afghanistan	-1.78322	226	PRIN1(EQL)
227	AFR	GuineaBissau	-1.87129	227	PRIN1(EQL)
228	AFR	Sierra Leone	-1.88600	228	PRIN1(EQL)
229	AFR	Burundi	-1.99246	229	PRIN1(EQL)
230	AFR	Congo, Dem. Rep.	-2.05727	230	PRIN1(EQL)
231	AFR	Liberia	-2.07670	231	PRIN1(EQL)

		TABLE 1.6 – SOCIETAL INTEGRATION INDEX, OPENNESS OF POLITICAL PROCESS, 2006			
OBS	REGION	COUNTRY	SCINTX	RANK	SOURCE
1	LAM	Brazil	0.89174	1.0	06(CALC(CIA))
2	MEA	Morocco	0.89102	2.0	06(CALC(CIA))
3	LAM	Neth. Antilles	0.88017	3.0	06(CALC(CIA))
4	DME	Israel	0.87250	4.0	06(CALC(CIA))
5	EEU	Serbia	0.86898	5.0	06(CALC(CIA))
6	MEA	Lebanon	0.86169	6.0	06(CALC(CIA))
7	DME	Belgium	0.85760	7.0	06(CALC(CIA))
8	SEA	Indonesia	0.85226	8.0	06(CALC(CIA))
9	EEU	Bosnia	0.84921	9.0	06(CALC(CIA))
10	LAM	Haiti	0.84912	10.0	06(CALC(CIA))
11	SAS	India	0.84382	11.0	06(CALC(CIA))
12	SEA	Hong Kong	0.84000	12.0	06(CALC(CIA))
13	USR	Lithuania	0.83990	13.0	06(CALC(CIA))
14	USR	Latvia	0.83340	14.0	06(CALC(CIA))
15	USR	Armenia	0.83084	15.0	06(CALC(CIA))
16	AFR	Liberia	0.82910	16.0	06(CALC(CIA))
17	LAM	Ecuador	0.82640	17.0	06(CALC(CIA))
18	USR	Estonia	0.82443	18.0	06(CALC(CIA))
19	DME	Netherlands	0.81804	19.0	06(CALC(CIA))
20	LAM	Martinique	0.81383	20.0	05(CALC(CIA))
21	LAM	Chile	0.80861	21.0	06(CALC(CIA))
22	SEA	Vanuatu	0.80843	22.0	06(CALC(CIA))
23	LAM	Colombia	0.80766	23.0	06(CALC(CIA))
24	EEU	Romania	0.80748	24.0	06(CALC(CIA))
25	AFR	Congo, Dem. Rep.	0.80491	25.0	06(CALC(CIA))
26	AFR	Reunion	0.80300	26.0	05(CALC(CIA))
27	DME	Italy	0.80280	27.0	06(CALC(CIA))
28	SAS	Sri Lanka	0.80111	28.0	06(CALC(CIA))
29	DME	Finland	0.79700	29.0	06(CALC(CIA))
30	EEU	Slovenia	0.79580	30.0	06(CALC(CIA))
31	AFR	Mauritania	0.79579	31.0	06(CALC(CIA))
32	DME	Denmark	0.79562	32.0	06(CALC(CIA))
33	EEU	Bulgaria	0.79253	33.0	06(CALC(CIA))
34	SEA	Papua New Guinea	0.79236	34.0	06(CALC(CIA))
35	EEU	Slovakia	0.79227	35.0	06(CALC(CIA))
36	DME	Switzerland	0.79035	36.0	06(CALC(CIA))
37	DME	Faeroe Islands	0.78906	37.0	06(CALC(CIA))
38	DME	Norway	0.78078	38.0	06(CALC(CIA))
39	SEA	New Caledonia	0.77709	39.0	06(CALC(CIA))
40	LAM	Guatemala	0.76831	40.0	06(CALC(CIA))
41	SAS	Pakistan	0.76603	41.0	06(CALC(CIA))
42	EEU	Poland	0.76531	42.0	06(CALC(CIA))
43	AFR	CAR	0.76004	43.0	06(CALC(CIA))
44	DME	Sweden	0.75899	44.0	06(CALC(CIA))
45	DME	Greenland	0.75546	45.0	06(CALC(CIA))
46	EEU	Macedonia	0.75361	46.0	06(CALC(CIA))

		TABLE 1.6 – SOCIETAL INTEGRATION INDEX, OPENNESS OF POLITICAL PROCESS, 2006			
OBS	*REGION*	*COUNTRY*	*SCINTX*	*RANK*	*SOURCE*
47	SEA	Philippines	0.75172	47.0	06(CALC(CIA))
48	LAM	Argentina	0.75008	48.0	06(CALC(CIA))
49	MEA	Cyprus	0.74362	49.0	06(CALC(CIA))
50	EEU	Croatia	0.74290	50.0	06(CALC(CIA))
51	DME	San Marino	0.73889	51.0	06(CALC(CIA))
52	DME	Luxembourg	0.73722	52.0	06(CALC(CIA))
53	LAM	Peru	0.73528	53.0	06(CALC(CIA))
54	AFR	Niger	0.73146	54.0	06(CALC(CIA))
55	DME	Iceland	0.73066	55.0	06(CALC(CIA))
56	MEA	Kuwait	0.72400	56.0	06(CALC(CIA))
57	AFR	Malawi	0.72244	57.0	06(CALC(CIA))
58	EEU	Albania	0.72163	58.0	06(CALC(CIA))
59	LAM	Mexico	0.71998	59.0	06(CALC(CIA))
60	USR	Uzbekistan	0.71417	60.0	06(CALC(CIA))
61	DME	Germany	0.70954	61.0	06(CALC(CIA))
62	MEA	Iraq	0.70815	62.0	06(CALC(CIA))
63	USR	Ukraine	0.70702	63.0	06(CALC(CIA))
64	EEU	Montenegro	0.70416	64.0	06(CALC(CIA))
65	DME	Austria	0.70405	65.0	06(CALC(CIA))
66	DME	Ireland	0.69938	66.0	06(CALC(CIA))
67	LAM	Guiana, French	0.69806	67.0	05(CALC(CIA))
68	MEA	Bahrain	0.69750	68.0	06(CALC(CIA))
69	LAM	Costa Rica	0.69498	69.0	06(CALC(CIA))
70	MEA	Algeria	0.69263	70.0	06(CALC(CIA))
71	DME	Canada	0.69192	71.0	06(CALC(CIA))
72	LAM	Nicaragua	0.68998	72.0	06(CALC(CIA))
73	LAM	Suriname	0.68743	73.0	06(CALC(CIA))
74	LAM	Paraguay	0.68531	74.0	06(CALC(CIA))
75	AFR	Burkina Faso	0.67722	75.0	06(CALC(CIA))
76	EEU	Czechia	0.67705	76.0	06(CALC(CIA))
77	SEA	Northern Mariana Is.	0.67284	77.0	06(CALC(CIA))
78	LAM	Panama	0.67193	78.0	06(CALC(CIA))
79	LAM	El Salvador	0.67120	79.0	06(CALC(CIA))
80	LAM	Montserrat	0.66667	80.0	06(CALC(CIA))
81	DME	New Zealand	0.66403	81.0	06(CALC(CIA))
82	SEA	Kiribati	0.66100	82.0	06(CALC(CIA))
83	AFR	Mayotte	0.65928	83.0	06(CALC(CIA))
84	AFR	San Tome & Principe	0.65785	84.0	06(CALC(CIA))
85	SEA	Taiwan	0.65698	85.0	06(CALC(CIA))
86	AFR	GuineaBissau	0.64560	86.0	06(CALC(CIA))
87	AFR	Zambia	0.64125	87.0	06(CALC(CIA))
88	AFR	Mali	0.63640	88.0	06(CALC(CIA))
89	SEA	Macao	0.63020	89.0	06(CALC(CIA))
90	AFR	Ivory Coast	0.62635	90.0	06(CALC(CIA))
91	AFR	Rwanda	0.62281	91.0	06(CALC(CIA))
92	EEU	Hungary	0.61722	92.0	06(CALC(CIA))

TABLE 1.6 – SOCIETAL INTEGRATION INDEX,
OPENNESS OF POLITICAL PROCESS, 2006

OBS	REGION	COUNTRY	SCINTX	RANK	SOURCE
93	SEA	Solomon Islands	0.61520	93.0	06(CALC(CIA))
94	DME	Portugal	0.60926	94.0	06(CALC(CIA))
95	LAM	Virgin Islands, US	0.60444	95.0	06(CALC(CIA))
96	DME	Spain	0.59927	96.0	06(CALC(CIA))
97	DME	Liechtenstein	0.59520	97.0	06(CALC(CIA))
98	DME	United Kingdom	0.59180	98.0	06(CALC(CIA))
99	AFR	Ethiopia	0.59115	99.0	06(CALC(CIA))
100	SEA	East Timor	0.59065	100.0	06(CALC(CIA))
101	SEA	Korea, South	0.58500	101.0	06(CALC(CIA))
102	LAM	Uruguay	0.58157	102.0	06(CALC(CIA))
103	LAM	Dominican Rep.	0.58023	103.0	06(CALC(CIA))
104	SAS	Nepal	0.57875	104.0	06(CALC(CIA))
105	LAM	Honduras	0.57800	105.0	06(CALC(CIA))
106	LAM	Aruba	0.57596	106.0	06(CALC(CIA))
107	LAM	Guyana	0.57183	107.0	06(CALC(CIA))
108	LAM	Anguilla	0.57143	108.0	06(CALC(CIA))
109	LAM	Bolivia	0.56935	109.0	06(CALC(CIA))
110	USR	Moldova	0.56740	110.0	06(CALC(CIA))
111	CPA	Cambodia	0.56501	111.0	06(CALC(CIA))
112	DME	Andorra	0.56122	112.0	06(CALC(CIA))
113	USR	Russia	0.55747	113.0	06(CALC(CIA))
114	DME	France	0.55712	114.0	06(CALC(CIA))
115	DME	Japan	0.55707	115.0	06(CALC(CIA))
116	AFR	Burundi	0.55681	116.0	06(CALC(CIA))
117	AFR	Angola	0.55248	117.0	06(CALC(CIA))
118	SEA	Fiji	0.55068	118.0	06(CALC(CIA))
119	CPA	Mongolia	0.54931	119.0	06(CALC(CIA))
120	SEA	French Polynesia	0.54848	120.0	06(CALC(CIA))
121	AFR	Kenya	0.54707	121.0	06(CALC(CIA))
122	AFR	Madagascar	0.54594	122.0	06(CALC(CIA))
123	LAM	St. Kitts & Nevis	0.54545	123.0	06(CALC(CIA))
124	AFR	Lesotho	0.54403	124.0	06(CALC(CIA))
125	DME	Greece	0.54340	125.0	06(CALC(CIA))
126	SAS	Bangladesh	0.54153	126.0	06(CALC(CIA))
127	AFR	Nigeria	0.53339	127.0	06(CALC(CIA))
128	AFR	Ghana	0.52839	128.0	06(CALC(CIA))
129	LAM	Dominica	0.52608	129.0	06(CALC(CIA))
130	LAM	Cayman Islands	0.52444	130.0	06(CALC(CIA))
131	AFR	Congo, Rep.	0.52267	131.0	06(CALC(CIA))
132	AFR	Mauritius	0.51918	132.0	06(CALC(CIA))
133	AFR	Gabon	0.51875	133.0	06(CALC(CIA))
134	AFR	Cape Verde	0.51273	134.0	06(CALC(CIA))
135	MEA	Iran	0.51203	135.0	06(CALC(CIA))
136	DME	Australia	0.50320	136.0	06(CALC(CIA))
137	LAM	Venezuela	0.49905	137.0	06(CALC(CIA))
138	DME	Malta	0.49893	138.0	06(CALC(CIA))
139	DME	Gibraltar	0.49778	140.0	06(CALC(CIA))

TABLE 1.6 – SOCIETAL INTEGRATION INDEX,
OPENNESS OF POLITICAL PROCESS, 2006

OBS	REGION	COUNTRY	SCINTX	RANK	SOURCE
140	LAM	Grenada	0.49778	140.0	06(CALC(CIA))
141	SEA	Guam	0.49778	140.0	06(CALC(CIA))
142	DME	United States	0.49746	142.0	06(CALC(CIA))
143	AFR	Uganda	0.49697	143.0	06(CALC(CIA))
144	SEA	Cook Islands	0.49653	144.0	06(CALC(CIA))
145	SEA	Niue	0.49500	145.0	06(CALC(CIA))
146	LAM	Trinidad & Tobago	0.49383	146.0	06(CALC(CIA))
147	MEA	Turkey	0.49114	147.0	06(CALC(CIA))
148	LAM	Jamaica	0.49111	148.0	06(CALC(CIA))
149	AFR	South Africa	0.48917	149.0	06(CALC(CIA))
150	LAM	Puerto Rico	0.48135	150.0	06(CALC(CIA))
151	AFR	Chad	0.47950	151.0	06(CALC(CIA))
152	DME	Bermuda	0.47531	152.0	06(CALC(CIA))
153	SEA	Turks & Caicos Is.	0.47337	153.5	06(CALG(CIA))
154	LAM	Virgin Islands, Brit.	0.47337	153.5	06(CALC(CIA))
155	AFR	Benin	0.46799	155.0	06(CALC(CIA))
156	AFR	Mozambique	0.46080	156.0	06(CALC(CIA))
157	AFR	Zimbabwe	0.46069	157.0	06(CALC(CIA))
158	LAM	St. Lucia	0.45675	158.0	06(CALC(CIA))
159	SEA	Wallis & Futuna	0.45500	159.0	06(CALC(CIA))
160	AFR	Comoros	0.44444	160.0	06(CALC(CIA))
161	MEA	Syria	0.44355	161.0	06(CALC(CIA))
162	SEA	Samoa, Western	0.44148	162.0	06(CALC(CIA))
163	AFR	Seychelles	0.43772	163.0	06(CALC(CIA))
164	LAM	Bahamas	0.43375	164.0	06(CALC(CIA))
165	AFR	Senegal	0.42764	165.0	06(CALC(CIA))
166	AFR	Cameroon	0.42605	166.0	06(CALC(CIA))
167	LAM	Guadeloupe	0.41404	167.0	05(CALC(CIA))
168	AFR	Guinea	0.40705	168.0	06(CALC(CIA))
169	AFR	Namibia	0.40471	169.0	06(CALC(CIA))
170	LAM	Belize	0.39952	170.0	06(CALC(CIA))
171	MEA	Yemen	0.39900	171.0	06(CALC(CIA))
172	AFR	Sierra Leone	0.39238	172.0	06(CALC(CIA))
173	USR	Kazakhstan	0.36937	173.0	06(CALC(CIA))
174	LAM	Antigua & Barbuda	0.35986	174.0	06(CALC(CIA))
175	AFR	Botswana	0.35950	175.0	06(CALC(CIA))
176	LAM	Barbados	0.35778	176.0	06(CALC(CIA))
177	SEA	Tonga	0.34568	177.0	06(CALC(CIA))
178	MEA	Tunisia	0.34260	178.0	06(CALC(CIA))
179	USR	Tajikistan	0.33107	179.0	06(CALC(CIA))
180	LAM	St. Vincent	0.32000	180.0	06(CALC(CIA))
181	USR	Azerbaijan	0.31132	181.0	06(CALC(CIA))
182	SEA	Nauru	0.27778	182.0	06(CALC(CIA))
183	DME	St. Pierre & Miquelon	0.27701	183.0	06(CALC(CIA))
184	MEA	Jordan	0.27372	184.0	06(CALC(CIA))
185	DME	Isle of Man	0.22569	185.0	06(CALC(CIA))

TABLE 1.6 – SOCIETAL INTEGRATION INDEX, OPENNESS OF POLITICAL PROCESS, 2006					
OBS	REGION	COUNTRY	SCINTX	RANK	SOURCE
186	AFR	Tanzania	0.21933	186.0	06(CALC(CIA))
187	DME	Monaco	0.21875	187.0	06(CALC(CIA))
188	AFR	Togo	0.20698	188.0	06(CALC(CIA))
189	USR	Georgia	0.18000	189.0	06(CALC(CIA))
190	SEA	Malaysia	0.17051	190.0	06(CALC(CIA))
191	AFR	Gambia	0.11892	191.0	06(CALC(CIA))
192	SEA	Singapore	0.04677	192.0	06(CALC(CIA))
193	MEA	Egypt	0.04101	193.0	05(CALC(CIA))
194	AFR	Equatorial Guinea	0.03920	194.0	06(CALC(CIA))
195	CPA	Laos	0.03418	195.0	06(CALC(CIA))
196	AFR	Sudan	0.02739	196.0	06(CALC(CIA))
197	SAS	Afghanistan	0.00000	214.0	06(CALC(CIA))
198	USR	Belarus	0.00000	214.0	06(CALC(CIA))
199	SAS	Bhutan	0.00000	214.0	06(CALC(CIA))
200	SEA	Brunei	0.00000	214.0	06(CALC(CIA))
201	CPA	Burma	0.00000	214.0	06(CALC(CIA))
202	CPA	China	0.00000	214.0	06(CALC(CIA))
203	LAM	Cuba	0.00000	214.0	06(CALC(CIA))
204	AFR	Djibouti	0.00000	214.0	06(CALC(CIA))
205	AFR	Eritrea	0.00000	214.0	06(CALC(CIA))
206	DME	Falkland Islands	0.00000	214.0	06(CALC(CIA))
207	MEA	Gaza Strip	0.00000	214.0	06(CALC(CIA))
208	DME	Guernsey	0.00000	214.0	06(CALC(CIA))
209	DME	Jersey	0.00000	214.0	06(CALC(CIA))
210	CPA	Korea, North	0.00000	214.0	06(CALC(CIA))
211	USR	Kyrgyzstan	0.00000	214.0	06(CALC(CIA))
212	MEA	Libya	0.00000	214.0	06(CALC(CIA))
213	SAS	Maldives	0.00000	214.0	06(CALC(CIA))
214	SEA	Marshall Islands	0.00000	214.0	06(CALC(CIA))
215	SEA	Micronesia	0.00000	214.0	06(CALC(CIA))
216	MEA	Oman	0.00000	214.0	06(CALC(CIA))
217	SEA	Palau	0.00000	214.0	06(CALC(CIA))
218	MEA	Qatar	0.00000	214.0	06(CALC(CIA))
219	SEA	Samoa, American	0.00000	214.0	06(CALC(CIA))
220	MEA	Saudi Arabia	0.00000	214.0	06(CALC(CIA))
221	AFR	Somalia	0.00000	214.0	06(CALC(CIA))
222	AFR	St. Helena	0.00000	214.0	06(CALC(CIA))
223	AFR	Swaziland	0.00000	214.0	06(CALC(CIA))
224	SEA	Thailand	0.00000	214.0	06(CALC(CIA))
225	SEA	Tokelau	0.00000	214.0	06(CALC(CIA))
226	USR	Turkmenistan	0.00000	214.0	06(CALC(CIA))
227	SEA	Tuvalu	0.00000	214.0	06(CALC(CIA))
228	MEA	UAE	0.00000	214.0	06(CALC(CIA))
229	CPA	Vietnam	0.00000	214.0	06(CALC(CIA))
230	MEA	West Bank	0.00000	214.0	06(CALC(CIA))
231	AFR	Western Sahara	0.00000	214.0	06(CALC(CIA))

TABLE 1.7 – CIVIL AND POLITICAL RIGHTS INDEX, 2006					
OBS	REGION	COUNTRY	CPRX	RANK	SOURCE
1	DME	Finland	9	1.5	06(FH)
2	DME	Iceland	9	1.5	06(FH)
3	DME	Denmark	10	4.0	06(FH)
4	DME	Norway	10	4.0	06(FH)
5	DME	Sweden	10	4.0	06(FH)
6	DME	Belgium	11	7.5	06(FH)
7	DME	Luxembourg	11	7.5	06(FH)
8	DME	Netherlands	11	7.5	06(FH)
9	DME	Switzerland	11	7.5	06(FH)
10	DME	Liechtenstein	13	10.5	06(FH)
11	DME	New Zealand	13	10.5	06(FH)
12	DME	Andorra	14	13.0	06(FH)
13	SEA	Palau	14	13.0	06(FH)
14	DME	Portugal	14	13.0	06(FH)
15	DME	Ireland	15	15.5	06(FH)
16	SEA	Marshall Islands	15	15.5	06(FH)
17	LAM	Bahamas	16	19.5	06(FH)
18	USR	Estonia	16	19.5	06(FH)
19	DME	Germany	16	19.5	06(FH)
20	DME	Monaco	16	19.5	06(FH)
21	LAM	St. Vincent	16	19.5	06(FH)
22	DME	United States	16	19.5	06(FH)
23	LAM	Barbados	17	24.0	06(FH)
24	LAM	Jamaica	17	24.0	06(FH)
25	DME	San Marino	17	24.0	06(FH)
26	DME	Canada	18	28.0	06(FH)
27	LAM	Costa Rica	18	28.0	06(FH)
28	USR	Lithuania	18	28.0	06(FH)
29	DME	Malta	18	28.0	06(FH)
30	LAM	St. Lucia	18	28.0	06(FH)
31	DME	Australia	19	32.5	06(FH)
32	LAM	Dominica	19	32.5	06(FH)
33	USR	Latvia	19	32.5	06(FH)
34	DME	United Kingdom	19	32.5	06(FH)
35	DME	Faeroe Islands	20	35.0	(REG)
36	EEU	Czechia	20	38.5	06(FH)
37	DME	Japan	20	38.5	06(FH)
38	SEA	Micronesia	20	38.5	06(FH)
39	EEU	Slovakia	20	38.5	06(FH)
40	EEU	Slovenia	20	38.5	06(FH)
41	SEA	Taiwan	20	38.5	06(FH)
42	LAM	Neth. Antilles	21	42.0	(REG)
43	DME	Austria	21	46.5	06(FH)
44	LAM	Belize	21	46.5	06(FH)
45	DME	France	21	46.5	06(FH)
46	EEU	Hungary	21	46.5	06(FH)
47	EEU	Poland	21	46.5	06(FH)

TABLE 1.7 – CIVIL AND POLITICAL RIGHTS INDEX, 2006

OBS	REGION	COUNTRY	CPRX	RANK	SOURCE
48	LAM	Puerto Rico	21	46.5	03(EST)
49	DME	Spain	21	46.5	06(FH)
50	LAM	St. Kitts & Nevis	21	46.5	06(FH)
51	DME	Greenland	22	51.0	(REG)
52	MEA	Cyprus	22	52.0	06(FH)
53	AFR	Reunion	23	53.0	(REG)
54	LAM	Grenada	23	54.5	06(FH)
55	LAM	Suriname	23	54.5	06(FH)
56	SEA	New Caledonia	24	56.0	(REG)
57	DME	Bermuda	24	57.0	(REG)
58	AFR	Mali	24	58.0	06(FH)
59	LAM	Martinique	25	59.0	(REG)
60	SEA	Vanuatu	25	60.0	06(FH)
61	LAM	Cayman Islands	26	61.0	(REG)
62	LAM	Chile	26	63.5	06(FH)
63	AFR	Mauritius	26	63.5	06(FH)
64	LAM	Trinidad & Tobago	26	63.5	06(FH)
65	SEA	Tuvalu	26	63.5	06(FH)
66	LAM	Guyana	27	66.5	06(FH)
67	AFR	South Africa	27	66.5	06(FH)
68	LAM	Virgin Islands, US	27	68.0	(REG)
69	SEA	Fiji	28	71.5	06(FH)
70	AFR	Ghana	28	71.5	06(FH)
71	DME	Greece	28	71.5	06(FH)
72	DME	Israel	28	71.5	06(FH)
73	SEA	Kiribati	28	71.5	06(FH)
74	LAM	Uruguay	28	71.5	06(FH)
75	SEA	Hong Kong	29	76.5	06(FH)
76	SEA	Papua New Guinea	29	76.5	06(FH)
77	SEA	Samoa, Western	29	76.5	06(FH)
78	AFR	San Tome & Principe	29	76.5	06(FH)
79	DME	Gibraltar	29	79.0	(REG)
80	LAM	Aruba	30	80.0	(REG)
81	AFR	Benin	30	83.0	06(FH)
82	SEA	Korea, South	30	83.0	06(FH)
83	AFR	Namibia	30	83.0	06(FH)
84	SEA	Nauru	30	83.0	06(FH)
85	SEA	Solomon Islands	30	83.0	06(FH)
86	SEA	Northern Mariana Is.	30	86.0	(REG)
87	LAM	Virgin Islands, Brit.	30	87.0	(REG)
88	SEA	French Polynesia	31	88.0	(REG)
89	AFR	Cape Verde	32	89.5	06(FH)
90	SEA	Tonga	32	89.5	06(FH)
91	LAM	Guiana, French	32	91.0	(REG)
92	SEA	Guam	33	92.0	(REG)
93	LAM	Bolivia	33	93.0	06(FH)
94	EEU	Bulgaria	34	94.5	06(FH)
95	CPA	Mongolia	34	94.5	06(FH)

	TABLE 1.7 – CIVIL AND POLITICAL RIGHTS INDEX, 2006				
OBS	*REGION*	*COUNTRY*	*CPRX*	*RANK*	*SOURCE*
96	AFR	Botswana	35	96.5	06(FH)
97	DME	Italy	35	96.5	06(FH)
98	LAM	Guadeloupe	36	98.0	(REG)
99	LAM	Dominican Rep.	37	99.5	06(FH)
100	SAS	India	37	99.5	06(FH)
101	LAM	Antigua & Barbuda	38	101.5	06(FH)
102	AFR	Burkina Faso	38	101.5	06(FH)
103	DME	Isle of Man	38	103.0	(REG)
104	LAM	Brazil	39	105.5	06(FH)
105	EEU	Croatia	39	105.5	06(FH)
106	SEA	East Timor	39	105.5	06(FH)
107	LAM	Peru	39	105.5	06(FH)
108	EEU	Montenegro	40	109.0	06(FH)
109	SEA	Philippines	40	109.0	06(FH)
110	EEU	Serbia	40	109.0	06(FH)
111	LAM	Anguilla	41	111.0	(REG)
112	LAM	Ecuador	41	112.0	06(FH)
113	DME	Jersey	41	113.0	(REG)
114	SEA	Turks & Caicos Is.	41	114.0	(REG)
115	AFR	Lesotho	42	115.0	06(FH)
116	AFR	Mayotte	42	116.0	(REG)
117	SEA	Cook Islands	43	117.0	(REG)
118	LAM	El Salvador	43	119.0	06(FH)
119	AFR	Mozambique	43	119.0	06(FH)
120	LAM	Panama	43	119.0	06(FH)
121	DME	Guernsey	44	121.0	(REG)
122	LAM	Nicaragua	44	123.0	06(FH)
123	EEU	Romania	44	123.0	06(FH)
124	AFR	Senegal	44	123.0	06(FH)
125	LAM	Argentina	45	125.5	06(FH)
126	EEU	Bosnia	45	125.5	06(FH)
127	LAM	Montserrat	46	127.0	(REG)
128	AFR	Comoros	47	128.5	06(FH)
129	AFR	GuineaBissau	47	128.5	06(FH)
130	SEA	Niue	47	130.0	(REG)
131	LAM	Mexico	48	131.5	06(FH)
132	MEA	Turkey	48	131.5	06(FH)
133	EEU	Macedonia	49	133.5	06(FH)
134	AFR	Madagascar	49	133.5	06(FH)
135	EEU	Albania	50	136.0	06(FH)
136	AFR	Tanzania	50	136.0	06(FH)
137	SEA	Thailand	50	136.0	06(FH)
138	DME	Falkland Islands	50	138.0	(REG)
139	AFR	Congo, Rep.	51	139.0	06(FH)
140	LAM	Honduras	52	140.5	06(FH)
141	AFR	Uganda	52	140.5	06(FH)
142	SEA	Wallis & Futuna	53	142.0	(REG)
143	DME	St. Pierre & Miquelon	53	143.0	(REG)

	TABLE 1.7 – CIVIL AND POLITICAL RIGHTS INDEX, 2006				
OBS	REGION	COUNTRY	CPRX	RANK	SOURCE
144	USR	Ukraine	53	144.0	06(FH)
145	AFR	Nigeria	54	145.0	06(FH)
146	AFR	Malawi	55	146.0	06(FH)
147	MEA	Kuwait	56	147.5	06(FH)
148	AFR	Niger	56	147.5	06(FH)
149	SEA	Samoa, American	56	149.0	(REG)
150	USR	Georgia	57	151.0	06(FH)
151	AFR	Mauritania	57	151.0	06(FH)
152	LAM	Paraguay	57	151.0	06(FH)
153	LAM	Guatemala	58	154.5	06(FH)
154	SEA	Indonesia	58	154.5	06(FH)
155	AFR	Kenya	58	154.5	06(FH)
156	SAS	Sri Lanka	58	154.5	06(FH)
157	AFR	Sierra Leone	59	157.0	06(FH)
158	MEA	Lebanon	60	158.5	06(FH)
159	AFR	Seychelles	60	158.5	06(FH)
160	MEA	Algeria	61	164.0	06(FH)
161	AFR	CAR	61	164.0	06(FH)
162	CPA	Cambodia	61	164.0	06(FH)
163	LAM	Colombia	61	164.0	06(FH)
164	MEA	Egypt	61	164.0	06(FH)
165	MEA	Jordan	61	164.0	06(FH)
166	MEA	Morocco	61	164.0	06(FH)
167	SAS	Pakistan	61	164.0	06(FH)
168	MEA	Qatar	61	164.0	06(FH)
169	USR	Armenia	64	170.5	06(FH)
170	USR	Kyrgyzstan	64	170.5	06(FH)
171	AFR	Liberia	64	170.5	06(FH)
172	AFR	Zambia	64	170.5	06(FH)
173	AFR	Angola	65	176.0	06(FH)
174	SAS	Bhutan	65	176.0	06(FH)
175	AFR	Cameroon	65	176.0	06(FH)
176	AFR	Ivory Coast	65	176.0	06(FH)
177	SEA	Malaysia	65	176.0	06(FH)
178	USR	Moldova	65	176.0	06(FH)
179	MEA	UAE	65	176.0	06(FH)
180	SEA	Singapore	66	180.0	06(FH)
181	AFR	Gabon	67	181.5	06(FH)
182	AFR	Guinea	67	181.5	06(FH)
183	SAS	Bangladesh	68	183.5	06(FH)
184	LAM	Haiti	68	183.5	06(FH)
185	SAS	Afghanistan	69	185.5	06(FH)
186	AFR	Djibouti	69	185.5	06(FH)
187	SAS	Maldives	70	187.5	06(FH)
188	MEA	Oman	70	187.5	06(FH)
189	MEA	Iraq	71	189.5	06(FH)
190	SEA	Macao	71	189.5	03(EST)
191	AFR	St. Helena	72	191.0	(REG)

TABLE 1.7 – CIVIL AND POLITICAL RIGHTS INDEX, 2006					
OBS	*REGION*	*COUNTRY*	*CPRX*	*RANK*	*SOURCE*
192	MEA	Bahrain	72	193.0	06(FH)
193	USR	Russia	72	193.0	06(FH)
194	LAM	Venezuela	72	193.0	06(FH)
195	USR	Azerbaijan	73	196.0	06(FH)
196	AFR	Chad	73	196.0	06(FH)
197	AFR	Gambia	73	196.0	06(FH)
198	AFR	Burundi	74	198.0	06(FH)
199	AFR	Ethiopia	75	199.5	06(FH)
200	USR	Kazakhstan	75	199.5	06(FH)
201	USR	Tajikistan	76	201.0	06(FH)
202	SEA	Brunei	77	203.0	06(FH)
203	SAS	Nepal	77	203.0	06(FH)
204	AFR	Swaziland	77	203.0	06(FH)
205	AFR	Togo	78	205.0	06(FH)
206	MEA	Saudi Arabia	79	206.5	06(FH)
207	CPA	Vietnam	79	206.5	06(FH)
208	SEA	Tokelau	81	208.0	(REG)
209	AFR	Congo, Dem. Rep.	81	210.0	06(FH)
210	CPA	Laos	81	210.0	06(FH)
211	MEA	Yemen	81	210.0	06(FH)
212	CPA	China	83	213.0	06(FH)
213	AFR	Somalia	83	213.0	06(FH)
214	MEA	Tunisia	83	213.0	06(FH)
215	MEA	Iran	84	215.5	06(FH)
216	MEA	Syria	84	215.5	06(FH)
217	AFR	Rwanda	85	217.5	06(FH)
218	AFR	Sudan	85	217.5	06(FH)
219	MEA	Gaza Strip	86	219.5	06(FH)
220	MEA	West Bank	86	219.5	06(FH)
221	USR	Belarus	88	221.5	06(FH)
222	AFR	Equatorial Guinea	88	221.5	06(FH)
223	USR	Uzbekistan	90	223.5	06(FH)
224	AFR	Zimbabwe	90	223.5	06(FH)
225	AFR	Eritrea	91	225.0	06(FH)
226	AFR	Western Sahara	93	226.0	03(EST)
227	CPA	Burma	96	228.5	06(FH)
228	LAM	Cuba	96	228.5	06(FH)
229	MEA	Libya	96	228.5	06(FH)
230	USR	Turkmenistan	96	228.5	06(FH)
231	CPA	Korea, North	97	231.0	06(FH)

OBS	REGION	COUNTRY	HDX	RANK	SOURCE
1	DME	Liechtenstein	1.043	1.0	(REG)
2	DME	Andorra	1.005	2.0	(REG)
3	DME	San Marino	0.988	3.0	(REG)
4	DME	Jersey	0.974	4.0	(REG)
5	SEA	Macao	0.972	5.0	(REG)
6	DME	Monaco	0.970	6.0	(REG)
7	DME	Iceland	0.968	7.5	05(UN)
8	DME	Norway	0.968	7.5	05(UN)
9	DME	Guernsey	0.967	9.0	(REG)
10	DME	Australia	0.962	10.0	05(UN)
11	DME	Canada	0.961	11.0	05(UN)
12	DME	Ireland	0.959	12.0	05(UN)
13	DME	Sweden	0.956	13.0	05(UN)
14	DME	Switzerland	0.955	14.0	05(UN)
15	DME	Japan	0.953	15.5	05(UN)
16	DME	Netherlands	0.953	15.5	05(UN)
17	DME	Finland	0.952	17.5	05(UN)
18	DME	France	0.952	17.5	05(UN)
19	DME	Gibraltar	0.951	19.0	(REG)
20	DME	United States	0.951	20.0	05(UN)
21	DME	Denmark	0.949	21.5	05(UN)
22	DME	Spain	0.949	21.5	05(UN)
23	DME	Bermuda	0.948	23.0	(REG)
24	DME	Austria	0.948	24.0	05(UN)
25	DME	Belgium	0.946	25.5	05(UN)
26	DME	United Kingdom	0.946	25.5	05(UN)
27	DME	Luxembourg	0.944	27.0	05(UN)
28	DME	New Zealand	0.943	28.0	05(UN)
29	DME	Italy	0.941	29.0	05(UN)
30	SEA	Hong Kong	0.937	30.0	05(UN)
31	DME	Germany	0.935	31.0	05(UN)
32	DME	Isle of Man	0.935	32.0	(REG)
33	DME	Israel	0.932	33.0	05(UN)
34	DME	Greece	0.926	34.0	05(UN)
35	DME	Faeroe Islands	0.923	35.0	(REG)
36	LAM	Cayman Islands	0.923	36.0	(REG)
37	SEA	Singapore	0.922	37.0	05(UN)
38	SEA	Korea, South	0.921	38.0	05(UN)
39	SEA	Taiwan	0.917	39.0	(REG)
40	EEU	Slovenia	0.917	40.0	05(UN)
41	LAM	Aruba	0.908	41.0	(REG)
42	MEA	Cyprus	0.903	42.0	05(UN)
43	DME	Falkland Islands	0.898	43.0	(REG)
44	AFR	Reunion	0.897	44.0	(REG)
45	DME	Portugal	0.897	45.0	05(UN)
46	SEA	Brunei	0.894	46.0	05(UN)
47	LAM	Barbados	0.892	47.0	05(UN)

TABLE 1.8 – HUMAN DEVELOPMENT INDEX, 2005

TABLE 1.8 – HUMAN DEVELOPMENT INDEX, 2005

OBS	REGION	COUNTRY	HDX	RANK	SOURCE
48	EEU	Czechia	0.891	48.5	05(UN)
49	MEA	Kuwait	0.891	48.5	05(UN)
50	LAM	Guadeloupe	0.881	50.0	(REG)
51	DME	Malta	0.878	51.0	05(UN)
52	MEA	Qatar	0.875	52.0	05(UN)
53	EEU	Hungary	0.874	53.0	05(UN)
54	SEA	Guam	0.871	54.0	(REG)
55	EEU	Poland	0.870	55.0	05(UN)
56	LAM	Argentina	0.869	56.0	05(UN)
57	MEA	UAE	0.868	57.0	05(UN)
58	LAM	Chile	0.867	58.0	05(UN)
59	LAM	Martinique	0.867	59.0	(REG)
60	MEA	Bahrain	0.866	60.0	05(UN)
61	SEA	French Polynesia	0.865	61.0	(REG)
62	EEU	Slovakia	0.863	62.0	05(UN)
63	LAM	Puerto Rico	0.863	63.0	(REG)
64	SEA	New Caledonia	0.862	64.0	(REG)
65	USR	Lithuania	0.862	65.0	05(UN)
66	USR	Estonia	0.860	66.0	05(UN)
67	SEA	Northern Mariana Is.	0.858	67.0	(REG)
68	LAM	Virgin Islands, US	0.857	68.0	(REG)
69	LAM	Virgin Islands, Brit.	0.856	69.0	(REG)
70	USR	Latvia	0.855	70.0	05(UN)
71	LAM	Uruguay	0.852	71.0	05(UN)
72	EEU	Croatia	0.850	72.0	05(UN)
73	LAM	Neth. Antilles	0.846	73.0	(REG)
74	LAM	Costa Rica	0.846	74.0	05(UN)
75	LAM	Bahamas	0.845	75.0	05(UN)
76	AFR	Seychelles	0.843	76.0	05(UN)
77	LAM	Cuba	0.838	77.0	05(UN)
78	SEA	Palau	0.837	78.0	(REG)
79	EEU	Serbia	0.837	79.0	(REG)
80	LAM	Mexico	0.829	80.0	05(UN)
81	EEU	Bulgaria	0.824	81.0	05(UN)
82	DME	Greenland	0.823	82.0	(REG)
83	EEU	Montenegro	0.821	83.0	(REG)
84	LAM	St. Kitts & Nevis	0.821	84.0	05(UN)
85	SEA	Tonga	0.819	85.0	05(UN)
86	DME	St. Pierre & Miquelon	0.818	86.0	(REG)
87	MEA	Libya	0.818	87.0	05(UN)
88	LAM	Antigua & Barbuda	0.815	88.0	05(UN)
89	MEA	Oman	0.814	89.5	05(UN)
90	LAM	Trinidad & Tobago	0.814	89.5	05(UN)
91	EEU	Romania	0.813	91.0	05(UN)
92	LAM	Panama	0.812	92.5	05(UN)
93	MEA	Saudi Arabia	0.812	92.5	05(UN)
94	SEA	Malaysia	0.811	94.0	05(UN)
95	USR	Belarus	0.804	95.5	05(UN)

\multicolumn{6}{|c|}{TABLE 1.8 – HUMAN DEVELOPMENT INDEX, 2005}

OBS	REGION	COUNTRY	HDX	RANK	SOURCE
96	AFR	Mauritius	0.804	95.5	05(UN)
97	EEU	Bosnia	0.803	97.0	05(UN)
98	USR	Russia	0.802	98.0	05(UN)
99	EEU	Albania	0.801	99.5	05(UN)
100	EEU	Macedonia	0.801	99.5	05(UN)
101	LAM	Brazil	0.800	101.0	05(UN)
102	LAM	Dominica	0.798	102.0	05(UN)
103	LAM	St. Lucia	0.795	103.0	05(UN)
104	USR	Kazakhstan	0.794	104.0	05(UN)
105	LAM	Venezuela	0.792	105.0	05(UN)
106	LAM	Guiana, French	0.792	106.0	(REG)
107	LAM	Colombia	0.791	107.0	05(UN)
108	SEA	Turks & Caicos Is.	0.791	108.0	(REG)
109	SEA	Samoa, American	0.791	109.0	(REG)
110	USR	Ukraine	0.788	110.0	05(UN)
111	SEA	Samoa, Western	0.785	111.0	05(UN)
112	SEA	Thailand	0.781	112.0	05(UN)
113	LAM	Dominican Rep.	0.779	113.0	05(UN)
114	LAM	Belize	0.778	114.0	05(UN)
115	CPA	China	0.777	115.5	05(UN)
116	LAM	Grenada	0.777	115.5	05(UN)
117	LAM	Montserrat	0.777	117.0	(REG)
118	SEA	Nauru	0.776	118.0	(REG)
119	USR	Armenia	0.775	119.5	05(UN)
120	MEA	Turkey	0.775	119.5	05(UN)
121	LAM	Suriname	0.774	121.0	05(UN)
122	MEA	Jordan	0.773	122.5	05(UN)
123	LAM	Peru	0.773	122.5	05(UN)
124	LAM	Ecuador	0.772	124.5	05(UN)
125	MEA	Lebanon	0.772	124.5	05(UN)
126	SEA	Philippines	0.771	126.0	05(UN)
127	MEA	Tunisia	0.766	127.0	05(UN)
128	SEA	Fiji	0.762	128.0	05(UN)
129	LAM	St. Vincent	0.761	129.0	05(UN)
130	MEA	Iran	0.759	130.0	05(UN)
131	LAM	Paraguay	0.755	131.0	05(UN)
132	USR	Georgia	0.754	132.0	05(UN)
133	LAM	Anguilla	0.751	133.0	(REG)
134	LAM	Guyana	0.750	134.0	05(UN)
135	USR	Azerbaijan	0.746	135.0	05(UN)
136	SAS	Sri Lanka	0.743	136.0	05(UN)
137	SAS	Maldives	0.741	137.0	05(UN)
138	SEA	Cook Islands	0.738	138.0	(REG)
139	AFR	Cape Verde	0.736	139.5	05(UN)
140	LAM	Jamaica	0.736	139.5	05(UN)
141	LAM	El Salvador	0.735	141.0	05(UN)
142	MEA	Algeria	0.733	142.5	05(UN)
143	CPA	Vietnam	0.733	142.5	05(UN)

TABLE 1.8 – HUMAN DEVELOPMENT INDEX, 2005

OBS	REGION	COUNTRY	HDX	RANK	SOURCE
144	SEA	Niue	0.731	144.0	(REG)
145	MEA	Gaza Strip	0.731	145.5	05(UN)
146	MEA	West Bank	0.731	145.5	05(UN)
147	SEA	Indonesia	0.728	147.0	05(UN)
148	MEA	Syria	0.724	148.0	05(UN)
149	USR	Turkmenistan	0.713	149.0	05(UN)
150	LAM	Nicaragua	0.710	150.0	05(UN)
151	MEA	Egypt	0.708	151.5	05(UN)
152	USR	Moldova	0.708	151.5	05(UN)
153	USR	Uzbekistan	0.702	153.0	05(UN)
154	LAM	Honduras	0.700	154.5	05(UN)
155	CPA	Mongolia	0.700	154.5	05(UN)
156	SEA	Wallis & Futuna	0.698	156.0	(REG)
157	USR	Kyrgyzstan	0.696	157.0	05(UN)
158	LAM	Bolivia	0.695	158.0	05(UN)
159	LAM	Guatemala	0.689	159.0	05(UN)
160	SEA	Micronesia	0.686	160.0	(REG)
161	AFR	St. Helena	0.683	161.0	(REG)
162	AFR	Gabon	0.677	162.0	05(UN)
163	AFR	South Africa	0.674	163.5	05(UN)
164	SEA	Vanuatu	0.674	163.5	05(UN)
165	USR	Tajikistan	0.673	165.0	05(UN)
166	SEA	Marshall Islands	0.660	166.0	(REG)
167	AFR	Botswana	0.654	167.5	05(UN)
168	AFR	San Tome & Principe	0.654	167.5	05(UN)
169	SEA	Tuvalu	0.652	169.0	(REG)
170	AFR	Namibia	0.650	170.0	05(UN)
171	MEA	Morocco	0.646	171.0	05(UN)
172	AFR	Equatorial Guinea	0.642	172.0	05(UN)
173	SEA	Kiribati	0.632	173.0	(REG)
174	AFR	Mayotte	0.629	174.0	(REG)
175	SAS	India	0.619	175.0	05(UN)
176	MEA	Iraq	0.615	176.0	(REG)
177	SEA	Solomon Islands	0.602	177.0	05(UN)
178	CPA	Laos	0.601	178.0	05(UN)
179	CPA	Cambodia	0.598	179.0	05(UN)
180	CPA	Korea, North	0.598	180.0	(REG)
181	CPA	Burma	0.583	181.0	05(UN)
182	SAS	Bhutan	0.579	182.0	05(UN)
183	SEA	Tokelau	0.570	183.0	(REG)
184	AFR	Comoros	0.561	184.0	05(UN)
185	AFR	Ghana	0.553	185.0	05(UN)
186	SAS	Pakistan	0.551	186.0	05(UN)
187	AFR	Mauritania	0.550	187.0	05(UN)
188	AFR	Lesotho	0.549	188.0	05(UN)
189	AFR	Congo, Rep.	0.548	189.0	05(UN)
190	SAS	Bangladesh	0.547	190.5	05(UN)
191	AFR	Swaziland	0.547	190.5	05(UN)

TABLE 1.8 – HUMAN DEVELOPMENT INDEX, 2005					
OBS	*REGION*	*COUNTRY*	*HDX*	*RANK*	*SOURCE*
192	SAS	Nepal	0.534	192.0	05(UN)
193	AFR	Madagascar	0.533	193.0	05(UN)
194	AFR	Cameroon	0.532	194.0	05(UN)
195	SEA	Papua New Guinea	0.530	195.0	05(UN)
196	LAM	Haiti	0.529	196.0	05(UN)
197	AFR	Sudan	0.526	197.0	05(UN)
198	AFR	Kenya	0.521	198.0	05(UN)
199	AFR	Djibouti	0.516	199.0	05(UN)
200	AFR	Western Sahara	0.515	200.0	(REG)
201	SEA	East Timor	0.514	201.0	05(UN)
202	AFR	Zimbabwe	0.513	202.0	05(UN)
203	AFR	Togo	0.512	203.0	05(UN)
204	MEA	Yemen	0.508	204.0	05(UN)
205	AFR	Uganda	0.505	205.0	05(UN)
206	AFR	Gambia	0.502	206.0	05(UN)
207	AFR	Senegal	0.499	207.0	05(UN)
208	AFR	Eritrea	0.483	208.0	05(UN)
209	AFR	Somalia	0.471	209.0	(REG)
210	AFR	Nigeria	0.470	210.0	05(UN)
211	AFR	Tanzania	0.467	211.0	05(UN)
212	AFR	Guinea	0.456	212.0	05(UN)
213	AFR	Rwanda	0.452	213.0	05(UN)
214	AFR	Angola	0.446	214.0	05(UN)
215	SAS	Afghanistan	0.442	215.0	(REG)
216	AFR	Benin	0.437	216.5	05(UN)
217	AFR	Malawi	0.437	216.5	05(UN)
218	AFR	Zambia	0.434	218.0	05(UN)
219	AFR	Ivory Coast	0.432	219.0	05(UN)
220	AFR	Burundi	0.413	220.0	05(UN)
221	AFR	Congo, Dem. Rep.	0.411	221.0	05(UN)
222	AFR	Ethiopia	0.406	222.0	05(UN)
223	AFR	Liberia	0.390	223.0	(REG)
224	AFR	Chad	0.388	224.0	05(UN)
225	AFR	CAR	0.384	225.5	05(UN)
226	AFR	Mozambique	0.384	225.5	05(UN)
227	AFR	Mali	0.380	227.0	05(UN)
228	AFR	GuineaBissau	0.374	228.5	05(UN)
229	AFR	Niger	0.374	228.5	05(UN)
230	AFR	Burkina Faso	0.370	230.0	05(UN)
231	AFR	Sierra Leone	0.336	231.0	05(UN)

TABLE 1.9 – GINI COEFFICIENT OF INCOME INEQUALITY, 2006

OBS	REGION	COUNTRY	GINI	RANK	SOURCE
1	CPA	Korea, North	20.00	1.0	06(EST)
2	LAM	Cuba	22.00	2.0	06(EST)
3	DME	Liechtenstein	23.47	3.0	(REG)
4	DME	Iceland	24.00	4.0	06(EST)
5	DME	Denmark	24.70	5.0	06(WB)
6	DME	Japan	24.85	6.0	06(WB)
7	DME	Sweden	25.00	7.0	06(WB)
8	EEU	Czechia	25.40	8.0	06(WB)
9	DME	Norway	25.79	9.0	06(WB)
10	EEU	Slovakia	25.81	10.0	06(WB)
11	DME	Finland	26.88	11.0	06(WB)
12	USR	Belarus	27.95	12.0	06(WB)
13	USR	Ukraine	28.24	13.0	06(WB)
14	DME	Germany	28.31	14.0	06(WB)
15	DME	Jersey	28.63	15.0	(REG)
16	EEU	Croatia	29.03	16.0	06(WB)
17	DME	Austria	29.15	17.0	06(WB)
18	EEU	Bulgaria	29.21	18.0	06(WB)
19	DME	Andorra	29.65	19.0	(REG)
20	AFR	Ethiopia	29.97	20.0	06(WB)
21	EEU	Serbia	30.02	21.0	06(WB)
22	EEU	Hungary	30.06	22.0	06(WB)
23	USR	Kyrgyzstan	30.31	23.0	06(WB)
24	DME	San Marino	30.48	24.0	(REG)
25	DME	Luxembourg	30.76	25.0	06(WB)
26	DME	Netherlands	30.90	26.0	06(WB)
27	EEU	Slovenia	30.94	27.0	06(WB)
28	DME	Bermuda	31.09	28.0	(REG)
29	EEU	Albania	31.10	29.0	06(WB)
30	SAS	Pakistan	31.18	30.0	06(WB)
31	DME	Guernsey	31.39	31.0	(REG)
32	EEU	Romania	31.54	32.0	06(WB)
33	SEA	Korea, South	31.59	33.0	06(WB)
34	DME	Monaco	32.09	34.0	(REG)
35	DME	Canada	32.56	35.0	06(WB)
36	SEA	Taiwan	32.60	36.0	02(CIA)
37	DME	France	32.74	37.0	06(WB)
38	CPA	Mongolia	32.80	38.0	06(WB)
39	DME	Belgium	32.97	39.0	06(WB)
40	SAS	Bangladesh	33.20	40.0	06(WB)
41	USR	Moldova	33.22	41.0	06(WB)
42	LAM	Montserrat	33.38	42.0	(REG)
43	USR	Tajikistan	33.59	43.0	06(WB)
44	DME	Switzerland	33.68	44.0	06(WB)
45	USR	Armenia	33.77	45.0	06(WB)
46	MEA	Cyprus	33.77	46.0	(REG)
47	USR	Kazakhstan	33.91	47.0	06(WB)

OBS	REGION	COUNTRY	GINI	RANK	SOURCE
		TABLE 1.9 – GINI COEFFICIENT OF INCOME INEQUALITY, 2006			
48	MEA	UAE	34.18	48.0	(REG)
49	DME	Greece	34.27	49.0	06(WB)
50	DME	Ireland	34.28	50.0	06(WB)
51	MEA	Egypt	34.41	51.0	06(WB)
52	MEA	Syria	34.55	52.0	(REG)
53	SEA	Samoa, American	34.57	53.0	(REG)
54	AFR	Tanzania	34.62	54.0	06(WB)
55	CPA	Laos	34.65	55.0	06(WB)
56	DME	Spain	34.66	56.0	06(WB)
57	DME	Isle of Man	34.85	57.0	(REG)
58	EEU	Poland	34.91	58.0	06(WB)
59	MEA	Qatar	35.09	59.0	(REG)
60	DME	Australia	35.19	60.0	06(WB)
61	DME	Gibraltar	35.30	61.0	(REG)
62	MEA	Algeria	35.30	62.0	06(WB)
63	DME	St. Pierre & Miquelon	35.42	63.0	(REG)
64	LAM	Virgin Islands, US	35.60	64.0	(REG)
65	AFR	Eritrea	35.66	65.0	(REG)
66	LAM	Cayman Islands	35.72	66.0	(REG)
67	USR	Latvia	35.75	67.0	06(WB)
68	SEA	Guam	35.76	68.0	(REG)
69	EEU	Bosnia	35.79	69.0	06(WB)
70	USR	Lithuania	35.83	70.0	06(WB)
71	DME	United Kingdom	35.97	71.0	06(WB)
72	USR	Estonia	36.03	72.5	06(WB)
73	DME	Italy	36.03	72.5	06(WB)
74	MEA	Kuwait	36.04	74.0	(REG)
75	AFR	St. Helena	36.15	75.0	(REG)
76	DME	New Zealand	36.17	76.0	06(WB)
77	MEA	West Bank	36.22	77.0	(REG)
78	AFR	Benin	36.48	78.0	06(WB)
79	LAM	Aruba	36.49	79.0	(REG)
80	USR	Azerbaijan	36.50	80.0	06(WB)
81	SEA	Tokelau	36.55	81.0	(REG)
82	USR	Uzbekistan	36.77	82.0	06(WB)
83	SEA	Brunei	36.78	83.0	(REG)
84	SAS	India	36.80	84.0	06(WB)
85	SEA	Nauru	36.82	85.0	(REG)
86	DME	Faeroe Islands	36.91	86.0	(REG)
87	CPA	Vietnam	37.05	87.0	06(WB)
88	SEA	Northern Mariana Is.	37.14	88.0	(REG)
89	DME	Falkland Islands	37.15	89.0	(REG)
90	MEA	Gaza Strip	37.22	90.0	(REG)
91	SEA	New Caledonia	37.44	91.0	(REG)
92	SEA	French Polynesia	37.66	92.0	(REG)
93	MEA	Yemen	37.70	93.0	06(WB)
94	LAM	Martinique	37.82	94.0	(REG)
95	MEA	Bahrain	37.85	95.0	(REG)

TABLE 1.9 – GINI COEFFICIENT OF INCOME INEQUALITY, 2006					
OBS	REGION	COUNTRY	GINI	RANK	SOURCE
96	DME	Malta	37.91	96.0	(REG)
97	SEA	Tuvalu	38.13	97.0	(REG)
98	MEA	Iran	38.35	98.0	06(WB)
99	MEA	Oman	38.39	99.0	(REG)
100	DME	Portugal	38.45	100.0	06(WB)
101	EEU	Montenegro	38.45	101.0	(REG)
102	MEA	Libya	38.56	102.0	(REG)
103	AFR	Guinea	38.60	103.0	06(WB)
104	AFR	Reunion	38.76	104.0	(REG)
105	MEA	Jordan	38.84	105.0	06(WB)
106	LAM	Trinidad & Tobago	38.88	106.0	06(WB)
107	CPA	Burma	38.89	107.0	(REG)
108	EEU	Macedonia	38.98	108.0	06(WB)
109	AFR	Malawi	39.00	109.0	06(WB)
110	AFR	Mauritania	39.02	110.0	06(WB)
111	LAM	Guadeloupe	39.15	111.0	(REG)
112	DME	Israel	39.20	112.0	06(WB)
113	AFR	Congo, Dem. Rep.	39.22	113.0	(REG)
114	SEA	Indonesia	39.41	114.0	06(WB)
115	MEA	Morocco	39.50	115.0	06(WB)
116	AFR	Burkina Faso	39.51	116.0	06(WB)
117	AFR	Togo	39.55	117.0	(REG)
118	LAM	Guiana, French	39.60	118.0	(REG)
119	AFR	Somalia	39.77	119.0	(REG)
120	MEA	Tunisia	39.80	120.0	06(WB)
121	AFR	Seychelles	39.87	121.0	(REG)
122	AFR	Western Sahara	39.93	122.0	(REG)
123	USR	Russia	39.93	123.0	06(WB)
124	AFR	Sierra Leone	39.96	124.0	06(WB)
125	LAM	Neth. Antilles	40.04	125.0	(REG)
126	SEA	Wallis & Futuna	40.10	126.0	(REG)
127	AFR	Mali	40.10	127.0	06(WB)
128	SAS	Sri Lanka	40.17	128.0	06(WB)
129	LAM	Antigua & Barbuda	40.45	129.0	(REG)
130	SEA	Fiji	40.52	130.0	(REG)
131	USR	Turkmenistan	40.76	131.0	06(WB)
132	USR	Georgia	40.80	132.5	06(WB)
133	AFR	Ghana	40.80	132.5	06(WB)
134	DME	United States	40.81	134.0	06(WB)
135	SAS	Maldives	40.99	135.0	(REG)
136	LAM	Puerto Rico	41.05	136.0	(REG)
137	AFR	Senegal	41.25	137.0	06(WB)
138	LAM	Barbados	41.36	138.0	(REG)
139	SEA	Niue	41.37	139.0	(REG)
140	DME	Greenland	41.47	140.0	(REG)
141	AFR	Comoros	41.64	141.0	(REG)
142	CPA	Cambodia	41.71	142.0	06(WB)
143	AFR	Sudan	41.82	143.0	(REG)

TABLE 1.9 – GINI COEFFICIENT OF INCOME INEQUALITY, 2006					
OBS	REGION	COUNTRY	GINI	RANK	SOURCE
144	SEA	Thailand	41.98	144.0	06(WB)
145	SEA	Turks & Caicos Is.	42.20	145.0	(REG)
146	MEA	Saudi Arabia	42.30	146.0	(REG)
147	AFR	Mauritius	42.34	147.0	(REG)
148	AFR	Burundi	42.40	148.0	05(WB)
149	SEA	Palau	42.42	149.0	(REG)
150	SEA	Singapore	42.48	150.0	06(WB)
151	AFR	Kenya	42.50	151.0	06(WB)
152	AFR	Liberia	42.54	152.0	(REG)
153	LAM	St. Lucia	42.58	153.0	06(WB)
154	SEA	Tonga	42.66	154.0	(REG)
155	LAM	Belize	42.79	155.0	(REG)
156	LAM	Virgin Islands, Brit.	42.82	156.0	(REG)
157	LAM	Dominica	42.85	157.0	(REG)
158	MEA	Iraq	42.91	158.0	(REG)
159	LAM	Bahamas	43.07	159.0	(REG)
160	LAM	Nicaragua	43.11	160.0	06(WB)
161	LAM	Guyana	43.20	161.0	06(WB)
162	SEA	Macao	43.40	162.0	03(WB)
163	SEA	Hong Kong	43.44	163.0	06(WB)
164	LAM	Anguilla	43.51	164.0	(REG)
165	MEA	Turkey	43.64	165.0	06(WB)
166	AFR	Nigeria	43.70	166.0	06(WB)
167	SEA	Samoa, Western	43.79	167.0	(REG)
168	LAM	St. Vincent	43.84	168.0	(REG)
169	LAM	Grenada	43.89	169.0	(REG)
170	MEA	Lebanon	43.90	170.0	(REG)
171	SEA	East Timor	44.21	171.0	(REG)
172	LAM	St. Kitts & Nevis	44.49	172.0	(REG)
173	SEA	Vanuatu	44.51	173.0	(REG)
174	SEA	Philippines	44.53	174.0	06(WB)
175	AFR	Ivory Coast	44.58	175.0	06(WB)
176	AFR	Cameroon	44.60	176.0	05(WB)
177	SEA	Cook Islands	44.66	177.0	(REG)
178	AFR	Djibouti	45.29	178.0	(REG)
179	SEA	Solomon Islands	45.38	179.0	(REG)
180	AFR	San Tome & Principe	45.51	180.0	(REG)
181	LAM	Jamaica	45.51	181.0	06(WB)
182	AFR	Uganda	45.70	182.0	06(WB)
183	SAS	Afghanistan	45.77	183.0	(REG)
184	LAM	Mexico	46.05	184.0	06(WB)
185	LAM	Uruguay	46.14	185.0	06(WB)
186	AFR	Chad	46.28	186.0	(REG)
187	SAS	Bhutan	46.38	187.0	(REG)
188	AFR	Rwanda	46.79	188.0	06(WB)
189	CPA	China	46.90	189.0	06(WB)
190	LAM	Suriname	47.03	190.0	(REG)
191	AFR	GuineaBissau	47.05	191.0	06(WB)

TABLE 1.9 – GINI COEFFICIENT OF INCOME INEQUALITY, 2006

OBS	REGION	COUNTRY	GINI	RANK	SOURCE
192	SEA	Micronesia	47.13	192.0	(REG)
193	SAS	Nepal	47.17	193.0	06(WB)
194	SEA	Kiribati	47.27	194.0	(REG)
195	AFR	Mozambique	47.29	195.0	06(WB)
196	AFR	Gambia	47.36	196.0	06(WB)
197	AFR	Madagascar	47.45	197.0	06(WB)
198	LAM	Costa Rica	48.20	198.5	06(WB)
199	LAM	Venezuela	48.20	198.5	06(WB)
200	AFR	Mayotte	48.53	200.0	(REG)
201	AFR	Congo, Rep.	48.55	201.0	(REG)
202	SEA	Malaysia	49.15	202.0	06(WB)
203	LAM	Guatemala	49.39	203.0	06(WB)
204	LAM	Dominican Rep.	49.90	204.0	06(WB)
205	AFR	Zimbabwe	50.10	205.0	06(WB)
206	AFR	Gabon	50.19	206.0	(REG)
207	AFR	Swaziland	50.40	207.0	06(WB)
208	AFR	Cape Verde	50.52	208.0	06(WB)
209	AFR	Niger	50.54	209.0	06(WB)
210	SEA	Marshall Islands	50.58	210.0	(REG)
211	AFR	Zambia	50.80	211.0	06(WB)
212	SEA	Papua New Guinea	50.90	212.0	06(WB)
213	LAM	Argentina	51.32	213.0	06(WB)
214	LAM	Peru	52.02	214.0	06(WB)
215	LAM	El Salvador	52.36	215.0	06(WB)
216	AFR	Angola	52.41	216.0	(REG)
217	LAM	Ecuador	53.55	217.0	06(WB)
218	LAM	Honduras	53.84	218.0	06(WB)
219	LAM	Chile	54.92	219.0	06(WB)
220	AFR	Equatorial Guinea	55.03	220.0	(REG)
221	LAM	Panama	56.08	221.0	06(WB)
222	LAM	Colombia	56.23	222.0	06(WB)
223	LAM	Brazil	56.60	223.0	06(WB)
224	AFR	South Africa	57.78	224.0	06(WB)
225	LAM	Paraguay	58.36	225.0	06(WB)
226	LAM	Haiti	59.21	226.0	06(WB)
227	LAM	Bolivia	60.05	227.0	06(WB)
228	AFR	Botswana	60.51	228.0	06(WB)
229	AFR	CAR	61.33	229.0	06(WB)
230	AFR	Lesotho	63.20	230.0	06(WB)
231	AFR	Namibia	74.33	231.0	06(WB)

OBS	REGION	COUNTRY	PQLX	RANK	SOURCE
TABLE 1.10 – HUMAN RIGHTS INDEX, PRINCIPAL COMPONENT 1 OF THE POLITICAL QUALITY-OF-LIFE INDICATORS, 2006					
1	DME	Iceland	1.98387	1	PRIN1(PQL)
2	DME	Liechtenstein	1.96925	2	PRIN1(PQL)
3	DME	Denmark	1.96626	3	PRIN1(PQL)
4	DME	Norway	1.96415	4	PRIN1(PQL)
5	DME	Sweden	1.93498	5	PRIN1(PQL)
6	DME	Finland	1.92613	6	PRIN1(PQL)
7	DME	Netherlands	1.79006	7	PRIN1(PQL)
8	DME	Belgium	1.75108	8	PRIN1(PQL)
9	DME	San Marino	1.69539	9	PRIN1(PQL)
10	DME	Luxembourg	1.68453	10	PRIN1(PQL)
11	DME	Switzerland	1.67905	11	PRIN1(PQL)
12	DME	Andorra	1.62817	12	PRIN1(PQL)
13	DME	Germany	1.61601	13	PRIN1(PQL)
14	DME	Japan	1.53017	14	PRIN1(PQL)
15	EEU	Slovakia	1.52856	15	PRIN1(PQL)
16	DME	Austria	1.52475	16	PRIN1(PQL)
17	EEU	Slovenia	1.50897	17	PRIN1(PQL)
18	DME	Ireland	1.49871	18	PRIN1(PQL)
19	DME	Canada	1.49380	19	PRIN1(PQL)
20	EEU	Czechia	1.48711	20	PRIN1(PQL)
21	DME	New Zealand	1.39862	21	PRIN1(PQL)
22	DME	Faeroe Islands	1.33431	22	PRIN1(PQL)
23	USR	Estonia	1.31271	23	PRIN1(PQL)
24	SEA	Taiwan	1.30785	24	PRIN1(PQL)
25	USR	Lithuania	1.30386	25	PRIN1(PQL)
26	MEA	Cyprus	1.29297	26	PRIN1(PQL)
27	DME	France	1.26491	27	PRIN1(PQL)
28	USR	Latvia	1.26336	28	PRIN1(PQL)
29	DME	Spain	1.24342	29	PRIN1(PQL)
30	DME	Israel	1.22645	30	PRIN1(PQL)
31	DME	United Kingdom	1.22402	31	PRIN1(PQL)
32	EEU	Hungary	1.21710	32	PRIN1(PQL)
33	EEU	Poland	1.21673	33	PRIN1(PQL)
34	DME	Australia	1.19266	34	PRIN1(PQL)
35	AFR	Reunion	1.17074	35	PRIN1(PQL)
36	DME	Bermuda	1.17036	36	PRIN1(PQL)
37	DME	Italy	1.14326	37	PRIN1(PQL)
38	DME	Portugal	1.13502	38	PRIN1(PQL)
39	LAM	Neth. Antilles	1.12315	39	PRIN1(PQL)
40	LAM	Martinique	1.10533	40	PRIN1(PQL)
41	SEA	Korea, South	1.08736	41	PRIN1(PQL)
42	SEA	New Caledonia	1.08509	42	PRIN1(PQL)
43	EEU	Bulgaria	1.06822	43	PRIN1(PQL)
44	DME	Monaco	1.05574	44	PRIN1(PQL)
45	SEA	Hong Kong	1.05417	45	PRIN1(PQL)
46	EEU	Serbia	1.04819	46	PRIN1(PQL)

		TABLE 1.10 – HUMAN RIGHTS INDEX, PRINCIPAL COMPONENT 1 OF THE POLITICAL QUALITY-OF-LIFE INDICATORS, 2006			
OBS	*REGION*	*COUNTRY*	*PQLX*	*RANK*	*SOURCE*
47	DME	United States	1.03992	47	PRIN1(PQL)
48	DME	Greece	1.00874	48	PRIN1(PQL)
49	EEU	Croatia	0.99351	49	PRIN1(PQL)
50	LAM	Cayman Islands	0.97876	50	PRIN1(PQL)
51	DME	Gibraltar	0.96552	51	PRIN1(PQL)
52	DME	Malta	0.91131	52	PRIN1(PQL)
53	LAM	Aruba	0.89730	53	PRIN1(PQL)
54	LAM	Virgin Islands, US	0.87775	54	PRIN1(PQL)
55	DME	Greenland	0.87153	55	PRIN1(PQL)
56	SEA	Northern Mariana Is.	0.84972	56	PRIN1(PQL)
57	EEU	Romania	0.80070	57	PRIN1(PQL)
58	LAM	Costa Rica	0.72402	58	PRIN1(PQL)
59	LAM	Barbados	0.70568	59	PRIN1(PQL)
60	SEA	French Polynesia	0.70508	60	PRIN1(PQL)
61	LAM	Puerto Rico	0.70158	61	PRIN1(PQL)
62	SEA	Guam	0.68890	62	PRIN1(PQL)
63	EEU	Bosnia	0.67062	63	PRIN1(PQL)
64	LAM	Bahamas	0.63514	64	PRIN1(PQL)
65	LAM	Guiana, French	0.59594	65	PRIN1(PQL)
66	EEU	Albania	0.58118	66	PRIN1(PQL)
67	EEU	Montenegro	0.56913	67	PRIN1(PQL)
68	LAM	Dominica	0.56837	68	PRIN1(PQL)
69	LAM	Trinidad & Tobago	0.56811	69	PRIN1(PQL)
70	USR	Ukraine	0.56622	70	PRIN1(PQL)
71	LAM	St. Kitts & Nevis	0.55969	71	PRIN1(PQL)
72	MEA	Kuwait	0.54639	72	PRIN1(PQL)
73	LAM	Chile	0.54414	73	PRIN1(PQL)
74	LAM	St. Lucia	0.51287	74	PRIN1(PQL)
75	LAM	Uruguay	0.49654	75	PRIN1(PQL)
76	LAM	Suriname	0.47945	76	PRIN1(PQL)
77	DME	Isle of Man	0.47790	77	PRIN1(PQL)
78	DME	Jersey	0.47449	78	PRIN1(PQL)
79	AFR	Mauritius	0.46330	79	PRIN1(PQL)
80	LAM	Guadeloupe	0.45870	80	PRIN1(PQL)
81	LAM	Montserrat	0.45833	81	PRIN1(PQL)
82	LAM	Virgin Islands, Brit.	0.45402	82	PRIN1(PQL)
83	SEA	Fiji	0.41133	83	PRIN1(PQL)
84	SEA	Vanuatu	0.40045	84	PRIN1(PQL)
85	EEU	Macedonia	0.39000	85	PRIN1(PQL)
86	CPA	Mongolia	0.38318	86	PRIN1(PQL)
87	LAM	Grenada	0.37954	87	PRIN1(PQL)
88	LAM	Belize	0.34687	88	PRIN1(PQL)
89	LAM	Guyana	0.33952	89	PRIN1(PQL)
90	LAM	Jamaica	0.32954	90	PRIN1(PQL)
91	DME	Guernsey	0.32113	91	PRIN1(PQL)
92	SAS	India	0.31887	92	PRIN1(PQL)
93	SEA	Philippines	0.30623	93	PRIN1(PQL)

TABLE 1.10 – HUMAN RIGHTS INDEX, PRINCIPAL COMPONENT 1
OF THE POLITICAL QUALITY-OF-LIFE INDICATORS, 2006

OBS	REGION	COUNTRY	PQLX	RANK	SOURCE
94	USR	Armenia	0.29372	94	PRIN1(PQL)
95	LAM	St. Vincent	0.27752	95	PRIN1(PQL)
96	LAM	Argentina	0.24811	96	PRIN1(PQL)
97	SEA	Samoa, Western	0.23145	97	PRIN1(PQL)
98	SEA	Nauru	0.22862	98	PRIN1(PQL)
99	LAM	Mexico	0.22332	99	PRIN1(PQL)
100	SEA	Palau	0.20433	100	PRIN1(PQL)
101	SEA	Tonga	0.19327	101	PRIN1(PQL)
102	LAM	Brazil	0.17469	102	PRIN1(PQL)
103	LAM	Antigua & Barbuda	0.15652	103	PRIN1(PQL)
104	SEA	Macao	0.14352	104	PRIN1(PQL)
105	SEA	Indonesia	0.13452	105	PRIN1(PQL)
106	MEA	Bahrain	0.10474	106	PRIN1(PQL)
107	SEA	Turks & Caicos Is.	0.10070	107	PRIN1(PQL)
108	SAS	Sri Lanka	0.09338	108	PRIN1(PQL)
109	LAM	Ecuador	0.09157	109	PRIN1(PQL)
110	AFR	San Tome & Principe	0.08321	110	PRIN1(PQL)
111	LAM	Anguilla	0.08246	111	PRIN1(PQL)
112	LAM	Peru	0.07985	112	PRIN1(PQL)
113	MEA	Lebanon	0.07941	113	PRIN1(PQL)
114	LAM	Nicaragua	0.05692	114	PRIN1(PQL)
115	MEA	Algeria	0.04685	115	PRIN1(PQL)
116	LAM	Dominican Rep.	0.02993	116	PRIN1(PQL)
117	SEA	Kiribati	-0.00591	117	PRIN1(PQL)
118	DME	St. Pierre & Miquelon	-0.04172	118	PRIN1(PQL)
119	AFR	Seychelles	-0.07570	119	PRIN1(PQL)
120	AFR	Cape Verde	-0.07813	120	PRIN1(PQL)
121	MEA	Turkey	-0.08465	121	PRIN1(PQL)
122	MEA	Morocco	-0.08736	122	PRIN1(PQL)
123	LAM	Panama	-0.09001	123	PRIN1(PQL)
124	SEA	Niue	-0.10485	124	PRIN1(PQL)
125	SEA	Solomon Islands	-0.10767	125	PRIN1(PQL)
126	SEA	Cook Islands	-0.10934	126	PRIN1(PQL)
127	AFR	Ghana	-0.14580	127	PRIN1(PQL)
128	DME	Falkland Islands	-0.15028	128	PRIN1(PQL)
129	USR	Moldova	-0.16025	129	PRIN1(PQL)
130	LAM	El Salvador	-0.16878	130	PRIN1(PQL)
131	SAS	Pakistan	-0.20299	131	PRIN1(PQL)
132	SEA	Papua New Guinea	-0.24974	132	PRIN1(PQL)
133	USR	Russia	-0.27165	133	PRIN1(PQL)
134	SEA	Wallis & Futuna	-0.28919	134	PRIN1(PQL)
135	AFR	Mayotte	-0.31826	135	PRIN1(PQL)
136	LAM	Colombia	-0.33176	136	PRIN1(PQL)
137	MEA	Qatar	-0.33819	137	PRIN1(PQL)
138	AFR	Mauritania	-0.34269	138	PRIN1(PQL)
139	SEA	Tuvalu	-0.34911	139	PRIN1(PQL)
140	LAM	Guatemala	-0.36317	140	PRIN1(PQL)

TABLE 1.10 – HUMAN RIGHTS INDEX, PRINCIPAL COMPONENT 1
OF THE POLITICAL QUALITY-OF-LIFE INDICATORS, 2006

OBS	REGION	COUNTRY	PQLX	RANK	SOURCE
141	USR	Kazakhstan	-0.36352	141	PRIN1(PQL)
142	AFR	Mali	-0.36808	142	PRIN1(PQL)
143	AFR	South Africa	-0.39212	143	PRIN1(PQL)
144	MEA	UAE	-0.40119	144	PRIN1(PQL)
145	AFR	Benin	-0.40508	145	PRIN1(PQL)
146	MEA	Jordan	-0.41480	146	PRIN1(PQL)
147	SEA	Micronesia	-0.43160	147	PRIN1(PQL)
148	LAM	Bolivia	-0.43350	148	PRIN1(PQL)
149	SEA	Samoa, American	-0.44328	149	PRIN1(PQL)
150	SEA	East Timor	-0.48428	150	PRIN1(PQL)
151	SEA	Singapore	-0.49066	151	PRIN1(PQL)
152	SEA	Marshall Islands	-0.51105	152	PRIN1(PQL)
153	LAM	Paraguay	-0.54665	153	PRIN1(PQL)
154	USR	Georgia	-0.55085	154	PRIN1(PQL)
155	LAM	Honduras	-0.56860	155	PRIN1(PQL)
156	SEA	Thailand	-0.58531	156	PRIN1(PQL)
157	USR	Uzbekistan	-0.58648	157	PRIN1(PQL)
158	AFR	Burkina Faso	-0.58825	158	PRIN1(PQL)
159	USR	Azerbaijan	-0.59012	159	PRIN1(PQL)
160	AFR	Comoros	-0.59181	160	PRIN1(PQL)
161	MEA	Iran	-0.60033	161	PRIN1(PQL)
162	LAM	Venezuela	-0.61602	162	PRIN1(PQL)
163	CPA	Cambodia	-0.62832	163	PRIN1(PQL)
164	SEA	Brunei	-0.63707	164	PRIN1(PQL)
165	MEA	Syria	-0.64427	165	PRIN1(PQL)
166	SAS	Bangladesh	-0.64675	166	PRIN1(PQL)
167	MEA	Iraq	-0.65311	167	PRIN1(PQL)
168	AFR	Malawi	-0.66807	168	PRIN1(PQL)
169	LAM	Cuba	-0.66916	169	PRIN1(PQL)
170	MEA	Egypt	-0.69198	170	PRIN1(PQL)
171	USR	Kyrgyzstan	-0.69453	171	PRIN1(PQL)
172	AFR	Senegal	-0.69826	172	PRIN1(PQL)
173	USR	Tajikistan	-0.71701	173	PRIN1(PQL)
174	MEA	Oman	-0.75904	174	PRIN1(PQL)
175	AFR	Madagascar	-0.76920	175	PRIN1(PQL)
176	USR	Belarus	-0.79170	176	PRIN1(PQL)
177	MEA	Tunisia	-0.79226	177	PRIN1(PQL)
178	AFR	Kenya	-0.81023	178	PRIN1(PQL)
179	AFR	Botswana	-0.81402	179	PRIN1(PQL)
180	SEA	Malaysia	-0.82382	180	PRIN1(PQL)
181	AFR	Congo, Rep.	-0.82758	181	PRIN1(PQL)
182	AFR	Gabon	-0.85319	182	PRIN1(PQL)
183	AFR	Uganda	-0.89329	183	PRIN1(PQL)
184	AFR	Tanzania	-0.90845	184	PRIN1(PQL)
185	AFR	Nigeria	-0.91661	185	PRIN1(PQL)
186	AFR	Liberia	-0.94493	186	PRIN1(PQL)
187	AFR	Ethiopia	-0.97567	187	PRIN1(PQL)

TABLE 1.10 – HUMAN RIGHTS INDEX, PRINCIPAL COMPONENT 1
OF THE POLITICAL QUALITY-OF-LIFE INDICATORS, 2006

OBS	REGION	COUNTRY	PQLX	RANK	SOURCE
188	AFR	GuineaBissau	-1.01142	188	PRIN1(PQL)
189	SAS	Maldives	-1.02285	189	PRIN1(PQL)
190	MEA	Saudi Arabia	-1.05053	190	PRIN1(PQL)
191	AFR	St. Helena	-1.05384	191	PRIN1(PQL)
192	CPA	Vietnam	-1.08629	192	PRIN1(PQL)
193	AFR	Lesotho	-1.09030	193	PRIN1(PQL)
194	AFR	Cameroon	-1.10708	194	PRIN1(PQL)
195	AFR	Namibia	-1.11142	195	PRIN1(PQL)
196	AFR	Mozambique	-1.11977	196	PRIN1(PQL)
197	AFR	Congo, Dem. Rep.	-1.12905	197	PRIN1(PQL)
198	AFR	Ivory Coast	-1.14111	198	PRIN1(PQL)
199	LAM	Haiti	-1.16552	199	PRIN1(PQL)
200	AFR	Guinea	-1.16923	200	PRIN1(PQL)
201	AFR	Niger	-1.19231	201	PRIN1(PQL)
202	MEA	West Bank	-1.19418	202	PRIN1(PQL)
203	MEA	Gaza Strip	-1.22515	203	PRIN1(PQL)
204	CPA	Korea, North	-1.22907	204	PRIN1(PQL)
205	MEA	Libya	-1.23234	205	PRIN1(PQL)
206	SAS	Nepal	-1.23744	206	PRIN1(PQL)
207	MEA	Yemen	-1.27697	207	PRIN1(PQL)
208	AFR	Zambia	-1.29430	208	PRIN1(PQL)
209	CPA	Laos	-1.34307	209	PRIN1(PQL)
210	CPA	China	-1.35456	210	PRIN1(PQL)
211	AFR	Burundi	-1.36185	211	PRIN1(PQL)
212	AFR	Sierra Leone	-1.38124	212	PRIN1(PQL)
213	AFR	Angola	-1.42831	213	PRIN1(PQL)
214	AFR	Togo	-1.47646	214	PRIN1(PQL)
215	SAS	Bhutan	-1.50440	215	PRIN1(PQL)
216	SEA	Tokelau	-1.50944	216	PRIN1(PQL)
217	AFR	Rwanda	-1.53097	217	PRIN1(PQL)
218	AFR	CAR	-1.56255	218	PRIN1(PQL)
219	USR	Turkmenistan	-1.56400	219	PRIN1(PQL)
220	AFR	Chad	-1.60994	220	PRIN1(PQL)
221	AFR	Djibouti	-1.70231	221	PRIN1(PQL)
222	AFR	Gambia	-1.74662	222	PRIN1(PQL)
223	AFR	Zimbabwe	-1.74743	223	PRIN1(PQL)
224	CPA	Burma	-1.83233	224	PRIN1(PQL)
225	AFR	Sudan	-1.83433	225	PRIN1(PQL)
226	AFR	Eritrea	-1.89119	226	PRIN1(PQL)
227	AFR	Somalia	-1.90261	227	PRIN1(PQL)
228	SAS	Afghanistan	-1.90361	228	PRIN1(PQL)
229	AFR	Swaziland	-1.92984	229	PRIN1(PQL)
230	AFR	Western Sahara	-1.98105	230	PRIN1(PQL)
231	AFR	Equatorial Guinea	-1.99472	231	PRIN1(PQL)

TABLE 1.11 – ECONOMICO-POLITICAL QUALITY-OF-LIFE
INDEX, PRINCIPAL COMPONENT 1 OF THE ECONOMIC AND
POLITICAL QUALITY-OF-LIFE INDICATORS, 2006

OBS	REGION	COUNTRY	EPQLX	RANK	SOURCE
1	DME	Liechtenstein	1.91995	1	PRIN1(EPQL)
2	DME	Andorra	1.88858	2	PRIN1(EPQL)
3	DME	Iceland	1.82750	3	PRIN1(EPQL)
4	DME	Norway	1.79300	4	PRIN1(EPQL)
5	DME	San Marino	1.71998	5	PRIN1(EPQL)
6	DME	Japan	1.71184	6	PRIN1(EPQL)
7	DME	Sweden	1.70999	7	PRIN1(EPQL)
8	DME	Luxembourg	1.67544	8	PRIN1(EPQL)
9	DME	Switzerland	1.63675	9	PRIN1(EPQL)
10	DME	Finland	1.61662	10	PRIN1(EPQL)
11	DME	Denmark	1.57401	11	PRIN1(EPQL)
12	DME	Netherlands	1.54051	12	PRIN1(EPQL)
13	DME	Belgium	1.51056	13	PRIN1(EPQL)
14	DME	Austria	1.49291	14	PRIN1(EPQL)
15	DME	Germany	1.46916	15	PRIN1(EPQL)
16	DME	Ireland	1.46862	16	PRIN1(EPQL)
17	DME	Canada	1.46278	17	PRIN1(EPQL)
18	DME	France	1.45200	18	PRIN1(EPQL)
19	DME	Australia	1.42622	19	PRIN1(EPQL)
20	SEA	Hong Kong	1.41098	20	PRIN1(EPQL)
21	DME	Bermuda	1.40833	21	PRIN1(EPQL)
22	DME	Monaco	1.40495	22	PRIN1(EPQL)
23	DME	Spain	1.39692	23	PRIN1(EPQL)
24	DME	Italy	1.37434	24	PRIN1(EPQL)
25	DME	Jersey	1.35286	25	PRIN1(EPQL)
26	DME	United Kingdom	1.32630	26	PRIN1(EPQL)
27	DME	New Zealand	1.30777	27	PRIN1(EPQL)
28	MEA	Cyprus	1.29012	28	PRIN1(EPQL)
29	DME	Guernsey	1.28857	29	PRIN1(EPQL)
30	DME	Gibraltar	1.28851	30	PRIN1(EPQL)
31	DME	Greece	1.27872	31	PRIN1(EPQL)
32	LAM	Cayman Islands	1.27471	32	PRIN1(EPQL)
33	EEU	Slovenia	1.27216	33	PRIN1(EPQL)
34	DME	Faeroe Islands	1.25301	34	PRIN1(EPQL)
35	DME	United States	1.23008	35	PRIN1(EPQL)
36	DME	Israel	1.22829	36	PRIN1(EPQL)
37	EEU	Czechia	1.19247	37	PRIN1(EPQL)
38	DME	Portugal	1.14891	38	PRIN1(EPQL)
39	SEA	Korea, South	1.13922	39	PRIN1(EPQL)
40	SEA	Taiwan	1.12180	40	PRIN1(EPQL)
41	DME	Isle of Man	1.09710	41	PRIN1(EPQL)
42	SEA	Macao	1.09272	42	PRIN1(EPQL)
43	LAM	Aruba	1.07712	43	PRIN1(EPQL)
44	SEA	Singapore	1.03973	44	PRIN1(EPQL)
45	DME	Malta	1.02433	45	PRIN1(EPQL)
46	AFR	Reunion	0.97211	46	PRIN1(EPQL)
47	MEA	Kuwait	0.97140	47	PRIN1(EPQL)

	TABLE 1.11 – ECONOMICO-POLITICAL QUALITY-OF-LIFE INDEX, PRINCIPAL COMPONENT 1 OF THE ECONOMIC AND POLITICAL QUALITY-OF-LIFE INDICATORS, 2006				
OBS	REGION	COUNTRY	EPQLX	RANK	SOURCE
48	LAM	Martinique	0.94845	48	PRIN1(EPQL)
49	LAM	Virgin Islands, US	0.94558	49	PRIN1(EPQL)
50	EEU	Slovakia	0.93474	50	PRIN1(EPQL)
51	MEA	UAE	0.91473	51	PRIN1(EPQL)
52	USR	Estonia	0.87314	52	PRIN1(EPQL)
53	EEU	Hungary	0.87160	53	PRIN1(EPQL)
54	SEA	New Caledonia	0.84454	54	PRIN1(EPQL)
55	LAM	Guadeloupe	0.84258	55	PRIN1(EPQL)
56	LAM	Puerto Rico	0.83289	56	PRIN1(EPQL)
57	EEU	Poland	0.82808	57	PRIN1(EPQL)
58	EEU	Croatia	0.81936	58	PRIN1(EPQL)
59	SEA	Guam	0.80162	59	PRIN1(EPQL)
60	LAM	Virgin Islands, Brit.	0.78353	60	PRIN1(EPQL)
61	LAM	Neth. Antilles	0.77186	61	PRIN1(EPQL)
62	SEA	Northern Mariana Is.	0.75672	62	PRIN1(EPQL)
63	SEA	French Polynesia	0.74876	63	PRIN1(EPQL)
64	MEA	Qatar	0.74236	64	PRIN1(EPQL)
65	USR	Lithuania	0.73254	65	PRIN1(EPQL)
66	DME	Falkland Islands	0.71805	66	PRIN1(EPQL)
67	SEA	Brunei	0.71603	67	PRIN1(EPQL)
68	USR	Latvia	0.68998	68	PRIN1(EPQL)
69	LAM	Barbados	0.68668	69	PRIN1(EPQL)
70	MEA	Bahrain	0.67066	70	PRIN1(EPQL)
71	LAM	Bahamas	0.63948	71	PRIN1(EPQL)
72	DME	Greenland	0.60317	72	PRIN1(EPQL)
73	LAM	Chile	0.58266	73	PRIN1(EPQL)
74	LAM	Costa Rica	0.55336	74	PRIN1(EPQL)
75	EEU	Serbia	0.54084	75	PRIN1(EPQL)
76	LAM	Guiana, French	0.50280	76	PRIN1(EPQL)
77	EEU	Bulgaria	0.48695	77	PRIN1(EPQL)
78	LAM	Antigua & Barbuda	0.43937	78	PRIN1(EPQL)
79	LAM	Uruguay	0.42996	79	PRIN1(EPQL)
80	SEA	Palau	0.41220	80	PRIN1(EPQL)
81	DME	St. Pierre & Miquelon	0.40887	81	PRIN1(EPQL)
82	EEU	Montenegro	0.40447	82	PRIN1(EPQL)
83	LAM	St. Lucia	0.38419	83	PRIN1(EPQL)
84	LAM	St. Kitts & Nevis	0.38300	84	PRIN1(EPQL)
85	EEU	Romania	0.36331	85	PRIN1(EPQL)
86	LAM	Dominica	0.35449	86	PRIN1(EPQL)
87	MEA	Oman	0.35093	87	PRIN1(EPQL)
88	AFR	Mauritius	0.34129	88	PRIN1(EPQL)
89	LAM	Trinidad & Tobago	0.32386	89	PRIN1(EPQL)
90	AFR	Seychelles	0.31519	90	PRIN1(EPQL)
91	LAM	Montserrat	0.30558	91	PRIN1(EPQL)
92	LAM	Cuba	0.29293	92	PRIN1(EPQL)
93	SEA	Turks & Caicos Is.	0.29175	93	PRIN1(EPQL)
94	EEU	Albania	0.28933	94	PRIN1(EPQL)

TABLE 1.11 – ECONOMICO-POLITICAL QUALITY-OF-LIFE
INDEX, PRINCIPAL COMPONENT 1 OF THE ECONOMIC AND
POLITICAL QUALITY-OF-LIFE INDICATORS, 2006

OBS	REGION	COUNTRY	EPQLX	RANK	SOURCE
95	LAM	Argentina	0.28687	95	PRIN1(EPQL)
96	EEU	Bosnia	0.28369	96	PRIN1(EPQL)
97	SEA	Samoa, American	0.27061	97	PRIN1(EPQL)
98	LAM	Anguilla	0.20835	98	PRIN1(EPQL)
99	LAM	Mexico	0.20146	99	PRIN1(EPQL)
100	EEU	Macedonia	0.19177	100	PRIN1(EPQL)
101	LAM	Belize	0.18174	101	PRIN1(EPQL)
102	SEA	Nauru	0.11951	102	PRIN1(EPQL)
103	LAM	St. Vincent	0.10364	103	PRIN1(EPQL)
104	MEA	Saudi Arabia	0.09826	104	PRIN1(EPQL)
105	LAM	Panama	0.09630	105	PRIN1(EPQL)
106	SEA	Malaysia	0.09423	106	PRIN1(EPQL)
107	LAM	Grenada	0.08588	107	PRIN1(EPQL)
108	LAM	Brazil	0.04261	108	PRIN1(EPQL)
109	SEA	Fiji	0.03090	109	PRIN1(EPQL)
110	LAM	Suriname	0.03085	110	PRIN1(EPQL)
111	SEA	Tonga	0.03081	111	PRIN1(EPQL)
112	SEA	Thailand	0.02870	112	PRIN1(EPQL)
113	USR	Ukraine	0.02659	113	PRIN1(EPQL)
114	USR	Russia	0.02165	114	PRIN1(EPQL)
115	LAM	Jamaica	0.02150	115	PRIN1(EPQL)
116	MEA	Lebanon	0.01553	116	PRIN1(EPQL)
117	LAM	Venezuela	0.01081	117	PRIN1(EPQL)
118	MEA	Turkey	0.00606	118	PRIN1(EPQL)
119	LAM	Ecuador	-0.01272	119	PRIN1(EPQL)
120	SEA	Cook Islands	-0.02082	120	PRIN1(EPQL)
121	MEA	Libya	-0.03676	121	PRIN1(EPQL)
122	USR	Belarus	-0.03985	122	PRIN1(EPQL)
123	SAS	Sri Lanka	-0.05030	123	PRIN1(EPQL)
124	SEA	Samoa, Western	-0.05645	124	PRIN1(EPQL)
125	USR	Armenia	-0.07001	125	PRIN1(EPQL)
126	LAM	Peru	-0.08269	126	PRIN1(EPQL)
127	LAM	Dominican Rep.	-0.10206	127	PRIN1(EPQL)
128	MEA	Algeria	-0.12068	128	PRIN1(EPQL)
129	USR	Kazakhstan	-0.14067	129	PRIN1(EPQL)
130	LAM	Colombia	-0.15401	130	PRIN1(EPQL)
131	MEA	Jordan	-0.17327	131	PRIN1(EPQL)
132	MEA	Tunisia	-0.17715	132	PRIN1(EPQL)
133	LAM	El Salvador	-0.19604	133	PRIN1(EPQL)
134	SEA	Niue	-0.19897	134	PRIN1(EPQL)
135	MEA	Syria	-0.20626	135	PRIN1(EPQL)
136	SEA	Philippines	-0.20793	136	PRIN1(EPQL)
137	SEA	Wallis & Futuna	-0.22154	137	PRIN1(EPQL)
138	MEA	Iran	-0.23066	138	PRIN1(EPQL)
139	SEA	Vanuatu	-0.24373	139	PRIN1(EPQL)
140	AFR	Cape Verde	-0.30593	140	PRIN1(EPQL)
141	SEA	Micronesia	-0.32684	141	PRIN1(EPQL)

TABLE 1.11 – ECONOMICO-POLITICAL QUALITY-OF-LIFE
INDEX, PRINCIPAL COMPONENT 1 OF THE ECONOMIC AND
POLITICAL QUALITY-OF-LIFE INDICATORS, 2006

OBS	REGION	COUNTRY	EPQLX	RANK	SOURCE
142	SEA	Indonesia	-0.32966	142	PRIN1(EPQL)
143	CPA	Mongolia	-0.33134	143	PRIN1(EPQL)
144	AFR	St. Helena	-0.34681	144	PRIN1(EPQL)
145	LAM	Nicaragua	-0.35875	145	PRIN1(EPQL)
146	SEA	Marshall Islands	-0.36021	146	PRIN1(EPQL)
147	USR	Moldova	-0.36260	147	PRIN1(EPQL)
148	USR	Georgia	-0.36283	148	PRIN1(EPQL)
149	MEA	Morocco	-0.36289	149	PRIN1(EPQL)
150	MEA	Egypt	-0.36843	150	PRIN1(EPQL)
151	SEA	Tuvalu	-0.37577	151	PRIN1(EPQL)
152	LAM	Guyana	-0.37638	152	PRIN1(EPQL)
153	LAM	Guatemala	-0.37654	153	PRIN1(EPQL)
154	LAM	Paraguay	-0.41237	154	PRIN1(EPQL)
155	SAS	Maldives	-0.41560	155	PRIN1(EPQL)
156	USR	Azerbaijan	-0.42424	156	PRIN1(EPQL)
157	MEA	West Bank	-0.44448	157	PRIN1(EPQL)
158	CPA	China	-0.44903	158	PRIN1(EPQL)
159	LAM	Honduras	-0.49942	159	PRIN1(EPQL)
160	MEA	Gaza Strip	-0.50973	160	PRIN1(EPQL)
161	CPA	Vietnam	-0.53956	161	PRIN1(EPQL)
162	AFR	South Africa	-0.55281	162	PRIN1(EPQL)
163	AFR	Gabon	-0.55717	163	PRIN1(EPQL)
164	SEA	Kiribati	-0.59085	164	PRIN1(EPQL)
165	SAS	India	-0.59673	165	PRIN1(EPQL)
166	AFR	Mayotte	-0.60156	166	PRIN1(EPQL)
167	MEA	Iraq	-0.67539	167	PRIN1(EPQL)
168	LAM	Bolivia	-0.68490	168	PRIN1(EPQL)
169	USR	Kyrgyzstan	-0.69470	169	PRIN1(EPQL)
170	AFR	Botswana	-0.70670	170	PRIN1(EPQL)
171	AFR	San Tome & Principe	-0.72457	171	PRIN1(EPQL)
172	USR	Uzbekistan	-0.73831	172	PRIN1(EPQL)
173	USR	Turkmenistan	-0.76062	173	PRIN1(EPQL)
174	SEA	Solomon Islands	-0.78673	174	PRIN1(EPQL)
175	SAS	Pakistan	-0.79045	175	PRIN1(EPQL)
176	CPA	Korea, North	-0.80528	176	PRIN1(EPQL)
177	AFR	Equatorial Guinea	-0.87429	177	PRIN1(EPQL)
178	AFR	Namibia	-0.89659	178	PRIN1(EPQL)
179	USR	Tajikistan	-0.89872	179	PRIN1(EPQL)
180	AFR	Mauritania	-0.91382	180	PRIN1(EPQL)
181	SAS	Bhutan	-0.92094	181	PRIN1(EPQL)
182	SEA	East Timor	-0.92350	182	PRIN1(EPQL)
183	SEA	Papua New Guinea	-0.95655	183	PRIN1(EPQL)
184	AFR	Comoros	-0.96550	184	PRIN1(EPQL)
185	AFR	Ghana	-0.97405	185	PRIN1(EPQL)
186	AFR	Senegal	-0.98741	186	PRIN1(EPQL)
187	SAS	Bangladesh	-1.00973	187	PRIN1(EPQL)
188	AFR	Congo, Rep.	-1.02916	188	PRIN1(EPQL)

	TABLE 1.11 – ECONOMICO-POLITICAL QUALITY-OF-LIFE INDEX, PRINCIPAL COMPONENT 1 OF THE ECONOMIC AND POLITICAL QUALITY-OF-LIFE INDICATORS, 2006				
OBS	*REGION*	*COUNTRY*	*EPQLX*	*RANK*	*SOURCE*
189	CPA	Cambodia	-1.05138	189	PRIN1(EPQL)
190	CPA	Laos	-1.05701	190	PRIN1(EPQL)
191	SEA	Tokelau	-1.10281	191	PRIN1(EPQL)
192	AFR	Benin	-1.12527	192	PRIN1(EPQL)
193	MEA	Yemen	-1.12687	193	PRIN1(EPQL)
194	AFR	Kenya	-1.21542	194	PRIN1(EPQL)
195	AFR	Cameroon	-1.22096	195	PRIN1(EPQL)
196	SAS	Nepal	-1.27236	196	PRIN1(EPQL)
197	AFR	Sudan	-1.27246	197	PRIN1(EPQL)
198	AFR	Mali	-1.28161	198	PRIN1(EPQL)
199	AFR	Madagascar	-1.29194	199	PRIN1(EPQL)
200	AFR	Djibouti	-1.30400	200	PRIN1(EPQL)
201	AFR	Tanzania	-1.30742	201	PRIN1(EPQL)
202	AFR	Swaziland	-1.31496	202	PRIN1(EPQL)
203	AFR	Nigeria	-1.33729	203	PRIN1(EPQL)
204	LAM	Haiti	-1.34331	204	PRIN1(EPQL)
205	AFR	Angola	-1.35874	205	PRIN1(EPQL)
206	AFR	Ivory Coast	-1.36313	206	PRIN1(EPQL)
207	AFR	Burkina Faso	-1.36731	207	PRIN1(EPQL)
208	AFR	Guinea	-1.39985	208	PRIN1(EPQL)
209	AFR	Uganda	-1.40825	209	PRIN1(EPQL)
210	AFR	Lesotho	-1.41543	210	PRIN1(EPQL)
211	AFR	Togo	-1.42645	211	PRIN1(EPQL)
212	CPA	Burma	-1.45663	212	PRIN1(EPQL)
213	AFR	Malawi	-1.46432	213	PRIN1(EPQL)
214	AFR	Gambia	-1.50817	214	PRIN1(EPQL)
215	AFR	Ethiopia	-1.52704	215	PRIN1(EPQL)
216	AFR	Eritrea	-1.54985	216	PRIN1(EPQL)
217	AFR	Zambia	-1.56717	217	PRIN1(EPQL)
218	AFR	Western Sahara	-1.61659	218	PRIN1(EPQL)
219	AFR	Chad	-1.61810	219	PRIN1(EPQL)
220	AFR	Mozambique	-1.63750	220	PRIN1(EPQL)
221	AFR	Zimbabwe	-1.67345	221	PRIN1(EPQL)
222	AFR	Niger	-1.69863	222	PRIN1(EPQL)
223	AFR	Somalia	-1.73557	223	PRIN1(EPQL)
224	AFR	Rwanda	-1.75119	224	PRIN1(EPQL)
225	AFR	GuineaBissau	-1.75570	225	PRIN1(EPQL)
226	AFR	Sierra Leone	-1.83201	226	PRIN1(EPQL)
227	SAS	Afghanistan	-1.83473	227	PRIN1(EPQL)
228	AFR	CAR	-1.85496	228	PRIN1(EPQL)
229	AFR	Liberia	-1.88246	229	PRIN1(EPQL)
230	AFR	Burundi	-1.89617	230	PRIN1(EPQL)
231	AFR	Congo, Dem. Rep.	-1.89915	231	PRIN1(EPQL)

2. BALANCE OF POWER

TABLE 2.1 – POPULATION, THOUSANDS, 2006					
OBS	REGION	COUNTRY	POP	RANK	SOURCE
1	CPA	China	1,311,381	1	06(E)
2	SAS	India	1,119,538	2	06(E)
3	DME	United States	299,330	3	06(E)
4	SEA	Indonesia	222,731	4	06(E)
5	LAM	Brazil	186,771	5	06(E)
6	SAS	Pakistan	156,770	6	06(E)
7	USR	Russia	142,394	7	06(E)
8	SAS	Bangladesh	138,835	8	06(E)
9	AFR	Nigeria	134,375	9	06(E)
10	DME	Japan	127,716	10	06(E)
11	LAM	Mexico	104,038	11	06(E)
12	SEA	Philippines	85,563	12	06(E)
13	CPA	Vietnam	83,458	13	06(E)
14	DME	Germany	82,442	14	06(E)
15	AFR	Ethiopia	74,778	15	06(E)
16	MEA	Turkey	72,932	16	06(E)
17	MEA	Egypt	72,034	17	06(E)
18	MEA	Iran	69,341	18	06(E)
19	SEA	Thailand	64,632	19	06(E)
20	DME	France	61,114	20	06(E)
21	DME	United Kingdom	60,501	21	06(E)
22	AFR	Congo, Dem. Rep.	59,320	22	06(E)
23	DME	Italy	58,888	23	06(E)
24	SEA	Korea, South	47,983	24	06(E)
25	AFR	South Africa	47,391	25	06(E)
26	CPA	Burma	47,383	26	06(E)
27	USR	Ukraine	46,757	27	06(E)
28	DME	Spain	44,561	28	06(E)
29	LAM	Colombia	43,593	29	06(E)
30	LAM	Argentina	38,971	30	06(E)
31	EEU	Poland	38,136	31	06(E)
32	AFR	Tanzania	37,445	32	06(E)
33	AFR	Sudan	36,992	33	06(E)
34	AFR	Kenya	34,059	34	06(E)
35	MEA	Algeria	33,354	35	06(E)
36	DME	Canada	32,547	36	06(E)
37	MEA	Morocco	30,275	37	06(E)
38	MEA	Iraq	28,513	38	06(E)
39	AFR	Uganda	28,196	39	06(E)
40	SAS	Nepal	27,678	40	06(E)

TABLE 2.1 – POPULATION, THOUSANDS, 2006					
OBS	*REGION*	*COUNTRY*	*POP*	*RANK*	*SOURCE*
41	LAM	Peru	27,515	41	06(E)
42	LAM	Venezuela	27,216	42	06(E)
43	SEA	Malaysia	26,640	43	06(E)
44	USR	Uzbekistan	26,383	44	06(E)
45	SAS	Afghanistan	24,592	45	06(E)
46	MEA	Saudi Arabia	23,687	46	06(E)
47	SEA	Taiwan	22,815	47	06(E)
48	CPA	Korea, North	22,583	48	06(E)
49	AFR	Ghana	22,410	49	06(E)
50	EEU	Romania	21,577	50	06(E)
51	DME	Australia	20,680	51	06(E)
52	MEA	Yemen	20,676	52	06(E)
53	SAS	Sri Lanka	19,879	53	06(E)
54	AFR	Mozambique	19,687	54	06(E)
55	AFR	Madagascar	19,105	55	06(E)
56	MEA	Syria	18,542	56	06(E)
57	AFR	Ivory Coast	17,655	57	06(E)
58	AFR	Cameroon	17,341	58	06(E)
59	LAM	Chile	16,436	59	06(E)
60	DME	Netherlands	16,343	60	06(E)
61	USR	Kazakhstan	15,242	61	06(E)
62	CPA	Cambodia	13,648	62	06(E)
63	AFR	Burkina Faso	13,558	63	06(E)
64	LAM	Ecuador	13,419	64	06(E)
65	LAM	Guatemala	13,019	65	06(E)
66	AFR	Malawi	13,014	66	06(E)
67	AFR	Niger	12,841	67	06(E)
68	AFR	Zimbabwe	12,237	68	06(E)
69	AFR	Angola	12,127	69	06(E)
70	AFR	Mali	11,717	70	06(E)
71	LAM	Cuba	11,294	71	06(E)
72	AFR	Zambia	11,288	72	06(E)
73	DME	Greece	11,130	73	06(E)
74	AFR	Senegal	10,961	74	06(E)
75	DME	Portugal	10,605	75	06(E)
76	DME	Belgium	10,517	76	06(E)
77	EEU	Czechia	10,260	77	06(E)
78	MEA	Tunisia	10,141	78	06(E)
79	EEU	Hungary	10,064	79	06(E)
80	EEU	Serbia	10,027	80	06(E)
81	AFR	Chad	9,944	81	06(E)
82	USR	Belarus	9,726	82	06(E)
83	AFR	Guinea	9,603	83	06(E)
84	LAM	Bolivia	9,354	84	06(E)
85	DME	Sweden	9,082	85	06(E)
86	LAM	Dominican Rep.	9,021	86	06(E)
87	LAM	Haiti	8,808	87	06(E)
88	AFR	Rwanda	8,771	88	06(E)

TABLE 2.1 – POPULATION, THOUSANDS, 2006					
OBS	REGION	COUNTRY	POP	RANK	SOURCE
89	AFR	Somalia	8,496	89	06(E)
90	USR	Azerbaijan	8,474	90	06(E)
91	DME	Austria	8,263	91	06(E)
92	AFR	Burundi	8,090	92	06(E)
93	AFR	Benin	7,687	93	06(E)
94	EEU	Bulgaria	7,681	94	06(E)
95	DME	Switzerland	7,533	95	06(E)
96	LAM	Honduras	7,329	96	06(E)
97	USR	Tajikistan	7,063	97	06(E)
98	SEA	Hong Kong	6,997	98	06(E)
99	LAM	El Salvador	6,991	99	06(E)
100	DME	Israel	6,801	100	06(E)
101	SEA	Papua New Guinea	6,001	101	06(E)
102	LAM	Paraguay	5,993	102	06(E)
103	MEA	Libya	5,968	103	06(E)
104	CPA	Laos	5,751	104	06(E)
105	AFR	Togo	5,549	105	06(E)
106	MEA	Jordan	5,505	106	06(E)
107	DME	Denmark	5,435	107	06(E)
108	EEU	Slovakia	5,391	108	06(E)
109	DME	Finland	5,265	109	06(E)
110	LAM	Nicaragua	5,233	110	06(E)
111	USR	Kyrgyzstan	5,192	111	06(E)
112	AFR	Sierra Leone	5,124	112	06(E)
113	USR	Turkmenistan	4,899	113	06(E)
114	AFR	Eritrea	4,787	114	06(E)
115	DME	Norway	4,659	115	06(E)
116	USR	Georgia	4,474	116	06(E)
117	EEU	Croatia	4,450	117	06(E)
118	SEA	Singapore	4,408	118	06(E)
119	LAM	Costa Rica	4,274	119	06(E)
120	DME	Ireland	4,250	120	06(E)
121	MEA	UAE	4,214	121	06(E)
122	USR	Moldova	4,192	122	06(E)
123	DME	New Zealand	4,141	123	06(E)
124	AFR	CAR	4,039	124	06(E)
125	LAM	Puerto Rico	3,927	125	06(E)
126	EEU	Bosnia	3,860	126	06(E)
127	MEA	Lebanon	3,834	127	06(E)
128	AFR	Congo, Rep.	3,702	128	06(E)
129	USR	Lithuania	3,392	129	06(E)
130	LAM	Uruguay	3,266	130	06(E)
131	LAM	Panama	3,191	131	06(E)
132	EEU	Albania	3,161	132	06(E)
133	AFR	Mauritania	3,158	133	06(E)
134	MEA	Kuwait	3,084	134	06(E)
135	AFR	Liberia	3,042	135	06(E)
136	USR	Armenia	2,976	136	06(E)

TABLE 2.1 – POPULATION, THOUSANDS, 2006

OBS	REGION	COUNTRY	POP	RANK	SOURCE
137	MEA	West Bank	2,697	137	06(E)
138	LAM	Jamaica	2,667	138	06(E)
139	CPA	Mongolia	2,580	139	06(E)
140	MEA	Oman	2,516	140	06(E)
141	USR	Latvia	2,287	141	06(E)
142	EEU	Macedonia	2,041	142	06(E)
143	AFR	Lesotho	2,022	143	06(E)
144	EEU	Slovenia	2,006	144	06(E)
145	AFR	Namibia	1,959	145	06(E)
146	AFR	Botswana	1,760	146	06(E)
147	AFR	Gambia	1,556	147	06(E)
148	MEA	Gaza Strip	1,444	148	06(E)
149	AFR	GuineaBissau	1,442	149	06(E)
150	AFR	Gabon	1,406	150	06(E)
151	USR	Estonia	1,343	151	06(E)
152	LAM	Trinidad & Tobago	1,301	152	06(E)
153	AFR	Mauritius	1,255	153	06(E)
154	SEA	East Timor	1,032	154	06(E)
155	AFR	Swaziland	1,029	155	06(E)
156	MEA	Cyprus	1,004	156	06(E)
157	SEA	Fiji	855	157	06(E)
158	MEA	Qatar	838	158	06(E)
159	AFR	Reunion	791	159	06(E)
160	SAS	Bhutan	790	160	06(E)
161	LAM	Guyana	756	161	06(E)
162	MEA	Bahrain	727	162	06(E)
163	AFR	Comoros	632	163	06(E)
164	EEU	Montenegro	624	164	06(E)
165	AFR	Equatorial Guinea	515	165	06(E)
166	SEA	Macao	505	166	06(E)
167	LAM	Suriname	502	167	06(E)
168	AFR	Djibouti	487	168	06(E)
169	AFR	Cape Verde	485	169	06(E)
170	SEA	Solomon Islands	482	170	06(E)
171	DME	Luxembourg	461	171	06(E)
172	LAM	Guadeloupe	458	172	06(E)
173	DME	Malta	405	173	06(E)
174	LAM	Martinique	400	174	06(E)
175	SEA	Brunei	375	175	06(E)
176	AFR	Western Sahara	372	176	06(E)
177	LAM	Bahamas	327	177	06(E)
178	DME	Iceland	302	178	06(E)
179	LAM	Belize	301	179	06(E)
180	SAS	Maldives	300	180	06(E)
181	LAM	Barbados	270	181	06(E)
182	SEA	French Polynesia	258	182	06(E)
183	SEA	New Caledonia	238	183	06(E)
184	SEA	Vanuatu	215	184	06(E)

TABLE 2.1 – POPULATION, THOUSANDS, 2006					
OBS	REGION	COUNTRY	POP	RANK	SOURCE
185	LAM	Guiana, French	199	185	06(E)
186	LAM	Neth. Antilles	189	186	06(E)
187	AFR	Mayotte	188	187	06(E)
188	SEA	Samoa, Western	183	188	06(E)
189	SEA	Guam	172	189	06(E)
190	LAM	St. Lucia	165	190	06(E)
191	AFR	San Tome & Principe	152	191	06(E)
192	LAM	Virgin Islands, US	113	192	06(E)
193	SEA	Micronesia	108	193	06(E)
194	LAM	Grenada	107	194	06(E)
195	SEA	Tonga	102	195	06(E)
196	LAM	Aruba	101	196	06(E)
197	LAM	St. Vincent	97	197	06(E)
198	SEA	Kiribati	94	198	06(E)
199	DME	Jersey	88	199	06(E)
200	AFR	Seychelles	83	200	06(E)
201	DME	Isle of Man	78	201	06(E)
202	LAM	Antigua & Barbuda	78	202	06(E)
203	DME	Andorra	78	203	06(E)
204	SEA	Northern Mariana Is.	76	204	06(E)
205	LAM	Dominica	70	205	06(E)
206	SEA	Samoa, American	67	206	06(E)
207	DME	Bermuda	66	207	06(E)
208	DME	Guernsey	64	208	06(E)
209	SEA	Marshall Islands	60	209	06(E)
210	DME	Greenland	57	210	06(E)
211	LAM	St. Kitts & Nevis	49	211	06(E)
212	DME	Faeroe Islands	48	212	06(E)
213	LAM	Cayman Islands	45	213	06(CIA)
214	DME	Liechtenstein	35	214	06(E)
215	DME	Monaco	33	215	06(E)
216	DME	San Marino	30	216	06(E)
217	DME	Gibraltar	28	217	06(CIA)
218	LAM	Virgin Islands, Brit.	23	218	06(CIA)
219	SEA	Cook Islands	21	219	06(CIA)
220	SEA	Turks & Caicos Is.	21	220	06(CIA)
221	SEA	Palau	20	221	06(E)
222	SEA	Wallis & Futuna	16	222	06(CIA)
223	LAM	Anguilla	13	223	06(CIA)
224	SEA	Tuvalu	11	224	06(E)
225	SEA	Nauru	10	225	06(E)
226	LAM	Montserrat	9	226	06(CIA)
227	AFR	St. Helena	8	227	06(CIA)
228	DME	St. Pierre & Miquelon	7	228	06(CIA)
229	DME	Falkland Islands	3	229	06(CIA)
230	SEA	Niue	2	230	06(CIA)
231	SEA	Tokelau	1	231	06(CIA)

TABLE 2.2 – GDP AT PURCHASING POWER PARITIES, MILLIONS OF DOLLARS, 2006					
OBS	REGION	COUNTRY	GDPPPP	RANK	SOURCE
1	DME	United States	13,163,870	1	06(WB)
2	CPA	China	6,091,977	2	06(WB)
3	DME	Japan	4,081,442	3	06(WB)
4	SAS	India	2,740,066	4	06(WB)
5	DME	Germany	2,662,508	5	06(WB)
6	DME	United Kingdom	2,003,433	6	06(WB)
7	DME	France	1,959,745	7	06(WB)
8	USR	Russia	1,868,980	8	06(WB)
9	DME	Italy	1,709,548	9	06(WB)
10	LAM	Brazil	1,694,335	10	06(WB)
11	LAM	Mexico	1,269,089	11	06(WB)
12	DME	Spain	1,264,047	12	06(WB)
13	DME	Canada	1,198,654	13	06(WB)
14	SEA	Korea, South	1,113,038	14	06(WB)
15	SEA	Indonesia	770,479	15	06(WB)
16	DME	Australia	735,879	16	06(WB)
17	MEA	Iran	694,362	17	06(WB)
18	SEA	Taiwan	661,635	18	POP*GPCPPP
19	MEA	Turkey	614,258	19	06(WB)
20	DME	Netherlands	597,402	20	06(WB)
21	EEU	Poland	565,699	21	06(WB)
22	MEA	Saudi Arabia	527,951	22	06(WB)
23	SEA	Thailand	482,081	23	06(WB)
24	LAM	Argentina	469,006	24	06(WB)
25	AFR	South Africa	430,652	25	06(WB)
26	SAS	Pakistan	375,400	26	06(WB)
27	MEA	Egypt	367,366	27	06(WB)
28	DME	Belgium	353,570	28	06(WB)
29	DME	Greece	349,817	29	06(WB)
30	SEA	Malaysia	327,364	30	06(WB)
31	DME	Sweden	310,602	31	06(WB)
32	LAM	Venezuela	298,862	32	06(WB)
33	DME	Austria	298,521	33	06(WB)
34	USR	Ukraine	290,654	34	06(WB)
35	LAM	Colombia	290,568	35	06(WB)
36	DME	Switzerland	278,628	36	06(WB)
37	SEA	Philippines	271,976	37	06(WB)
38	SEA	Hong Kong	267,849	38	06(WB)
39	DME	Norway	233,368	39	06(WB)
40	AFR	Nigeria	233,189	40	06(WB)
41	EEU	Czechia	227,154	41	06(WB)
42	EEU	Romania	225,220	42	06(WB)
43	DME	Portugal	220,084	43	06(WB)
44	LAM	Chile	214,110	44	06(WB)
45	MEA	Algeria	211,682	45	06(WB)
46	MEA	UAE	209,436	46	POP*GPCPPP
47	SEA	Singapore	200,467	47	06(WB)

		TABLE 2.2 – GDP AT PURCHASING POWER PARITIES, MILLIONS OF DOLLARS, 2006			
OBS	REGION	COUNTRY	GDPPPP	RANK	SOURCE
48	CPA	Vietnam	198,757	48	06(WB)
49	LAM	Peru	195,654	49	06(WB)
50	DME	Denmark	194,042	50	06(WB)
51	EEU	Hungary	183,996	51	06(WB)
52	SAS	Bangladesh	180,144	52	06(WB)
53	DME	Finland	173,903	53	06(WB)
54	DME	Ireland	171,862	54	06(WB)
55	DME	Israel	169,847	55	06(WB)
56	USR	Kazakhstan	150,511	56	06(WB)
57	MEA	Kuwait	134,311	57	POP*GPCPPP
58	MEA	Morocco	119,398	58	06(WB)
59	DME	New Zealand	106,780	59	06(WB)
60	EEU	Slovakia	95,573	60	06(WB)
61	USR	Belarus	94,718	61	06(WB)
62	LAM	El Salvador	94,330	62	06(WB)
63	MEA	Iraq	82,688	63	POP*GPCPPP
64	MEA	Syria	81,998	64	06(WB)
65	EEU	Bulgaria	79,036	65	06(WB)
66	LAM	Puerto Rico	75,791	66	POP*GPCPPP
67	SAS	Sri Lanka	74,507	67	06(WB)
68	AFR	Angola	73,422	68	06(WB)
69	AFR	Sudan	72,825	69	06(WB)
70	MEA	Libya	70,181	70	06(WB)
71	EEU	Serbia	70,176	71	06(WB)
72	MEA	Tunisia	69,473	72	06(WB)
73	LAM	Guatemala	67,424	73	06(WB)
74	EEU	Croatia	63,550	74	06(WB)
75	USR	Uzbekistan	58,165	75	06(WB)
76	LAM	Ecuador	57,419	76	05(WB)
77	LAM	Dominican Rep.	56,396	77	06(WB)
78	AFR	Kenya	53,606	78	06(WB)
79	USR	Lithuania	53,421	79	06(WB)
80	USR	Azerbaijan	53,278	80	06(WB)
81	MEA	Oman	51,201	81	POP*GPCPPP
82	MEA	Qatar	49,855	82	POP*GPCPPP
83	MEA	Yemen	49,203	83	06(WB)
84	AFR	Ethiopia	49,093	84	06(WB)
85	EEU	Slovenia	48,877	85	06(WB)
86	LAM	Cuba	44,047	86	POP*GPCPPP
87	LAM	Costa Rica	42,071	87	06(WB)
88	USR	Turkmenistan	41,642	88	POP*GPCPPP
89	CPA	Korea, North	40,649	89	POP*GPCPPP
90	CPA	Burma	39,707	90	POP*GPCPPP
91	MEA	Lebanon	39,504	91	06(WB)
92	AFR	Tanzania	39,262	92	06(WB)
93	AFR	Cameroon	37,965	93	06(WB)
94	LAM	Bolivia	36,828	94	06(WB)

		TABLE 2.2 – GDP AT PURCHASING POWER PARITIES, MILLIONS OF DOLLARS, 2006			
OBS	*REGION*	*COUNTRY*	*GDPPPP*	*RANK*	*SOURCE*
95	USR	Latvia	35,112	95	06(WB)
96	DME	Luxembourg	34,925	96	06(WB)
97	LAM	Uruguay	33,817	97	06(WB)
98	AFR	Ivory Coast	31,208	98	06(WB)
99	LAM	Panama	30,426	99	06(WB)
100	AFR	Ghana	28,646	100	06(WB)
101	SAS	Nepal	27,602	101	06(WB)
102	AFR	Uganda	26,692	102	06(WB)
103	MEA	Jordan	25,628	103	06(WB)
104	EEU	Bosnia	25,475	104	06(WB)
105	USR	Estonia	25,462	105	06(WB)
106	LAM	Honduras	24,688	106	06(WB)
107	AFR	Zimbabwe	24,474	107	POP*GPCPPP
108	MEA	Bahrain	24,319	108	POP*GPCPPP
109	LAM	Paraguay	24,267	109	06(WB)
110	SAS	Afghanistan	23,927	110	06(WB)
111	LAM	Trinidad & Tobago	23,536	111	06(WB)
112	AFR	Botswana	23,241	112	06(WB)
113	CPA	Cambodia	22,982	113	06(WB)
114	SEA	Macao	20,987	114	06(WB)
115	LAM	Jamaica	20,183	115	06(WB)
116	MEA	Cyprus	19,960	116	06(WB)
117	AFR	Senegal	19,141	117	06(WB)
118	SEA	Brunei	19,059	118	06(WB)
119	EEU	Albania	18,673	119	06(WB)
120	AFR	Gabon	18,625	120	06(WB)
121	AFR	Reunion	18,376	121	POP*GPCPPP
122	USR	Georgia	17,776	122	06(WB)
123	AFR	Congo, Dem. Rep.	17,036	123	06(WB)
124	AFR	Madagascar	16,821	124	06(WB)
125	AFR	Burkina Faso	16,226	125	06(WB)
126	EEU	Macedonia	15,986	126	06(WB)
127	AFR	Mozambique	15,492	127	06(WB)
128	AFR	Chad	15,474	128	06(WB)
129	LAM	Nicaragua	15,428	129	06(WB)
130	AFR	Zambia	14,729	130	06(WB)
131	USR	Armenia	14,683	131	06(WB)
132	AFR	Equatorial Guinea	13,462	132	06(WB)
133	AFR	Mauritius	13,250	133	06(WB)
134	AFR	Congo, Rep.	12,866	134	06(WB)
135	AFR	Mali	12,664	135	06(WB)
136	LAM	Haiti	11,564	136	06(WB)
137	CPA	Laos	11,404	137	06(WB)
138	SEA	Papua New Guinea	11,269	138	06(WB)
139	DME	Iceland	11,143	139	06(WB)
140	AFR	Benin	11,063	140	06(WB)
141	LAM	Guadeloupe	11,022	141	POP*GPCPPP

	TABLE 2.2 – GDP AT PURCHASING POWER PARITIES, MILLIONS OF DOLLARS, 2006				
OBS	REGION	COUNTRY	GDPPPP	RANK	SOURCE
142	USR	Tajikistan	10,689	142	06(WB)
143	AFR	Guinea	10,550	143	06(WB)
144	AFR	Namibia	9,863	144	06(WB)
145	AFR	Malawi	9,496	145	06(WB)
146	USR	Kyrgyzstan	9,415	146	06(WB)
147	USR	Moldova	9,109	147	06(WB)
148	DME	Malta	8,818	148	06(WB)
149	AFR	Niger	8,638	149	06(WB)
150	MEA	West Bank	8,616	150	POP*GPCPPP
151	CPA	Mongolia	7,448	151	POP*GPCPPP
152	LAM	Bahamas	7,031	152	POP*GPCPPP
153	AFR	Rwanda	6,987	153	06(WB)
154	LAM	Martinique	5,760	154	POP*GPCPPP
155	AFR	Mauritania	5,753	155	06(WB)
156	EEU	Montenegro	5,430	156	06(WB)
157	AFR	Swaziland	5,315	157	06(WB)
158	AFR	Somalia	5,098	158	POP*GPCPPP
159	DME	Jersey	5,033	159	POP*GPCPPP
160	AFR	Togo	4,971	160	06(WB)
161	MEA	Gaza Strip	4,613	161	POP*GPCPPP
162	DME	Bermuda	4,578	162	POP*GPCPPP
163	SEA	French Polynesia	4,515	163	POP*GPCPPP
164	SEA	Fiji	3,790	164	06(WB)
165	AFR	Sierra Leone	3,615	165	06(WB)
166	LAM	Suriname	3,594	166	06(WB)
167	SEA	New Caledonia	3,570	167	POP*GPCPPP
168	LAM	Barbados	3,305	168	POP*GPCPPP
169	AFR	Eritrea	3,201	169	06(WB)
170	DME	Andorra	3,034	170	POP*GPCPPP
171	LAM	Neth. Antilles	3,024	171	POP*GPCPPP
172	AFR	CAR	2,945	172	06(WB)
173	AFR	Lesotho	2,872	173	06(WB)
174	DME	Guernsey	2,841	174	POP*GPCPPP
175	DME	Isle of Man	2,744	175	POP*GPCPPP
176	AFR	Burundi	2,723	176	06(WB)
177	LAM	Guyana	2,621	177	06(WB)
178	SAS	Bhutan	2,601	178	06(WB)
179	SEA	Guam	2,580	179	POP*GPCPPP
180	DME	Liechtenstein	2,479	180	POP*GPCPPP
181	LAM	Belize	2,335	181	06(WB)
182	LAM	Aruba	2,273	182	POP*GPCPPP
183	SEA	East Timor	2,203	183	06(WB)
184	LAM	Cayman Islands	1,990	184	POP*GPCPPP
185	AFR	Gambia	1,880	185	06(WB)
186	LAM	St. Lucia	1,659	186	06(WB)
187	LAM	Guiana, French	1,652	187	POP*GPCPPP
188	LAM	Virgin Islands, US	1,639	188	POP*GPCPPP

		TABLE 2.2 – GDP AT PURCHASING POWER PARITIES, MILLIONS OF DOLLARS, 2006			
OBS	REGION	COUNTRY	GDPPPP	RANK	SOURCE
189	AFR	Djibouti	1,609	189	06(WB)
190	SAS	Maldives	1,504	190	06(WB)
191	DME	Faeroe Islands	1,491	191	POP*GPCPPP
192	AFR	Cape Verde	1,399	192	06(WB)
193	LAM	Antigua & Barbuda	1,394	193	06(WB)
194	AFR	Seychelles	1,287	194	06(WB)
195	AFR	Liberia	1,195	195	06(WB)
196	DME	Greenland	1,144	196	POP*GPCPPP
197	DME	Gibraltar	1,067	197	POP*GPCPPP
198	DME	San Marino	1,030	198	POP*GPCPPP
199	LAM	Grenada	1,018	199	06(WB)
200	DME	Monaco	984	200	POP*GPCPPP
201	SEA	Samoa, Western	954	201	06(WB)
202	SEA	Northern Mariana Is.	953	202	POP*GPCPPP
203	AFR	Mayotte	921	203	POP*GPCPPP
204	SEA	Solomon Islands	890	204	06(WB)
205	LAM	Virgin Islands, Brit.	889	205	POP*GPCPPP
206	SEA	Vanuatu	832	206	06(WB)
207	AFR	Guinea Bissau	786	207	06(WB)
208	LAM	St. Kitts & Nevis	720	208	06(WB)
209	AFR	Comoros	702	209	06(WB)
210	LAM	St. Vincent	678	210	POP*GPCPPP
211	LAM	Dominica	669	211	06(WB)
212	SEA	Micronesia	627	212	06(WB)
213	SEA	Tonga	540	213	06(WB)
214	SEA	Marshall Islands	420	214	06(WB)
215	SEA	Samoa, American	389	215	POP*GPCPPP
216	SEA	Kiribati	370	216	06(WB)
217	AFR	Western Sahara	369	217	POP*GPCPPP
218	SEA	Palau	287	218	06(WB)
219	SEA	Turks & Caicos Is.	243	219	POP*GPCPPP
220	AFR	San Tome & Principe	236	220	06(WB)
221	SEA	Cook Islands	195	221	POP*GPCPPP
222	LAM	Anguilla	119	222	POP*GPCPPP
223	DME	Falkland Islands	74	223	POP*GPCPPP
224	SEA	Wallis & Futuna	61	224	POP*GPCPPP
225	SEA	Nauru	51	225	POP*GPCPPP
226	DME	St. Pierre & Miquelon	49	226	POP*GPCPPP
227	LAM	Montserrat	32	227	POP*GPCPPP
228	AFR	St. Helena	19	228	POP*GPCPPP
229	SEA	Tuvalu	17	229	POP*GPCPPP
230	SEA	Niue	13	230	POP*GPCPPP
231	SEA	Tokelau	1	231	POP*GPCPPP

TABLE 2.3 – GNI AT MARKET EXCHANGE RATES, MILLIONS OF DOLLARS, 2006

OBS	REGION	COUNTRY	GDP	RANK	SOURCE
1	DME	United States	13,386,875	1	06(WB)
2	DME	Japan	4,934,676	2	06(WB)
3	DME	Germany	3,032,617	3	06(WB)
4	CPA	China	2,620,951	4	06(WB)
5	DME	United Kingdom	2,455,691	5	06(WB)
6	DME	France	2,306,714	6	06(WB)
7	DME	Italy	1,882,544	7	06(WB)
8	DME	Spain	1,206,169	8	06(WB)
9	DME	Canada	1,196,626	9	06(WB)
10	SAS	India	909,138	10	06(WB)
11	LAM	Brazil	892,639	11	06(WB)
12	SEA	Korea, South	856,565	12	06(WB)
13	USR	Russia	822,328	13	06(WB)
14	LAM	Mexico	815,741	14	06(WB)
15	DME	Australia	742,254	15	06(WB)
16	DME	Netherlands	703,484	16	06(WB)
17	DME	Switzerland	434,844	17	06(WB)
18	DME	Belgium	405,419	18	06(WB)
19	DME	Sweden	395,411	19	06(WB)
20	MEA	Turkey	393,903	20	06(WB)
21	SEA	Taiwan	379,413	21	POP*GPC
22	MEA	Saudi Arabia	331,041	22	06(WB)
23	DME	Austria	329,183	23	06(WB)
24	DME	Norway	318,919	24	06(WB)
25	SEA	Indonesia	315,845	25	06(WB)
26	EEU	Poland	312,994	26	06(WB)
27	DME	Greece	305,308	27	06(WB)
28	DME	Denmark	283,316	28	06(WB)
29	AFR	South Africa	255,389	29	06(WB)
30	DME	Finland	217,803	30	06(WB)
31	MEA	Iran	205,040	31	06(WB)
32	LAM	Argentina	201,347	32	06(WB)
33	SEA	Hong Kong	199,107	33	06(WB)
34	SEA	Thailand	193,734	34	06(WB)
35	DME	Ireland	191,315	35	06(WB)
36	DME	Portugal	189,017	36	06(WB)
37	MEA	UAE	173,120	37	POP*GPC
38	LAM	Venezuela	163,959	38	06(WB)
39	SEA	Malaysia	146,754	39	06(WB)
40	DME	Israel	142,199	40	06(WB)
41	LAM	Colombia	141,982	41	06(WB)
42	EEU	Czechia	131,404	42	06(WB)
43	SEA	Singapore	128,816	43	06(WB)
44	SAS	Pakistan	126,711	44	06(WB)
45	MEA	Kuwait	123,712	45	POP*GPC
46	SEA	Philippines	120,190	46	06(WB)

TABLE 2.3 – GNI AT MARKET EXCHANGE RATES, MILLIONS OF DOLLARS, 2006					
OBS	REGION	COUNTRY	GDP	RANK	SOURCE
47	DME	New Zealand	111,958	47	06(WB)
48	LAM	Chile	111,869	48	06(WB)
49	EEU	Hungary	109,461	49	06(WB)
50	EEU	Romania	104,382	50	06(WB)
51	MEA	Algeria	101,206	51	06(WB)
52	MEA	Egypt	100,912	52	06(WB)
53	USR	Ukraine	90,740	53	06(WB)
54	AFR	Nigeria	90,025	54	06(WB)
55	LAM	Peru	82,201	55	06(WB)
56	SAS	Bangladesh	70,475	56	06(WB)
57	MEA	Morocco	65,793	57	06(WB)
58	USR	Kazakhstan	59,175	58	06(WB)
59	CPA	Vietnam	58,506	59	06(WB)
60	LAM	Puerto Rico	57,805	60	POP*GPC
61	MEA	Qatar	55,358	61	POP*GPC
62	EEU	Slovakia	51,807	62	06(WB)
63	LAM	Cuba	51,625	63	POP*GPC
64	MEA	Iraq	48,472	64	POP*GPC
65	MEA	Libya	44,011	65	06(WB)
66	EEU	Croatia	41,348	66	06(WB)
67	LAM	El Salvador	38,481	67	06(WB)
68	EEU	Slovenia	37,445	68	06(WB)
69	LAM	Ecuador	34,667	69	05(WB)
70	USR	Belarus	33,760	70	06(WB)
71	LAM	Guatemala	33,725	71	06(WB)
72	DME	Luxembourg	32,904	72	06(WB)
73	AFR	Angola	32,646	73	06(WB)
74	EEU	Bulgaria	30,669	74	06(WB)
75	MEA	Syria	30,333	75	06(WB)
76	MEA	Tunisia	30,091	76	06(WB)
77	AFR	Sudan	30,086	77	06(WB)
78	EEU	Serbia	29,961	78	06(WB)
79	MEA	Oman	28,368	79	POP*GPC
80	LAM	Dominican Rep.	27,954	80	06(WB)
81	USR	Lithuania	26,917	81	06(WB)
82	SAS	Sri Lanka	26,001	82	06(WB)
83	CPA	Korea, North	25,022	83	POP*GPC
84	MEA	Lebanon	22,640	84	06(WB)
85	LAM	Costa Rica	21,894	85	06(WB)
86	AFR	Kenya	21,335	86	06(WB)
87	USR	Latvia	18,525	87	06(WB)
88	AFR	Cameroon	18,060	88	06(WB)
89	MEA	Cyprus	17,948	89	06(WB)
90	LAM	Uruguay	17,591	90	06(WB)
91	LAM	Trinidad & Tobago	16,612	91	06(WB)
92	AFR	Ivory Coast	16,578	92	06(WB)
93	MEA	Yemen	16,444	93	06(WB)

TABLE 2.3 – GNI AT MARKET EXCHANGE RATES, MILLIONS OF DOLLARS, 2006

OBS	REGION	COUNTRY	GDP	RANK	SOURCE
94	LAM	Panama	16,442	94	06(WB)
95	USR	Uzbekistan	16,179	95	06(WB)
96	SEA	Macao	15,760	96	POP*GPC
97	USR	Azerbaijan	15,639	97	06(WB)
98	USR	Estonia	15,302	98	06(WB)
99	AFR	Reunion	15,132	99	POP*GPC
100	DME	Iceland	15,078	100	06(WB)
101	MEA	Bahrain	14,983	101	POP*GPC
102	MEA	Jordan	14,653	102	06(WB)
103	AFR	Tanzania	13,404	103	06(WB)
104	CPA	Burma	13,267	104	POP*GPC
105	AFR	Ethiopia	12,874	105	06(WB)
106	EEU	Bosnia	12,689	106	06(WB)
107	AFR	Ghana	11,778	107	06(WB)
108	AFR	Botswana	10,358	108	06(WB)
109	LAM	Bolivia	10,293	109	06(WB)
110	SEA	Brunei	10,287	110	06(WB)
111	LAM	Jamaica	9,504	111	06(WB)
112	EEU	Albania	9,295	112	06(WB)
113	LAM	Guadeloupe	9,178	113	POP*GPC
114	AFR	Senegal	9,117	114	06(WB)
115	AFR	Uganda	8,996	115	06(WB)
116	LAM	Honduras	8,844	116	06(WB)
117	SAS	Nepal	8,790	117	06(WB)
118	LAM	Paraguay	8,461	118	06(WB)
119	SAS	Afghanistan	8,092	119	06(WB)
120	AFR	Congo, Dem. Rep.	7,742	120	06(WB)
121	AFR	Zambia	7,413	121	06(WB)
122	AFR	Gabon	7,032	122	06(WB)
123	USR	Georgia	7,008	123	06(WB)
124	CPA	Cambodia	6,990	124	06(WB)
125	AFR	Mauritius	6,812	125	06(WB)
126	AFR	Namibia	6,573	126	06(WB)
127	AFR	Mozambique	6,453	127	06(WB)
128	EEU	Macedonia	6,260	128	06(WB)
129	AFR	Burkina Faso	6,249	129	06(WB)
130	DME	Malta	6,216	130	06(WB)
131	LAM	Bahamas	6,072	131	POP*GPC
132	USR	Turkmenistan	6,045	132	POP*GPC
133	LAM	Martinique	5,892	133	POP*GPC
134	DME	Jersey	5,828	134	POP*GPC
135	USR	Armenia	5,788	135	06(WB)
136	SEA	French Polynesia	5,616	136	POP*GPC
137	AFR	Mali	5,546	137	06(WB)
138	AFR	Madagascar	5,343	138	06(WB)
139	LAM	Nicaragua	5,163	139	06(WB)
140	DME	Bermuda	5,144	140	POP*GPC

	TABLE 2.3 – GNI AT MARKET EXCHANGE RATES, MILLIONS OF DOLLARS, 2006				
OBS	REGION	COUNTRY	GDP	RANK	SOURCE
141	SEA	New Caledonia	4,745	141	POP*GPC
142	AFR	Chad	4,708	142	06(WB)
143	AFR	Benin	4,665	143	06(WB)
144	SEA	Papua New Guinea	4,603	144	06(WB)
145	AFR	Equatorial Guinea	4,216	145	06(WB)
146	LAM	Haiti	4,044	146	06(WB)
147	AFR	Congo, Rep.	3,887	147	POP*GPC
148	MEA	West Bank	3,776	148	POP*GPC
149	AFR	Guinea	3,713	149	06(WB)
150	AFR	Niger	3,665	150	06(WB)
151	USR	Moldova	3,650	151	06(WB)
152	SEA	Guam	3,633	152	POP*GPC
153	DME	Andorra	3,498	153	POP*GPC
154	LAM	Neth. Antilles	3,344	154	POP*GPC
155	AFR	Malawi	3,143	155	06(WB)
156	SEA	Fiji	3,098	156	06(WB)
157	LAM	Virgin Islands, US	3,085	157	POP*GPC
158	LAM	Barbados	3,049	158	POP*GPC
159	DME	Liechtenstein	2,907	159	POP*GPC
160	DME	Guernsey	2,890	160	POP*GPC
161	CPA	Laos	2,890	161	06(WB)
162	AFR	Swaziland	2,737	162	06(WB)
163	DME	Isle of Man	2,662	163	POP*GPC
164	USR	Kyrgyzstan	2,609	164	06(WB)
165	CPA	Mongolia	2,580	165	POP*GPC
166	USR	Tajikistan	2,572	166	06(WB)
167	EEU	Montenegro	2,481	167	06(WB)
168	AFR	Rwanda	2,341	168	06(WB)
169	AFR	Somalia	2,328	169	POP*GPC
170	AFR	Mauritania	2,325	170	06(WB)
171	AFR	Togo	2,265	171	06(WB)
172	LAM	Aruba	2,184	172	POP*GPC
173	LAM	Cayman Islands	2,169	173	POP*GPC
174	MEA	Gaza Strip	2,022	174	POP*GPC
175	AFR	Lesotho	1,957	175	06(WB)
176	LAM	Suriname	1,918	176	06(WB)
177	LAM	Guiana, French	1,799	177	POP*GPC
178	AFR	Zimbabwe	1,603	178	POP*GPC
179	DME	Greenland	1,601	179	POP*GPC
180	AFR	CAR	1,499	180	06(WB)
181	DME	Faeroe Islands	1,476	181	POP*GPC
182	AFR	Sierra Leone	1,353	182	06(WB)
183	DME	San Marino	1,291	183	06(WB)
184	DME	Monaco	1,172	184	POP*GPC
185	LAM	Belize	1,114	185	06(WB)
186	AFR	Cape Verde	1,105	186	06(WB)
187	SEA	Northern Mariana Is.	1,017	187	POP*GPC

TABLE 2.3 – GNI AT MARKET EXCHANGE RATES, MILLIONS OF DOLLARS, 2006					
OBS	REGION	COUNTRY	GDP	RANK	SOURCE
188	LAM	Antigua & Barbuda	929	188	06(WB)
189	SAS	Bhutan	928	189	06(WB)
190	DME	Gibraltar	916	190	POP*GPC
191	SAS	Maldives	903	191	06(WB)
192	AFR	Eritrea	888	192	06(WB)
193	LAM	St. Lucia	883	193	POP*GPC
194	SEA	East Timor	865	194	06(WB)
195	AFR	Djibouti	864	195	06(WB)
196	LAM	Guyana	849	196	06(WB)
197	AFR	Burundi	815	197	06(WB)
198	LAM	Virgin Islands, Brit.	765	198	POP*GPC
199	AFR	Seychelles	751	199	06(WB)
200	SEA	Samoa, American	606	200	POP*GPC
201	AFR	Mayotte	523	201.0	POP*GPC
202	LAM	Grenada	498	202.0	POP*GPC
203	AFR	Gambia	488	203.0	06(WB)
204	AFR	Liberia	469	204.0	06(WB)
205	LAM	St. Kitts & Nevis	447	205.0	POP*GPC
206	SEA	Samoa, Western	421	206.0	06(WB)
207	AFR	Comoros	406	207.0	06(WB)
208	SEA	Vanuatu	373	208.0	06(WB)
209	LAM	St. Vincent	342	209.0	POP*GPC
210	SEA	Solomon Islands	333	210.0	06(WB)
211	AFR	GuineaBissau	307	211.0	06(WB)
212	LAM	Dominica	289	212.0	POP*GPC
213	SEA	Micronesia	264	213.0	06(WB)
214	SEA	Tonga	225	214.0	06(WB)
215	SEA	Marshall Islands	195	215.0	06(WB)
216	SEA	Palau	161	216.0	06(WB)
217	SEA	Turks & Caicos Is.	155	217.0	POP*GPC
218	SEA	Kiribati	124	218.5	06(WB)
219	AFR	San Tome & Principe	124	218.5	06(WB)
220	SEA	Cook Islands	117	220.0	POP*GPC
221	AFR	Western Sahara	112	221.0	POP*GPC
222	SEA	Nauru	79	222.0	POP*GPC
223	LAM	Anguilla	70	223.0	POP*GPC
224	DME	Falkland Islands	57	224.0	POP*GPC
225	SEA	Wallis & Futuna	29	225.0	POP*GPC
226	DME	St. Pierre & Miquelon	28	226.0	POP*GPC
227	SEA	Tuvalu	26	227.0	POP*GPC
228	LAM	Montserrat	15	228.0	POP*GPC
229	AFR	St. Helena	8	229.0	POP*GPC
230	SEA	Niue	7	230.0	POP*GPC
231	SEA	Tokelau	0	231.0	POP*GPC

OBS	REGION	COUNTRY	ARMY	RANK	SOURCE
— TABLE 2.4 – ARMED FORCES PERSONNEL, THOUSANDS, 2006

OBS	REGION	COUNTRY	ARMY	RANK	SOURCE
1	CPA	China	3,605	1.0	06(WB)
2	SAS	India	2,589	2.0	06(WB)
3	DME	United States	1,498	3.0	06(WB)
4	USR	Russia	1,446	4.0	06(WB)
5	CPA	Korea, North	1,295	5.0	06(WB)
6	SAS	Pakistan	923	6.0	06(WB)
7	MEA	Egypt	866	7.0	06(WB)
8	LAM	Brazil	754	8.0	06(WB)
9	SEA	Korea, South	692	9.0	06(WB)
10	MEA	Turkey	612	10.0	06(WB)
11	MEA	Iran	585	11.0	06(WB)
12	SEA	Indonesia	582	12.0	06(WB)
13	CPA	Burma	513	13.0	06(WB)
14	MEA	Iraq	495	14.5	06(WB)
15	CPA	Vietnam	495	14.5	06(WB)
16	DME	Italy	440	16.0	06(WB)
17	SEA	Thailand	420	17.0	06(WB)
18	MEA	Syria	401	18.0	06(WB)
19	LAM	Colombia	398	19.0	06(WB)
20	DME	France	354	20.0	06(WB)
21	MEA	Algeria	334	21.0	06(WB)
22	SEA	Taiwan	290	22.0	06(IISS)
23	LAM	Mexico	280	23.0	06(WB)
24	DME	Japan	252	24.0	06(WB)
25	DME	Germany	246	25.5	06(WB)
26	MEA	Morocco	246	25.5	06(WB)
27	MEA	Saudi Arabia	240	27.0	06(WB)
28	DME	Spain	222	28.0	06(WB)
29	USR	Ukraine	215	29.0	06(WB)
30	SAS	Bangladesh	214	30.0	06(WB)
31	SAS	Sri Lanka	213	31.0	06(WB)
32	AFR	Eritrea	202	32.0	05(WB)
33	LAM	Peru	198	33.0	06(WB)
34	CPA	Cambodia	191	34.0	06(WB)
35	DME	Israel	185	35.0	06(WB)
36	USR	Belarus	183	36.5	06(WB)
37	AFR	Ethiopia	183	36.5	05(WB)
38	DME	United Kingdom	181	38.0	06(WB)
39	SEA	Singapore	167	39.0	06(WB)
40	AFR	Nigeria	162	40.0	06(WB)
41	DME	Greece	161	41.0	06(WB)
42	EEU	Romania	154	42.0	06(WB)
43	EEU	Poland	148	43.0	06(WB)
44	SEA	Philippines	147	44.0	06(WB)
45	MEA	Yemen	138	45.0	06(WB)
46	SEA	Malaysia	134	46.0	06(WB)
47	SAS	Nepal	131	47.0	06(WB)
48	CPA	Laos	129	48.0	06(WB)

\multicolumn{6}{c}{TABLE 2.4 – ARMED FORCES PERSONNEL, THOUSANDS, 2006}
OBS	REGION	COUNTRY	ARMY	RANK	SOURCE
49	AFR	Sudan	123	49.0	05(WB)
50	MEA	Jordan	111	50.0	06(WB)
51	AFR	Angola	110	51.0	06(WB)
52	LAM	Argentina	107	52.0	06(WB)
53	LAM	Chile	103	53.5	06(WB)
54	AFR	South Africa	103	53.5	06(WB)
55	DME	Portugal	91	55.0	06(WB)
56	USR	Uzbekistan	87	56.0	06(WB)
57	LAM	Bolivia	83	57.0	06(WB)
58	USR	Azerbaijan	82	59.0	06(WB)
59	AFR	Burundi	82	59.0	05(WB)
60	LAM	Venezuela	82	59.0	05(WB)
61	USR	Kazakhstan	81	61.0	06(WB)
62	LAM	Cuba	76	63.0	06(WB)
63	MEA	Lebanon	76	63.0	06(WB)
64	MEA	Libya	76	63.0	06(WB)
65	EEU	Bulgaria	75	65.0	06(WB)
66	AFR	Congo, Dem. Rep.	65	66.5	05(WB)
67	LAM	Dominican Rep.	65	66.5	06(WB)
68	DME	Canada	64	68.0	06(WB)
69	LAM	Ecuador	57	69.0	06(WB)
70	AFR	Rwanda	53	70.0	05(WB)
71	SAS	Afghanistan	51	72.5	06(WB)
72	DME	Australia	51	72.5	06(WB)
73	MEA	UAE	51	72.5	06(WB)
74	AFR	Zimbabwe	51	72.5	06(WB)
75	AFR	Somalia	50	75.0	00(WB)
76	MEA	Tunisia	48	76.0	06(WB)
77	USR	Armenia	47	78.0	06(WB)
78	MEA	Oman	47	78.0	06(WB)
79	AFR	Uganda	47	78.0	05(WB)
80	DME	Netherlands	46	80.0	06(WB)
81	EEU	Hungary	44	81.0	06(WB)
82	DME	Austria	40	82.5	06(WB)
83	DME	Belgium	40	82.5	06(WB)
84	MEA	West Bank	37	84.0	06(WB)
85	AFR	Chad	35	85.5	05(WB)
86	LAM	Guatemala	35	85.5	06(WB)
87	USR	Georgia	33	87.0	06(WB)
88	DME	Finland	32	88.0	06(WB)
89	DME	Denmark	30	89.0	06(WB)
90	AFR	Kenya	29	90.0	05(WB)
91	LAM	El Salvador	28	91.5	06(WB)
92	AFR	Tanzania	28	91.5	05(WB)
93	EEU	Czechia	26	93.5	06(WB)
94	LAM	Paraguay	26	93.5	06(WB)
95	LAM	Uruguay	25	95.0	05(WB)
96	DME	Sweden	25	96.0	06(WB)

TABLE 2.4 – ARMED FORCES PERSONNEL, THOUSANDS, 2006					
OBS	REGION	COUNTRY	ARMY	RANK	SOURCE
97	USR	Lithuania	24	97.5	06(WB)
98	EEU	Serbia	24	97.5	06(WB)
99	AFR	Cameroon	23	100.0	05(WB)
100	MEA	Kuwait	23	100.0	06(WB)
101	DME	Switzerland	23	100.0	06(WB)
102	AFR	Madagascar	22	102.5	05(WB)
103	USR	Turkmenistan	22	102.5	06(WB)
104	EEU	Croatia	21	105.0	06(WB)
105	USR	Kyrgyzstan	21	105.0	06(WB)
106	AFR	Mauritania	21	105.0	06(WB)
107	LAM	Honduras	20	107.0	06(WB)
108	MEA	Gaza Strip	20	108.0	06(WB)
109	MEA	Bahrain	19	110.5	06(WB)
110	AFR	Ivory Coast	19	110.5	05(WB)
111	EEU	Macedonia	19	110.5	06(WB)
112	AFR	Senegal	19	110.5	06(WB)
113	USR	Latvia	17	114.0	06(WB)
114	EEU	Slovakia	17	114.0	06(WB)
115	USR	Tajikistan	17	114.0	06(WB)
116	CPA	Mongolia	16	117.5	06(WB)
117	EEU	Montenegro	16	117.5	06(WB)
118	DME	Norway	16	117.5	06(WB)
119	AFR	Zambia	16	117.5	06(WB)
120	AFR	Namibia	15	120.0	06(WB)
121	LAM	Nicaragua	14	121.0	06(WB)
122	AFR	Djibouti	13	122.5	05(WB)
123	AFR	Guinea	13	122.5	05(WB)
124	AFR	Congo, Rep.	12	125.5	05(WB)
125	AFR	Mali	12	125.5	06(WB)
126	LAM	Panama	12	125.5	06(IISS)
127	MEA	Qatar	12	125.5	06(IISS)
128	EEU	Albania	12	128.0	06(WB)
129	AFR	Burkina Faso	11	129.0	05(WB)
130	AFR	Botswana	11	131.5	06(WB)
131	AFR	Mozambique	11	131.5	06(WB)
132	AFR	Sierra Leone	11	131.5	06(WB)
133	EEU	Slovenia	11	131.5	06(WB)
134	MEA	Cyprus	11	134.0	06(WB)
135	LAM	Costa Rica	10	136.0	06(WB)
136	DME	Ireland	10	136.0	06(WB)
137	AFR	Niger	10	136.0	06(WB)
138	AFR	Togo	10	138.0	06(WB)
139	EEU	Bosnia	9	140.5	06(WB)
140	SEA	Brunei	9	140.5	06(WB)
141	AFR	GuineaBissau	9	140.5	06(WB)
142	DME	New Zealand	9	140.5	06(WB)
143	AFR	Benin	8	143.5	05(WB)
144	USR	Moldova	8	143.5	06(WB)

OBS	REGION	COUNTRY	ARMY	RANK	SOURCE
145	USR	Estonia	7	146.5	06(WB)
146	AFR	Gabon	7	146.5	05(WB)
147	AFR	Ghana	7	146.5	05(WB)
148	AFR	Malawi	7	146.5	06(WB)
149	SAS	Bhutan	6	149.0	00(WB)
150	SEA	Fiji	4	150.0	06(WB)
151	AFR	CAR	3	153.0	05(WB)
152	LAM	Jamaica	3	153.0	06(WB)
153	SEA	Papua New Guinea	3	153.0	06(WB)
154	AFR	Swaziland	3	153.0	00(E)
155	LAM	Trinidad & Tobago	3	153.0	06(WB)
156	AFR	Lesotho	2	158.0	06(WB)
157	AFR	Liberia	2	158.0	06(WB)
158	DME	Malta	2	158.0	06(WB)
159	AFR	Mauritius	2	158.0	05(WB)
160	LAM	Suriname	2	158.0	06(WB)
161	DME	Luxembourg	2	161.0	06(WB)
162	LAM	Belize	1	165.5	06(WB)
163	AFR	Cape Verde	1	165.5	05(WB)
164	SEA	East Timor	1	165.5	06(WB)
165	AFR	Equatorial Guinea	1	165.5	06(IISS)
166	LAM	Guyana	1	165.5	05(IISS)
167	LAM	Haiti	1	165.5	06(IISS)
168	SAS	Maldives	1	165.5	00(E)
169	AFR	San Tome & Principe	1	165.5	00(E)
170	LAM	Bahamas	1	170.0	06(WB)
171	AFR	Comoros	1	171.5	00(IISS)
172	AFR	Gambia	1	171.5	05(WB)
173	LAM	Barbados	1	173.0	06(WB)
174	AFR	Seychelles	1	174.5	05(WB)
175	SEA	Tonga	1	174.5	06(E)
176	LAM	Antigua & Barbuda	0	176.0	06(WB)
177	DME	Iceland	0	177.0	06(WB)
178	DME	Andorra	0	204.5	06(CIA)
179	LAM	Anguilla	0	204.5	06(CIA)
180	LAM	Aruba	0	204.5	06(CIA)
181	DME	Bermuda	0	204.5	06(CIA)
182	LAM	Cayman Islands	0	204.5	06(CIA)
183	SEA	Cook Islands	0	204.5	06(CIA)
184	LAM	Dominica	0	204.5	06(CIA)
185	DME	Faeroe Islands	0	204.5	06(CIA)
186	DME	Falkland Islands	0	204.5	06(CIA)
187	SEA	French Polynesia	0	204.5	06(CIA)
188	DME	Gibraltar	0	204.5	06(CIA)
189	DME	Greenland	0	204.5	06(CIA)
190	LAM	Grenada	0	204.5	06(CIA)
191	LAM	Guadeloupe	0	204.5	06(CIA)
192	SEA	Guam	0	204.5	06(CIA)

TABLE 2.4 – ARMED FORCES PERSONNEL, THOUSANDS, 2006

\multicolumn{6}{c}{TABLE 2.4 – ARMED FORCES PERSONNEL, THOUSANDS, 2006}

OBS	REGION	COUNTRY	ARMY	RANK	SOURCE
193	DME	Guernsey	0	204.5	06(CIA)
194	LAM	Guiana, French	0	204.5	06(CIA)
195	SEA	Hong Kong	0	204.5	06(CIA)
196	DME	Isle of Man	0	204.5	06(CIA)
197	DME	Jersey	0	204.5	06(CIA)
198	SEA	Kiribati	0	204.5	06(CIA)
199	DME	Liechtenstein	0	204.5	06(CIA)
200	SEA	Macao	0	204.5	06(CIA)
201	SEA	Marshall Islands	0	204.5	06(CIA)
202	LAM	Martinique	0	204.5	06(CIA)
203	AFR	Mayotte	0	204.5	06(CIA)
204	SEA	Micronesia	0	204.5	06(CIA)
205	DME	Monaco	0	204.5	06(CIA)
206	LAM	Montserrat	0	204.5	06(CIA)
207	SEA	Nauru	0	204.5	06(CIA)
208	LAM	Neth. Antilles	0	204.5	06(CIA)
209	SEA	New Caledonia	0	204.5	06(CIA)
210	SEA	Niue	0	204.5	06(CIA)
211	SEA	Northern Mariana Is.	0	204.5	06(CIA)
212	SEA	Palau	0	204.5	06(CIA)
213	LAM	Puerto Rico	0	204.5	06(CIA)
214	AFR	Reunion	0	204.5	06(CIA)
215	SEA	Samoa, American	0	204.5	06(CIA)
216	SEA	Samoa, Western	0	204.5	06(CIA)
217	DME	San Marino	0	204.5	06(CIA)
218	SEA	Solomon Islands	0	204.5	06(CIA)
219	AFR	St. Helena	0	204.5	06(CIA)
220	LAM	St. Kitts & Nevis	0	204.5	06(CIA)
221	LAM	St. Lucia	0	204.5	06(CIA)
222	DME	St. Pierre & Miquelon	0	204.5	06(CIA)
223	LAM	St. Vincent	0	204.5	06(CIA)
224	SEA	Tokelau	0	204.5	06(CIA)
225	SEA	Turks & Caicos Is.	0	204.5	06(CIA)
226	SEA	Tuvalu	0	204.5	06(CIA)
227	SEA	Vanuatu	0	204.5	06(CIA)
228	LAM	Virgin Islands, Brit.	0	204.5	06(CIA)
229	LAM	Virgin Islands, US	0	204.5	06(CIA)
230	SEA	Wallis & Futuna	0	204.5	06(CIA)
231	AFR	Western Sahara	0	204.5	06(CIA)

TABLE 2.5 – MILITARY EXPENDITURES AS SHARE OF GDP, PERCENT, 2006					
OBS	REGION	COUNTRY	MILGDP	RANK	SOURCE
1	CPA	Korea, North	25.00	1.0	02(IISS)
2	AFR	Eritrea	24.11	2.0	03(WB)
3	MEA	Oman	11.84	3.0	05(WB)
4	SAS	Afghanistan	9.93	4.0	05(WB)
5	MEA	Saudi Arabia	8.47	5.0	06(WB)
6	DME	Israel	8.36	6.0	06(WB)
7	AFR	Liberia	7.50	7.0	02(WB)
8	MEA	Gaza Strip	7.03	8.5	06(WB)
9	MEA	West Bank	7.03	8.5	06(WB)
10	SAS	Maldives	6.10	10.0	06(IISS)
11	MEA	Iraq	6.03	11.0	06(WB)
12	MEA	Yemen	6.02	12.0	05(WB)
13	CPA	Vietnam	5.60	13.0	06(IISS)
14	AFR	Burundi	5.46	14.0	06(WB)
15	AFR	Angola	5.40	15.0	05(WB)
16	MEA	Jordan	4.92	16.0	06(WB)
17	MEA	Kuwait	4.84	17.0	05(WB)
18	MEA	Iran	4.80	18.0	06(WB)
19	SEA	Singapore	4.69	19.0	06(WB)
20	MEA	Qatar	4.50	20.0	06(IISS)
21	AFR	Djibouti	4.28	21.0	02(WB)
22	DME	United States	4.15	22.0	06(WB)
23	MEA	Lebanon	4.14	23.0	06(WB)
24	AFR	GuineaBissau	4.02	24.5	05(WB)
25	USR	Russia	4.02	24.5	06(WB)
26	LAM	Cuba	4.00	26.5	06(IISS)
27	AFR	Somalia	4.00	26.5	02(IISS)
28	MEA	Syria	3.83	28.0	06(WB)
29	SAS	Pakistan	3.82	29.0	06(WB)
30	MEA	Morocco	3.66	30.0	06(WB)
31	LAM	Chile	3.63	31.0	06(WB)
32	LAM	Colombia	3.46	32.0	06(WB)
33	USR	Azerbaijan	3.31	33.0	06(WB)
34	SAS	Bhutan	3.30	34.0	02(IISS)
35	DME	Greece	3.24	35.0	06(WB)
36	USR	Georgia	3.10	36.0	06(WB)
37	USR	Kyrgyzstan	3.08	37.0	06(WB)
38	MEA	Bahrain	3.02	38.0	05(WB)
39	AFR	Botswana	3.00	39.0	05(WB)
40	AFR	Namibia	2.94	40.0	06(WB)
41	MEA	Turkey	2.85	41.0	06(WB)
42	AFR	Zimbabwe	2.80	42.0	06(IISS)
43	USR	Armenia	2.79	43.0	06(WB)
44	AFR	Rwanda	2.74	44.0	06(WB)
45	SEA	Korea, South	2.70	45.0	06(WB)
46	MEA	Algeria	2.68	46.0	06(WB)
47	MEA	Egypt	2.67	47.5	06(WB)

TABLE 2.5 – MILITARY EXPENDITURES AS SHARE OF GDP, PERCENT, 2006					
OBS	REGION	COUNTRY	MILGDP	RANK	SOURCE
48	SAS	India	2.67	47.5	06(WB)
49	AFR	Ethiopia	2.60	49.0	06(WB)
50	DME	United Kingdom	2.59	50.0	06(WB)
51	AFR	Mauritania	2.47	51.0	06(WB)
52	SEA	Brunei	2.44	52.5	06(WB)
53	SAS	Sri Lanka	2.44	52.5	06(WB)
54	DME	France	2.41	54.0	06(WB)
55	EEU	Montenegro	2.40	55.0	06(IISS)
56	AFR	Lesotho	2.36	56.0	05(WB)
57	EEU	Bulgaria	2.27	57.0	06(WB)
58	LAM	Ecuador	2.26	58.0	06(WB)
59	AFR	Mali	2.25	59.5	06(WB)
60	AFR	Zambia	2.25	59.5	04(WB)
61	AFR	Sudan	2.24	61.0	03(WB)
62	SEA	Taiwan	2.20	62.0	06(IISS)
63	USR	Tajikistan	2.17	63.0	04(WB)
64	EEU	Serbia	2.14	64.0	06(WB)
65	DME	Portugal	2.11	65.5	06(WB)
66	USR	Ukraine	2.11	65.5	06(WB)
67	AFR	Uganda	2.09	67.0	06(WB)
68	CPA	Laos	2.07	68.0	01(WB)
69	SEA	Malaysia	2.05	69.0	06(WB)
70	EEU	Macedonia	2.03	70.0	06(WB)
71	AFR	Guinea	2.02	71.0	04(WB)
72	EEU	Poland	1.97	72.5	06(WB)
73	MEA	UAE	1.97	72.5	05(WB)
74	CPA	China	1.95	74.0	06(WB)
75	AFR	Swaziland	1.94	75.0	04(WB)
76	AFR	Congo, Dem. Rep.	1.90	76.5	06(IISS)
77	EEU	Romania	1.90	76.5	06(WB)
78	SAS	Nepal	1.88	78.0	06(WB)
79	DME	Australia	1.80	80.0	06(WB)
80	LAM	Guyana	1.80	80.0	04(IISS)
81	AFR	Seychelles	1.80	80.0	06(WB)
82	EEU	Slovakia	1.73	82.0	06(WB)
83	EEU	Czechia	1.72	83.0	06(WB)
84	EEU	Slovenia	1.69	84.0	06(WB)
85	USR	Belarus	1.68	85.0	06(WB)
86	CPA	Cambodia	1.67	86.0	06(WB)
87	DME	Italy	1.66	87.0	06(WB)
88	AFR	Kenya	1.65	88.0	06(WB)
89	EEU	Croatia	1.63	89.5	06(WB)
90	USR	Latvia	1.63	89.5	06(WB)
91	EEU	Bosnia	1.62	91.0	05(WB)
92	AFR	Senegal	1.61	92.0	06(WB)
93	EEU	Albania	1.58	93.5	06(WB)
94	AFR	Togo	1.58	93.5	05(WB)
95	AFR	Ivory Coast	1.55	95.0	03(WB)

TABLE 2.5 – MILITARY EXPENDITURES AS SHARE OF GDP, PERCENT, 2006					
OBS	REGION	COUNTRY	MILGDP	RANK	SOURCE
96	MEA	Libya	1.51	96.0	06(WB)
97	LAM	Belize	1.50	98.0	06(IISS)
98	DME	Netherlands	1.50	98.0	06(WB)
99	DME	Norway	1.50	98.0	06(WB)
100	LAM	Brazil	1.47	100.0	06(WB)
101	LAM	Bolivia	1.45	101.0	06(WB)
102	USR	Estonia	1.44	102.0	06(WB)
103	MEA	Tunisia	1.42	103.0	06(WB)
104	DME	Denmark	1.41	104.5	06(WB)
105	DME	Sweden	1.41	104.5	06(WB)
106	AFR	Cameroon	1.40	106.0	06(WB)
107	AFR	Burkina Faso	1.38	107.5	06(WB)
108	AFR	South Africa	1.38	107.5	06(WB)
109	MEA	Cyprus	1.35	109.5	06(WB)
110	DME	Finland	1.35	109.5	06(WB)
111	DME	Germany	1.31	111.0	06(WB)
112	CPA	Burma	1.30	112.5	02(WB)
113	LAM	Suriname	1.30	112.5	06(IISS)
114	CPA	Mongolia	1.29	114.0	05(WB)
115	SEA	Indonesia	1.21	115.5	06(WB)
116	LAM	Peru	1.21	115.5	06(WB)
117	SEA	East Timor	1.20	117.5	04(CIA)
118	AFR	Gabon	1.20	117.5	06(WB)
119	EEU	Hungary	1.17	120.0	06(WB)
120	USR	Lithuania	1.17	120.0	06(WB)
121	LAM	Uruguay	1.17	120.0	06(WB)
122	DME	Canada	1.16	122.5	06(WB)
123	SEA	Fiji	1.16	122.5	04(WB)
124	LAM	Venezuela	1.15	124.0	06(WB)
125	AFR	Congo, Rep.	1.14	125.0	06(WB)
126	SAS	Bangladesh	1.13	126.5	06(WB)
127	DME	Belgium	1.13	126.5	06(WB)
128	AFR	CAR	1.12	128.5	05(WB)
129	AFR	Tanzania	1.12	128.5	06(WB)
130	AFR	Niger	1.11	130.5	04(WB)
131	SEA	Tonga	1.11	130.5	04(WB)
132	SEA	Thailand	1.10	132.0	06(WB)
133	DME	Spain	1.05	133.0	06(WB)
134	AFR	Benin	1.00	135.5	06(IISS)
135	LAM	Haiti	1.00	135.5	02(IISS)
136	DME	New Zealand	1.00	135.5	06(WB)
137	LAM	Panama	1.00	135.5	06(IISS)
138	AFR	Madagascar	0.98	138.0	06(WB)
139	AFR	Sierra Leone	0.97	139.5	06(WB)
140	USR	Turkmenistan	0.97	139.5	06(WB)
141	DME	Japan	0.95	141.0	06(WB)
142	USR	Kazakhstan	0.91	142.0	06(WB)
143	LAM	Argentina	0.90	144.5	06(WB)

TABLE 2.5 – MILITARY EXPENDITURES AS SHARE OF GDP, PERCENT, 2006

OBS	REGION	COUNTRY	MILGDP	RANK	SOURCE
144	AFR	Chad	0.90	144.5	06(WB)
145	AFR	San Tome & Principe	0.90	144.5	00(IISS)
146	DME	Switzerland	0.90	144.5	06(WB)
147	SEA	Philippines	0.87	147.0	06(WB)
148	DME	Austria	0.85	148.0	06(WB)
149	LAM	Barbados	0.83	149.0	04(WB)
150	LAM	Paraguay	0.81	150.0	06(WB)
151	DME	Luxembourg	0.80	151.5	06(WB)
152	AFR	Mozambique	0.80	151.5	06(IISS)
153	USR	Uzbekistan	0.75	153.0	06(WB)
154	AFR	Cape Verde	0.71	154.0	04(WB)
155	AFR	Ghana	0.70	155.0	06(WB)
156	AFR	Nigeria	0.69	156.0	06(WB)
157	LAM	Nicaragua	0.66	157.0	06(WB)
158	LAM	Bahamas	0.65	158.0	05(WB)
159	DME	Malta	0.64	159.0	06(WB)
160	LAM	Honduras	0.59	160.0	06(WB)
161	LAM	El Salvador	0.58	161.0	06(WB)
162	LAM	Jamaica	0.56	162.0	06(WB)
163	AFR	Malawi	0.54	163.0	03(WB)
164	DME	Ireland	0.53	164.0	06(WB)
165	SEA	Papua New Guinea	0.52	165.0	06(WB)
166	LAM	Dominican Rep.	0.51	166.0	06(WB)
167	LAM	Antigua & Barbuda	0.50	167.0	06(IISS)
168	AFR	Gambia	0.48	168.0	04(WB)
169	LAM	Guatemala	0.41	169.0	06(WB)
170	LAM	Costa Rica	0.40	170.0	06(IISS)
171	LAM	Mexico	0.38	171.0	06(WB)
172	DME	Iceland	0.30	172.5	05(E)
173	LAM	Trinidad & Tobago	0.30	172.5	06(IISS)
174	USR	Moldova	0.29	174.0	06(WB)
175	AFR	Comoros	0.20	175.5	00(IISS)
176	AFR	Mauritius	0.20	175.5	05(WB)
177	AFR	Equatorial Guinea	0.10	177.0	06(IISS)
178	DME	Andorra	0.00	204.5	06(CIA)
179	LAM	Anguilla	0.00	204.5	06(CIA)
180	LAM	Aruba	0.00	204.5	06(CIA)
181	DME	Bermuda	0.00	204.5	06(CIA)
182	LAM	Cayman Islands	0.00	204.5	06(CIA)
183	SEA	Cook Islands	0.00	204.5	06(CIA)
184	LAM	Dominica	0.00	204.5	06(CIA)
185	DME	Faeroe Islands	0.00	204.5	06(CIA)
186	DME	Falkland Islands	0.00	204.5	06(CIA)
187	SEA	French Polynesia	0.00	204.5	06(CIA)
188	DME	Gibraltar	0.00	204.5	06(CIA)
189	DME	Greenland	0.00	204.5	06(CIA)
190	LAM	Grenada	0.00	204.5	06(CIA)
191	LAM	Guadeloupe	0.00	204.5	06(CIA)

OBS	REGION	COUNTRY	MILGDP	RANK	SOURCE
	TABLE 2.5 – MILITARY EXPENDITURES AS SHARE OF GDP, PERCENT, 2006				
192	SEA	Guam	0.00	204.5	06(CIA)
193	DME	Guernsey	0.00	204.5	06(CIA)
194	LAM	Guiana, French	0.00	204.5	06(CIA)
195	SEA	Hong Kong	0.00	204.5	06(CIA)
196	DME	Isle of Man	0.00	204.5	06(CIA)
197	DME	Jersey	0.00	204.5	06(CIA)
198	SEA	Kiribati	0.00	204.5	06(CIA)
199	DME	Liechtenstein	0.00	204.5	06(CIA)
200	SEA	Macao	0.00	204.5	06(CIA)
201	SEA	Marshall Islands	0.00	204.5	06(CIA)
202	LAM	Martinique	0.00	204.5	06(CIA)
203	AFR	Mayotte	0.00	204.5	06(CIA)
204	SEA	Micronesia	0.00	204.5	06(CIA)
205	DME	Monaco	0.00	204.5	06(CIA)
206	LAM	Montserrat	0.00	204.5	06(CIA)
207	SEA	Nauru	0.00	204.5	06(CIA)
208	LAM	Neth. Antilles	0.00	204.5	06(CIA)
209	SEA	New Caledonia	0.00	204.5	06(CIA)
210	SEA	Niue	0.00	204.5	06(CIA)
211	SEA	Northern Mariana Is.	0.00	204.5	06(CIA)
212	SEA	Palau	0.00	204.5	06(CIA)
213	LAM	Puerto Rico	0.00	204.5	06(CIA)
214	AFR	Reunion	0.00	204.5	06(CIA)
215	SEA	Samoa, American	0.00	204.5	06(CIA)
216	SEA	Samoa, Western	0.00	204.5	06(CIA)
217	DME	San Marino	0.00	204.5	06(CIA)
218	SEA	Solomon Islands	0.00	204.5	06(CIA)
219	AFR	St. Helena	0.00	204.5	06(CIA)
220	LAM	St. Kitts & Nevis	0.00	204.5	06(CIA)
221	LAM	St. Lucia	0.00	204.5	06(CIA)
222	DME	St. Pierre & Miquelon	0.00	204.5	06(CIA)
223	LAM	St. Vincent	0.00	204.5	06(CIA)
224	SEA	Tokelau	0.00	204.5	06(CIA)
225	SEA	Turks & Caicos Is.	0.00	204.5	06(CIA)
226	SEA	Tuvalu	0.00	204.5	06(CIA)
227	SEA	Vanuatu	0.00	204.5	06(CIA)
228	LAM	Virgin Islands, Brit.	0.00	204.5	06(CIA)
229	LAM	Virgin Islands, US	0.00	204.5	06(CIA)
230	SEA	Wallis & Futuna	0.00	204.5	06(CIA)
231	AFR	Western Sahara	0.00	204.5	06(CIA)

\multicolumn{7}{c}{TABLE 2.6 – FOREIGN MILITARY AID, MILLIONS OF DOLLARS, 2006}

OBS	REGION	COUNTRY	MILAID	RANK	SOURCE
1	MEA	Iraq	5439.4	1.0	06(USAID)
2	DME	Israel	2257.2	2.0	06(USAID)
3	SAS	Afghanistan	1807.0	3.0	06(USAID)
4	MEA	Egypt	1288.2	4.0	06(USAID)
5	SAS	Pakistan	299.0	5.0	06(USAID)
6	MEA	Jordan	210.9	6.0	06(USAID)
7	AFR	Sudan	149.8	7.0	06(USAID)
8	LAM	Colombia	90.8	8.0	06(USAID)
9	SEA	Philippines	32.6	9.0	06(USAID)
10	EEU	Poland	31.8	10.0	06(USAID)
11	AFR	Liberia	22.1	11.0	06(USAID)
12	MEA	Turkey	17.9	12.0	06(USAID)
13	MEA	Bahrain	16.2	13.0	06(USAID)
14	USR	Ukraine	15.8	14.0	06(USAID)
15	MEA	Oman	15.0	15.0	06(USAID)
16	EEU	Romania	14.4	16.0	06(USAID)
17	MEA	Morocco	14.3	17.0	06(USAID)
18	USR	Georgia	13.8	18.0	06(USAID)
19	LAM	El Salvador	11.7	19.0	06(USAID)
20	EEU	Bulgaria	11.5	20.0	06(USAID)
21	MEA	Tunisia	10.3	21.0	06(USAID)
22	EEU	Bosnia	9.9	22.0	06(USAID)
23	MEA	Yemen	9.3	23.0	06(USAID)
24	USR	Latvia	7.3	24.0	06(USAID)
25	EEU	Czechia	6.0	25.0	06(USAID)
26	USR	Armenia	5.9	26.0	06(USAID)
27	USR	Estonia	5.7	28.0	06(USAID)
28	USR	Kazakhstan	5.7	28.0	06(USAID)
29	USR	Lithuania	5.7	28.0	06(USAID)
30	USR	Azerbaijan	5.3	30.0	06(USAID)
31	EEU	Macedonia	5.1	31.0	06(USAID)
32	EEU	Slovakia	4.9	32.0	06(USAID)
33	EEU	Albania	4.8	33.0	06(USAID)
34	MEA	Lebanon	4.5	34.0	06(USAID)
35	AFR	Djibouti	4.3	35.0	06(USAID)
36	EEU	Hungary	4.2	36.0	06(USAID)
37	SEA	Thailand	3.9	37.0	06(USAID)
38	CPA	Mongolia	3.8	38.0	06(USAID)
39	USR	Kyrgyzstan	3.4	39.0	06(USAID)
40	AFR	Ethiopia	2.6	40.0	06(USAID)
41	USR	Moldova	2.5	41.0	06(USAID)
42	LAM	Dominican Rep.	2.3	42.0	06(USAID)
43	LAM	Honduras	2.1	43.0	06(USAID)
44	SAS	Bangladesh	1.9	45.0	06(USAID)
45	SEA	Indonesia	1.9	45.0	06(USAID)
46	LAM	Panama	1.9	45.0	06(USAID)
47	AFR	Nigeria	1.8	47.0	06(USAID)

TABLE 2.6 – FOREIGN MILITARY AID, MILLIONS OF DOLLARS, 2006

OBS	REGION	COUNTRY	MILAID	RANK	SOURCE
48	AFR	Senegal	1.6	48.0	06(USAID)
49	LAM	Jamaica	1.5	50.0	06(USAID)
50	SAS	Sri Lanka	1.5	50.0	06(USAID)
51	USR	Tajikistan	1.5	50.0	06(USAID)
52	EEU	Slovenia	1.4	52.0	06(USAID)
53	SAS	India	1.3	54.0	06(USAID)
54	LAM	Nicaragua	1.3	54.0	06(USAID)
55	USR	Turkmenistan	1.3	54.0	06(USAID)
56	LAM	Chile	1.2	57.0	06(USAID)
57	SEA	East Timor	1.2	57.0	06(USAID)
58	LAM	Haiti	1.2	57.0	06(USAID)
59	LAM	Argentina	1.1	59.5	06(USAID)
60	AFR	Ghana	1.1	59.5	06(USAID)
61	CPA	Cambodia	1.0	61.5	06(USAID)
62	USR	Russia	1.0	61.5	06(USAID)
63	SEA	Malaysia	0.9	63.0	06(USAID)
64	MEA	Algeria	0.8	64.5	06(USAID)
65	AFR	Botswana	0.8	64.5	06(USAID)
66	SEA	Fiji	0.7	66.0	06(USAID)
67	DME	Greece	0.6	68.0	06(USAID)
68	SAS	Nepal	0.6	68.0	06(USAID)
69	DME	Portugal	0.6	68.0	06(USAID)
70	AFR	Angola	0.5	72.0	06(USAID)
71	LAM	Bahamas	0.5	72.0	06(USAID)
72	LAM	Belize	0.5	72.0	06(USAID)
73	EEU	Croatia	0.5	72.0	06(USAID)
74	LAM	Guatemala	0.5	72.0	06(USAID)
75	AFR	Guinea	0.4	76.0	06(USAID)
76	LAM	Guyana	0.4	76.0	06(USAID)
77	SEA	Tonga	0.4	76.0	06(USAID)
78	AFR	Chad	0.3	82.5	06(USAID)
79	AFR	Congo, Dem. Rep.	0.3	82.5	06(USAID)
80	AFR	Malawi	0.3	82.5	06(USAID)
81	SEA	Papua New Guinea	0.3	82.5	06(USAID)
82	AFR	Rwanda	0.3	82.5	06(USAID)
83	AFR	San Tome & Principe	0.3	82.5	06(USAID)
84	AFR	Sierra Leone	0.3	82.5	06(USAID)
85	LAM	Suriname	0.3	82.5	06(USAID)
86	AFR	Uganda	0.3	82.5	06(USAID)
87	AFR	Zambia	0.3	82.5	06(USAID)
88	AFR	Cameroon	0.2	90.5	06(USAID)
89	AFR	Congo, Rep.	0.2	90.5	06(USAID)
90	AFR	Gabon	0.2	90.5	06(USAID)
91	AFR	Madagascar	0.2	90.5	06(USAID)
92	SAS	Maldives	0.2	90.5	06(USAID)
93	AFR	Mozambique	0.2	90.5	06(USAID)
94	USR	Belarus	0.1	100.5	06(USAID)
95	AFR	Benin	0.1	100.5	06(USAID)

TABLE 2.6 – FOREIGN MILITARY AID, MILLIONS OF DOLLARS, 2006					
OBS	REGION	COUNTRY	MILAID	RANK	SOURCE
96	AFR	Burkina Faso	0.1	100.5	06(USAID)
97	AFR	Burundi	0.1	100.5	06(USAID)
98	AFR	CAR	0.1	100.5	06(USAID)
99	AFR	Cape Verde	0.1	100.5	06(USAID)
100	AFR	Comoros	0.1	100.5	06(USAID)
101	AFR	Gambia	0.1	100.5	06(USAID)
102	AFR	GuineaBissau	0.1	100.5	06(USAID)
103	AFR	Mauritius	0.1	100.5	06(USAID)
104	AFR	Seychelles	0.1	100.5	06(USAID)
105	SEA	Solomon Islands	0.1	100.5	06(USAID)
106	AFR	Swaziland	0.1	100.5	06(USAID)
107	SEA	Vanuatu	0.1	100.5	06(USAID)
108	DME	Andorra	0.0	169.5	06(USAID)
109	LAM	Anguilla	0.0	169.5	06(USAID)
110	LAM	Antigua & Barbuda	0.0	169.5	06(USAID)
111	LAM	Aruba	0.0	169.5	06(USAID)
112	DME	Australia	0.0	169.5	06(USAID)
113	DME	Austria	0.0	169.5	06(USAID)
114	LAM	Barbados	0.0	169.5	06(USAID)
115	DME	Belgium	0.0	169.5	06(USAID)
116	DME	Bermuda	0.0	169.5	06(USAID)
117	SAS	Bhutan	0.0	169.5	06(USAID)
118	LAM	Bolivia	0.0	169.5	06(USAID)
119	LAM	Brazil	0.0	169.5	06(USAID)
120	SEA	Brunei	0.0	169.5	06(USAID)
121	CPA	Burma	0.0	169.5	06(USAID)
122	DME	Canada	0.0	169.5	06(USAID)
123	LAM	Cayman Islands	0.0	169.5	06(USAID)
124	CPA	China	0.0	169.5	06(USAID)
125	SEA	Cook Islands	0.0	169.5	06(USAID)
126	LAM	Costa Rica	0.0	169.5	06(USAID)
127	LAM	Cuba	0.0	169.5	06(USAID)
128	MEA	Cyprus	0.0	169.5	06(USAID)
129	DME	Denmark	0.0	169.5	06(USAID)
130	LAM	Dominica	0.0	169.5	06(USAID)
131	LAM	Ecuador	0.0	169.5	06(USAID)
132	AFR	Equatorial Guinea	0.0	169.5	06(USAID)
133	AFR	Eritrea	0.0	169.5	06(USAID)
134	DME	Faeroe Islands	0.0	169.5	06(USAID)
135	DME	Falkland Islands	0.0	169.5	06(USAID)
136	DME	Finland	0.0	169.5	06(USAID)
137	DME	France	0.0	169.5	06(USAID)
138	SEA	French Polynesia	0.0	169.5	06(USAID)
139	MEA	Gaza Strip	0.0	169.5	06(USAID)
140	DME	Germany	0.0	169.5	06(USAID)
141	DME	Gibraltar	0.0	169.5	06(USAID)
142	DME	Greenland	0.0	169.5	06(USAID)
143	LAM	Grenada	0.0	169.5	06(USAID)

OBS	REGION	COUNTRY	MILAID	RANK	SOURCE
	TABLE 2.6 – FOREIGN MILITARY AID, MILLIONS OF DOLLARS, 2006				
144	LAM	Guadeloupe	0.0	169.5	06(USAID)
145	SEA	Guam	0.0	169.5	06(USAID)
146	DME	Guernsey	0.0	169.5	06(USAID)
147	LAM	Guiana, French	0.0	169.5	06(USAID)
148	SEA	Hong Kong	0.0	169.5	06(USAID)
149	DME	Iceland	0.0	169.5	06(USAID)
150	MEA	Iran	0.0	169.5	06(USAID)
151	DME	Ireland	0.0	169.5	06(USAID)
152	DME	Isle of Man	0.0	169.5	06(USAID)
153	DME	Italy	0.0	169.5	06(USAID)
154	AFR	Ivory Coast	0.0	169.5	06(USAID)
155	DME	Japan	0.0	169.5	06(USAID)
156	DME	Jersey	0.0	169.5	06(USAID)
157	AFR	Kenya	0.0	169.5	06(USAID)
158	SEA	Kiribati	0.0	169.5	06(USAID)
159	CPA	Korea, North	0.0	169.5	06(USAID)
160	SEA	Korea, South	0.0	169.5	06(USAID)
161	MEA	Kuwait	0.0	169.5	06(USAID)
162	CPA	Laos	0.0	169.5	06(USAID)
163	AFR	Lesotho	0.0	169.5	06(USAID)
164	MEA	Libya	0.0	169.5	06(USAID)
165	DME	Liechtenstein	0.0	169.5	06(USAID)
166	DME	Luxembourg	0.0	169.5	06(USAID)
167	SEA	Macao	0.0	169.5	06(USAID)
168	AFR	Mali	0.0	169.5	06(USAID)
169	DME	Malta	0.0	169.5	06(USAID)
170	SEA	Marshall Islands	0.0	169.5	06(USAID)
171	LAM	Martinique	0.0	169.5	06(USAID)
172	AFR	Mauritania	0.0	169.5	06(USAID)
173	AFR	Mayotte	0.0	169.5	06(USAID)
174	LAM	Mexico	0.0	169.5	06(USAID)
175	SEA	Micronesia	0.0	169.5	06(USAID)
176	DME	Monaco	0.0	169.5	06(USAID)
177	EEU	Montenegro	0.0	169.5	06(USAID)
178	LAM	Montserrat	0.0	169.5	06(USAID)
179	AFR	Namibia	0.0	169.5	06(USAID)
180	SEA	Nauru	0.0	169.5	06(USAID)
181	LAM	Neth. Antilles	0.0	169.5	06(USAID)
182	DME	Netherlands	0.0	169.5	06(USAID)
183	SEA	New Caledonia	0.0	169.5	06(USAID)
184	DME	New Zealand	0.0	169.5	06(USAID)
185	AFR	Niger	0.0	169.5	06(USAID)
186	SEA	Niue	0.0	169.5	06(USAID)
187	SEA	Northern Mariana Is.	0.0	169.5	06(USAID)
188	DME	Norway	0.0	169.5	06(USAID)
189	SEA	Palau	0.0	169.5	06(USAID)
190	LAM	Paraguay	0.0	169.5	06(USAID)
191	LAM	Peru	0.0	169.5	06(USAID)

	TABLE 2.6 – FOREIGN MILITARY AID, MILLIONS OF DOLLARS, 2006				
OBS	*REGION*	*COUNTRY*	*MILAID*	*RANK*	*SOURCE*
192	LAM	Puerto Rico	0.0	169.5	06(USAID)
193	MEA	Qatar	0.0	169.5	06(USAID)
194	AFR	Reunion	0.0	169.5	06(USAID)
195	SEA	Samoa, American	0.0	169.5	06(USAID)
196	SEA	Samoa, Western	0.0	169.5	06(USAID)
197	DME	San Marino	0.0	169.5	06(USAID)
198	MEA	Saudi Arabia	0.0	169.5	06(USAID)
199	EEU	Serbia	0.0	169.5	06(USAID)
200	SEA	Singapore	0.0	169.5	06(USAID)
201	AFR	Somalia	0.0	169.5	06(USAID)
202	AFR	South Africa	0.0	169.5	06(USAID)
203	DME	Spain	0.0	169.5	06(USAID)
204	AFR	St. Helena	0.0	169.5	06(USAID)
205	LAM	St. Kitts & Nevis	0.0	169.5	06(USAID)
206	LAM	St. Lucia	0.0	169.5	06(USAID)
207	DME	St. Pierre & Miquelon	0.0	169.5	06(USAID)
208	LAM	St. Vincent	0.0	169.5	06(USAID)
209	DME	Sweden	0.0	169.5	06(USAID)
210	DME	Switzerland	0.0	169.5	06(USAID)
211	MEA	Syria	0.0	169.5	06(USAID)
212	SEA	Taiwan	0.0	169.5	06(USAID)
213	AFR	Tanzania	0.0	169.5	06(USAID)
214	AFR	Togo	0.0	169.5	06(USAID)
215	SEA	Tokelau	0.0	169.5	06(USAID)
216	LAM	Trinidad & Tobago	0.0	169.5	06(USAID)
217	SEA	Turks & Caicos Is.	0.0	169.5	06(USAID)
218	SEA	Tuvalu	0.0	169.5	06(USAID)
219	MEA	UAE	0.0	169.5	06(USAID)
220	DME	United Kingdom	0.0	169.5	06(USAID)
221	DME	United States	0.0	169.5	06(USAID)
222	LAM	Uruguay	0.0	169.5	06(USAID)
223	USR	Uzbekistan	0.0	169.5	06(USAID)
224	LAM	Venezuela	0.0	169.5	06(USAID)
225	CPA	Vietnam	0.0	169.5	06(USAID)
226	LAM	Virgin Islands, Brit.	0.0	169.5	06(USAID)
227	LAM	Virgin Islands, US	0.0	169.5	06(USAID)
228	SEA	Wallis & Futuna	0.0	169.5	06(USAID)
229	MEA	West Bank	0.0	169.5	06(USAID)
230	AFR	Western Sahara	0.0	169.5	06(USAID)
231	AFR	Zimbabwe	0.0	169.5	06(USAID)

TABLE 2.7 – MILITARY EXPENDITURES AT PURCHASING POWER PARITIES
PLUS FOREIGN MILITARY AID, MILLIONS OF DOLLARS, 2006

OBS	REGION	COUNTRY	MILXPP	RANK	SOURCE
1	DME	United States	546,301	1.0	GDPPPP*MILGDP+MILAID
2	CPA	China	118,794	2.0	GDPPPP*MILGDP+MILAID
3	USR	Russia	75,134	3.0	GDPPPP*MILGDP+MILAID
4	SAS	India	73,161	4.0	GDPPPP*MILGDP+MILAID
5	DME	United Kingdom	51,889	5.0	GDPPPP*MILGDP+MILAID
6	DME	France	47,230	6.0	GDPPPP*MILGDP+MILAID
7	MEA	Saudi Arabia	44,717	7.0	GDPPPP*MILGDP+MILAID
8	DME	Japan	38,774	8.0	GDPPPP*MILGDP+MILAID
9	DME	Germany	34,879	9.0	GDPPPP*MILGDP+MILAID
10	MEA	Iran	33,329	10.0	GDPPPP*MILGDP+MILAID
11	SEA	Korea, South	30,052	11.0	GDPPPP*MILGDP+MILAID
12	DME	Italy	28,378	12.0	GDPPPP*MILGDP+MILAID
13	LAM	Brazil	24,907	13.0	GDPPPP*MILGDP+MILAID
14	MEA	Turkey	17,524	14.0	GDPPPP*MILGDP+MILAID
15	DME	Israel	16,456	15.0	GDPPPP*MILGDP+MILAID
16	SAS	Pakistan	14,639	16.0	GDPPPP*MILGDP+MILAID
17	SEA	Taiwan	14,556	17.0	GDPPPP*MILGDP+MILAID
18	DME	Canada	13,904	18.0	GDPPPP*MILGDP+MILAID
19	DME	Spain	13,272	19.0	GDPPPP*MILGDP+MILAID
20	DME	Australia	13,246	20.0	GDPPPP*MILGDP+MILAID
21	DME	Greece	11,335	21.0	GDPPPP*MILGDP+MILAID
22	EEU	Poland	11,176	22.0	GDPPPP*MILGDP+MILAID
23	CPA	Vietnam	11,130	23.0	GDPPPP*MILGDP+MILAID
24	MEA	Egypt	11,097	24.0	GDPPPP*MILGDP+MILAID
25	MEA	Iraq	10,425	25.0	GDPPPP*MILGDP+MILAID
26	CPA	Korea, North	10,162	26.0	GDPPPP*MILGDP+MILAID
27	LAM	Colombia	10,144	27.0	GDPPPP*MILGDP+MILAID
28	SEA	Singapore	9,402	28.0	GDPPPP*MILGDP+MILAID
29	SEA	Indonesia	9,325	29.0	GDPPPP*MILGDP+MILAID
30	DME	Netherlands	8,961	30.0	GDPPPP*MILGDP+MILAID
31	LAM	Chile	7,773	31.0	GDPPPP*MILGDP+MILAID
32	SEA	Malaysia	6,712	32.0	GDPPPP*MILGDP+MILAID
33	MEA	Kuwait	6,501	33.0	GDPPPP*MILGDP+MILAID
34	USR	Ukraine	6,149	34.0	GDPPPP*MILGDP+MILAID
35	MEA	Oman	6,077	35.0	GDPPPP*MILGDP+MILAID
36	AFR	South Africa	5,943	36.0	GDPPPP*MILGDP+MILAID
37	MEA	Algeria	5,674	37.0	GDPPPP*MILGDP+MILAID
38	SEA	Thailand	5,307	38.0	GDPPPP*MILGDP+MILAID
39	LAM	Mexico	4,823	39.0	GDPPPP*MILGDP+MILAID
40	DME	Portugal	4,644	40.0	GDPPPP*MILGDP+MILAID
41	MEA	Morocco	4,384	41.0	GDPPPP*MILGDP+MILAID
42	DME	Sweden	4,379	42.0	GDPPPP*MILGDP+MILAID
43	EEU	Romania	4,294	43.0	GDPPPP*MILGDP+MILAID
44	LAM	Argentina	4,222	44.0	GDPPPP*MILGDP+MILAID
45	SAS	Afghanistan	4,183	45.0	GDPPPP*MILGDP+MILAID
46	MEA	UAE	4,126	46.0	GDPPPP*MILGDP+MILAID

TABLE 2.7 – MILITARY EXPENDITURES AT PURCHASING POWER PARITIES PLUS FOREIGN MILITARY AID, MILLIONS OF DOLLARS, 2006

OBS	REGION	COUNTRY	MILXPP	RANK	SOURCE
47	DME	Belgium	3,995	47.0	GDPPPP*MILGDP+MILAID
48	AFR	Angola	3,965	48.0	GDPPPP*MILGDP+MILAID
49	EEU	Czechia	3,913	49.0	GDPPPP*MILGDP+MILAID
50	DME	Norway	3,501	50.0	GDPPPP*MILGDP+MILAID
51	LAM	Venezuela	3,437	51.0	GDPPPP*MILGDP+MILAID
52	MEA	Syria	3,141	52.0	GDPPPP*MILGDP+MILAID
53	MEA	Yemen	2,971	53.0	GDPPPP*MILGDP+MILAID
54	DME	Denmark	2,736	54.0	GDPPPP*MILGDP+MILAID
55	DME	Austria	2,537	55.0	GDPPPP*MILGDP+MILAID
56	DME	Switzerland	2,508	56.0	GDPPPP*MILGDP+MILAID
57	SEA	Philippines	2,399	57.0	GDPPPP*MILGDP+MILAID
58	LAM	Peru	2,367	58.0	GDPPPP*MILGDP+MILAID
59	DME	Finland	2,348	59.0	GDPPPP*MILGDP+MILAID
60	MEA	Qatar	2,243	60.0	GDPPPP*MILGDP+MILAID
61	EEU	Hungary	2,157	61.0	GDPPPP*MILGDP+MILAID
62	SAS	Bangladesh	2,038	62.0	GDPPPP*MILGDP+MILAID
63	SAS	Sri Lanka	1,819	63.0	GDPPPP*MILGDP+MILAID
64	EEU	Bulgaria	1,806	64.0	GDPPPP*MILGDP+MILAID
65	AFR	Sudan	1,781	65.0	GDPPPP*MILGDP+MILAID
66	USR	Azerbaijan	1,769	66.0	GDPPPP*MILGDP+MILAID
67	LAM	Cuba	1,762	67.0	GDPPPP*MILGDP+MILAID
68	EEU	Slovakia	1,658	68.0	GDPPPP*MILGDP+MILAID
69	MEA	Lebanon	1,640	69.0	GDPPPP*MILGDP+MILAID
70	AFR	Nigeria	1,611	70.0	GDPPPP*MILGDP+MILAID
71	USR	Belarus	1,591	71.0	GDPPPP*MILGDP+MILAID
72	EEU	Serbia	1,502	72.0	GDPPPP*MILGDP+MILAID
73	MEA	Jordan	1,472	73.0	GDPPPP*MILGDP+MILAID
74	USR	Kazakhstan	1,375	74.0	GDPPPP*MILGDP+MILAID
75	LAM	Ecuador	1,298	75.0	GDPPPP*MILGDP+MILAID
76	AFR	Ethiopia	1,279	76.0	GDPPPP*MILGDP+MILAID
77	DME	New Zealand	1,068	77.0	GDPPPP*MILGDP+MILAID
78	MEA	Libya	1,060	78.0	GDPPPP*MILGDP+MILAID
79	EEU	Croatia	1,036	79.0	GDPPPP*MILGDP+MILAID
80	MEA	Tunisia	997	80.0	GDPPPP*MILGDP+MILAID
81	DME	Ireland	911	81.0	GDPPPP*MILGDP+MILAID
82	AFR	Kenya	884	82.0	GDPPPP*MILGDP+MILAID
83	EEU	Slovenia	827	83.0	GDPPPP*MILGDP+MILAID
84	AFR	Eritrea	772	84.0	GDPPPP*MILGDP+MILAID
85	MEA	Bahrain	751	85.0	GDPPPP*MILGDP+MILAID
86	AFR	Botswana	698	86.0	GDPPPP*MILGDP+MILAID
87	AFR	Zimbabwe	685	87.0	GDPPPP*MILGDP+MILAID
88	USR	Lithuania	631	88.0	GDPPPP*MILGDP+MILAID
89	MEA	West Bank	606	89.0	GDPPPP*MILGDP+MILAID
90	USR	Latvia	580	90.0	GDPPPP*MILGDP+MILAID
91	USR	Georgia	565	91.0	GDPPPP*MILGDP+MILAID
92	LAM	El Salvador	559	92.0	GDPPPP*MILGDP+MILAID
93	AFR	Uganda	558	93.0	GDPPPP*MILGDP+MILAID

TABLE 2.7 – MILITARY EXPENDITURES AT PURCHASING POWER PARITIES
PLUS FOREIGN MILITARY AID, MILLIONS OF DOLLARS, 2006

OBS	REGION	COUNTRY	MILXPP	RANK	SOURCE
94	LAM	Bolivia	534	94.0	GDPPPP*MILGDP+MILAID
95	AFR	Cameroon	532	95.0	GDPPPP*MILGDP+MILAID
96	SAS	Nepal	520	96.0	GDPPPP*MILGDP+MILAID
97	CPA	Burma	516	97.0	GDPPPP*MILGDP+MILAID
98	AFR	Ivory Coast	484	98.0	GDPPPP*MILGDP+MILAID
99	SEA	Brunei	465	99.0	GDPPPP*MILGDP+MILAID
100	AFR	Tanzania	440	100.0	GDPPPP*MILGDP+MILAID
101	USR	Uzbekistan	436	101.0	GDPPPP*MILGDP+MILAID
102	EEU	Bosnia	423	102.0	GDPPPP*MILGDP+MILAID
103	USR	Armenia	416	103.0	GDPPPP*MILGDP+MILAID
104	USR	Turkmenistan	405	104.0	GDPPPP*MILGDP+MILAID
105	LAM	Uruguay	396	105.0	GDPPPP*MILGDP+MILAID
106	CPA	Cambodia	385	106.0	GDPPPP*MILGDP+MILAID
107	USR	Estonia	372	107.0	GDPPPP*MILGDP+MILAID
108	AFR	Zambia	332	108.0	GDPPPP*MILGDP+MILAID
109	EEU	Macedonia	330	109.0	GDPPPP*MILGDP+MILAID
110	MEA	Gaza Strip	324	110.0	GDPPPP*MILGDP+MILAID
111	AFR	Congo, Dem. Rep.	324	111.0	GDPPPP*MILGDP+MILAID
112	AFR	Senegal	310	112.0	GDPPPP*MILGDP+MILAID
113	LAM	Panama	306	113.0	GDPPPP*MILGDP+MILAID
114	EEU	Albania	300	114.0	GDPPPP*MILGDP+MILAID
115	USR	Kyrgyzstan	293	115.0	GDPPPP*MILGDP+MILAID
116	AFR	Namibia	290	116.0	GDPPPP*MILGDP+MILAID
117	LAM	Dominican Rep.	290	117.0	GDPPPP*MILGDP+MILAID
118	AFR	Mali	285	118.0	GDPPPP*MILGDP+MILAID
119	DME	Luxembourg	279	119.0	GDPPPP*MILGDP+MILAID
120	LAM	Guatemala	277	120.0	GDPPPP*MILGDP+MILAID
121	MEA	Cyprus	269	121.0	GDPPPP*MILGDP+MILAID
122	CPA	Laos	236	122.0	GDPPPP*MILGDP+MILAID
123	USR	Tajikistan	233	123.0	GDPPPP*MILGDP+MILAID
124	AFR	Burkina Faso	224	124.0	GDPPPP*MILGDP+MILAID
125	AFR	Gabon	224	125.0	GDPPPP*MILGDP+MILAID
126	AFR	Guinea	214	126.0	GDPPPP*MILGDP+MILAID
127	AFR	Somalia	204	127.0	GDPPPP*MILGDP+MILAID
128	AFR	Ghana	202	128.0	GDPPPP*MILGDP+MILAID
129	LAM	Paraguay	197	129.0	GDPPPP*MILGDP+MILAID
130	AFR	Rwanda	192	130.0	GDPPPP*MILGDP+MILAID
131	LAM	Costa Rica	168	131.0	GDPPPP*MILGDP+MILAID
132	AFR	Madagascar	165	132.0	GDPPPP*MILGDP+MILAID
133	AFR	Burundi	149	133.0	GDPPPP*MILGDP+MILAID
134	LAM	Honduras	148	134.0	GDPPPP*MILGDP+MILAID
135	AFR	Congo, Rep.	147	135.0	GDPPPP*MILGDP+MILAID
136	AFR	Mauritania	142	136.0	GDPPPP*MILGDP+MILAID
137	AFR	Chad	140	137.0	GDPPPP*MILGDP+MILAID
138	EEU	Montenegro	130	138.0	GDPPPP*MILGDP+MILAID

TABLE 2.7 – MILITARY EXPENDITURES AT PURCHASING POWER PARITIES PLUS FOREIGN MILITARY AID, MILLIONS OF DOLLARS, 2006

OBS	REGION	COUNTRY	MILXPP	RANK	SOURCE
139	AFR	Mozambique	124	139.0	GDPPPP*MILGDP+MILAID
140	LAM	Haiti	117	140.0	GDPPPP*MILGDP+MILAID
141	LAM	Jamaica	115	141.0	GDPPPP*MILGDP+MILAID
142	AFR	Liberia	112	142.0	GDPPPP*MILGDP+MILAID
143	AFR	Benin	111	143.0	GDPPPP*MILGDP+MILAID
144	AFR	Swaziland	103	144.0	GDPPPP*MILGDP+MILAID
145	LAM	Nicaragua	103	145.0	GDPPPP*MILGDP+MILAID
146	CPA	Mongolia	100	146.0	GDPPPP*MILGDP+MILAID
147	AFR	Niger	96	147.0	GDPPPP*MILGDP+MILAID
148	SAS	Maldives	92	148.0	GDPPPP*MILGDP+MILAID
149	SAS	Bhutan	86	149.0	GDPPPP*MILGDP+MILAID
150	AFR	Togo	79	150.0	GDPPPP*MILGDP+MILAID
151	AFR	Djibouti	73	151.0	GDPPPP*MILGDP+MILAID
152	LAM	Trinidad & Tobago	71	152.0	GDPPPP*MILGDP+MILAID
153	AFR	Lesotho	68	153.0	GDPPPP*MILGDP+MILAID
154	SEA	Papua New Guinea	59	154.0	GDPPPP*MILGDP+MILAID
155	DME	Malta	56	155.0	GDPPPP*MILGDP+MILAID
156	AFR	Malawi	52	156.0	GDPPPP*MILGDP+MILAID
157	LAM	Guyana	48	157.0	GDPPPP*MILGDP+MILAID
158	LAM	Suriname	47	158.0	GDPPPP*MILGDP+MILAID
159	LAM	Bahamas	46	159.0	GDPPPP*MILGDP+MILAID
160	SEA	Fiji	45	160.0	GDPPPP*MILGDP+MILAID
161	LAM	Belize	36	161.0	GDPPPP*MILGDP+MILAID
162	AFR	Sierra Leone	35	162.0	GDPPPP*MILGDP+MILAID
163	DME	Iceland	33	163.0	GDPPPP*MILGDP+MILAID
164	AFR	CAR	33	164.0	GDPPPP*MILGDP+MILAID
165	AFR	GuineaBissau	32	165.0	GDPPPP*MILGDP+MILAID
166	USR	Moldova	29	166.0	GDPPPP*MILGDP+MILAID
167	SEA	East Timor	28	167.0	GDPPPP*MILGDP+MILAID
168	LAM	Barbados	27	168.0	GDPPPP*MILGDP+MILAID
169	AFR	Mauritius	27	169.0	GDPPPP*MILGDP+MILAID
170	AFR	Seychelles	23	170.0	GDPPPP*MILGDP+MILAID
171	AFR	Equatorial Guinea	13	171.0	GDPPPP*MILGDP+MILAID
172	AFR	Cape Verde	10	172.0	GDPPPP*MILGDP+MILAID
173	AFR	Gambia	9	173.0	GDPPPP*MILGDP+MILAID
174	LAM	Antigua & Barbuda	7	174.0	GDPPPP*MILGDP+MILAID
175	SEA	Tonga	6	175.0	GDPPPP*MILGDP+MILAID
176	AFR	San Tome & Principe	2	176.0	GDPPPP*MILGDP+MILAID
177	AFR	Comoros	2	177.0	GDPPPP*MILGDP+MILAID
178	SEA	Solomon Islands	0	178.5	GDPPPP*MILGDP+MILAID
179	SEA	Vanuatu	0	178.5	GDPPPP*MILGDP+MILAID
180	DME	Andorra	0	205.5	GDPPPP*MILGDP+MILAID

		TABLE 2.7 – MILITARY EXPENDITURES AT PURCHASING POWER PARITIES PLUS FOREIGN MILITARY AID, MILLIONS OF DOLLARS, 2006			
OBS	REGION	COUNTRY	MILXPP	RANK	SOURCE
181	LAM	Anguilla	0	205.5	GDPPPP*MILGDP+MILAID
182	LAM	Aruba	0	205.5	GDPPPP*MILGDP+MILAID
183	DME	Bermuda	0	205.5	GDPPPP*MILGDP+MILAID
184	LAM	Cayman Islands	0	205.5	GDPPPP*MILGDP+MILAID
185	SEA	Cook Islands	0	205.5	GDPPPP*MILGDP+MILAID
186	LAM	Dominica	0	205.5	GDPPPP*MILGDP+MILAID
187	DME	Faeroe Islands	0	205.5	GDPPPP*MILGDP+MILAID
188	DME	Falkland Islands	0	205.5	GDPPPP*MILGDP+MILAID
189	SEA	French Polynesia	0	205.5	GDPPPP*MILGDP+MILAID
190	DME	Gibraltar	0	205.5	GDPPPP*MILGDP+MILAID
191	DME	Greenland	0	205.5	GDPPPP*MILGDP+MILAID
192	LAM	Grenada	0	205.5	GDPPPP*MILGDP+MILAID
193	LAM	Guadeloupe	0	205.5	GDPPPP*MILGDP+MILAID
194	SEA	Guam	0	205.5	GDPPPP*MILGDP+MILAID
195	DME	Guernsey	0	205.5	GDPPPP*MILGDP+MILAID
196	LAM	Guiana, French	0	205.5	GDPPPP*MILGDP+MILAID
197	SEA	Hong Kong	0	205.5	GDPPPP*MILGDP+MILAID
198	DME	Isle of Man	0	205.5	GDPPPP*MILGDP+MILAID
199	DME	Jersey	0	205.5	GDPPPP*MILGDP+MILAID
200	SEA	Kiribati	0	205.5	GDPPPP*MILGDP+MILAID
201	DME	Liechtenstein	0	205.5	GDPPPP*MILGDP+MILAID
202	SEA	Macao	0	205.5	GDPPPP*MILGDP+MILAID
203	SEA	Marshall Islands	0	205.5	GDPPPP*MILGDP+MILAID
204	LAM	Martinique	0	205.5	GDPPPP*MILGDP+MILAID
205	AFR	Mayotte	0	205.5	GDPPPP*MILGDP+MILAID
206	SEA	Micronesia	0	205.5	GDPPPP*MILGDP+MILAID
207	DME	Monaco	0	205.5	GDPPPP*MILGDP+MILAID
208	LAM	Montserrat	0	205.5	GDPPPP*MILGDP+MILAID
209	SEA	Nauru	0	205.5	GDPPPP*MILGDP+MILAID
210	LAM	Neth. Antilles	0	205.5	GDPPPP*MILGDP+MILAID
211	SEA	New Caledonia	0	205.5	GDPPPP*MILGDP+MILAID
212	SEA	Niue	0	205.5	GDPPPP*MILGDP+MILAID
213	SEA	Northern Mariana Is.	0	205.5	GDPPPP*MILGDP+MILAID
214	SEA	Palau	0	205.5	GDPPPP*MILGDP+MILAID
215	LAM	Puerto Rico	0	205.5	GDPPPP*MILGDP+MILAID
216	AFR	Reunion	0	205.5	GDPPPP*MILGDP+MILAID
217	SEA	Samoa, American	0	205.5	GDPPPP*MILGDP+MILAID
218	SEA	Samoa, Western	0	205.5	GDPPPP*MILGDP+MILAID

OBS	REGION	COUNTRY	MILXPP	RANK	SOURCE
		TABLE 2.7 – MILITARY EXPENDITURES AT PURCHASING POWER PARITIES PLUS FOREIGN MILITARY AID, MILLIONS OF DOLLARS, 2006			
219	DME	San Marino	0	205.5	GDPPPP*MILGDP+MILAID
220	AFR	St. Helena	0	205.5	GDPPPP*MILGDP+MILAID
221	LAM	St. Kitts & Nevis	0	205.5	GDPPPP*MILGDP+MILAID
222	LAM	St. Lucia	0	205.5	GDPPPP*MILGDP+MILAID
223	DME	St. Pierre & Miquelon	0	205.5	GDPPPP*MILGDP+MILAID
224	LAM	St. Vincent	0	205.5	GDPPPP*MILGDP+MILAID
225	SEA	Tokelau	0	205.5	GDPPPP*MILGDP+MILAID
226	SEA	Turks & Caicos Is.	0	205.5	GDPPPP*MILGDP+MILAID
227	SEA	Tuvalu	0	205.5	GDPPPP*MILGDP+MILAID
228	LAM	Virgin Islands, Brit.	0	205.5	GDPPPP*MILGDP+MILAID
229	LAM	Virgin Islands, US	0	205.5	GDPPPP*MILGDP+MILAID
230	SEA	Wallis & Futuna	0	205.5	GDPPPP*MILGDP+MILAID
231	AFR	Western Sahara	0	205.5	GDPPPP*MILGDP+MILAID

		TABLE 2.8 – MILITARY EXPENDITURES AT MARKET EXCHANGE RATES PLUS FOREIGN MILITARY AID, MILLIONS OF DOLLARS, 2006			
OBS	REGION	COUNTRY	MILEXP	RANK	SOURCE
1	DME	United States	555,555	1.0	GDP*MILGDP+MILAID
2	DME	United Kingdom	63,602	2.0	GDP*MILGDP+MILAID
3	DME	France	55,592	3.0	GDP*MILGDP+MILAID
4	CPA	China	51,109	4.0	GDP*MILGDP+MILAID
5	DME	Japan	46,879	5.0	GDP*MILGDP+MILAID
6	DME	Germany	39,727	6.0	GDP*MILGDP+MILAID
7	USR	Russia	33,059	7.0	GDP*MILGDP+MILAID
8	DME	Italy	31,250	8.0	GDP*MILGDP+MILAID
9	MEA	Saudi Arabia	28,039	9.0	GDP*MILGDP+MILAID
10	SAS	India	24,275	10.0	GDP*MILGDP+MILAID
11	SEA	Korea, South	23,127	11.0	GDP*MILGDP+MILAID
12	DME	Israel	14,145	12.0	GDP*MILGDP+MILAID
13	DME	Canada	13,881	13.0	GDP*MILGDP+MILAID
14	DME	Australia	13,361	14.0	GDP*MILGDP+MILAID
15	LAM	Brazil	13,122	15.0	GDP*MILGDP+MILAID
16	DME	Spain	12,665	16.0	GDP*MILGDP+MILAID
17	MEA	Turkey	11,244	17.0	GDP*MILGDP+MILAID
18	DME	Netherlands	10,552	18.0	GDP*MILGDP+MILAID
19	DME	Greece	9,893	19.0	GDP*MILGDP+MILAID
20	MEA	Iran	9,842	20.0	GDP*MILGDP+MILAID
21	MEA	Iraq	8,362	21.0	GDP*MILGDP+MILAID
22	SEA	Taiwan	8,347	22.0	GDP*MILGDP+MILAID
23	CPA	Korea, North	6,255	23.0	GDP*MILGDP+MILAID
24	EEU	Poland	6,198	24.0	GDP*MILGDP+MILAID
25	SEA	Singapore	6,041	25.0	GDP*MILGDP+MILAID
26	MEA	Kuwait	5,988	26.0	GDP*MILGDP+MILAID
27	DME	Sweden	5,575	27.0	GDP*MILGDP+MILAID
28	SAS	Pakistan	5,139	28.0	GDP*MILGDP+MILAID
29	LAM	Colombia	5,003	29.0	GDP*MILGDP+MILAID
30	DME	Norway	4,784	30.0	GDP*MILGDP+MILAID
31	DME	Belgium	4,581	31.0	GDP*MILGDP+MILAID
32	LAM	Chile	4,062	32.0	GDP*MILGDP+MILAID
33	DME	Denmark	3,995	33.0	GDP*MILGDP+MILAID
34	DME	Portugal	3,989	34.0	GDP*MILGDP+MILAID
35	MEA	Egypt	3,983	35.0	GDP*MILGDP+MILAID
36	DME	Switzerland	3,914	36.0	GDP*MILGDP+MILAID
37	SEA	Indonesia	3,824	37.0	GDP*MILGDP+MILAID
38	AFR	South Africa	3,524	38.0	GDP*MILGDP+MILAID
39	MEA	UAE	3,410	39.0	GDP*MILGDP+MILAID
40	MEA	Oman	3,374	40.0	GDP*MILGDP+MILAID
41	CPA	Vietnam	3,276	41.0	GDP*MILGDP+MILAID
42	LAM	Mexico	3,100	42.0	GDP*MILGDP+MILAID
43	SEA	Malaysia	3,009	43.0	GDP*MILGDP+MILAID
44	DME	Finland	2,940	44.0	GDP*MILGDP+MILAID
45	DME	Austria	2,798	45.0	GDP*MILGDP+MILAID
46	MEA	Algeria	2,713	46.0	GDP*MILGDP+MILAID

TABLE 2.8 – MILITARY EXPENDITURES AT MARKET EXCHANGE RATES PLUS FOREIGN MILITARY AID, MILLIONS OF DOLLARS, 2006

OBS	REGION	COUNTRY	MILEXP	RANK	SOURCE
47	SAS	Afghanistan	2,611	47.0	GDP*MILGDP+MILAID
48	MEA	Qatar	2,491	48.0	GDP*MILGDP+MILAID
49	MEA	Morocco	2,422	49.0	GDP*MILGDP+MILAID
50	EEU	Czechia	2,266	50.0	GDP*MILGDP+MILAID
51	SEA	Thailand	2,135	51.0	GDP*MILGDP+MILAID
52	LAM	Cuba	2,065	52.0	GDP*MILGDP+MILAID
53	EEU	Romania	1,998	53.0	GDP*MILGDP+MILAID
54	USR	Ukraine	1,930	54.0	GDP*MILGDP+MILAID
55	LAM	Venezuela	1,886	55.0	GDP*MILGDP+MILAID
56	LAM	Argentina	1,813	56.0	GDP*MILGDP+MILAID
57	AFR	Angola	1,763	57.0	GDP*MILGDP+MILAID
58	EEU	Hungary	1,285	58.0	GDP*MILGDP+MILAID
59	MEA	Syria	1,162	59.0	GDP*MILGDP+MILAID
60	DME	New Zealand	1,120	60.0	GDP*MILGDP+MILAID
61	SEA	Philippines	1,078	61.0	GDP*MILGDP+MILAID
62	DME	Ireland	1,014	62.0	GDP*MILGDP+MILAID
63	MEA	Yemen	999	63.0	GDP*MILGDP+MILAID
64	LAM	Peru	995	64.0	GDP*MILGDP+MILAID
65	MEA	Lebanon	942	65.0	GDP*MILGDP+MILAID
66	MEA	Jordan	932	66.0	GDP*MILGDP+MILAID
67	EEU	Slovakia	901	67.0	GDP*MILGDP+MILAID
68	AFR	Sudan	824	68.0	GDP*MILGDP+MILAID
69	SAS	Bangladesh	798	69.0	GDP*MILGDP+MILAID
70	LAM	Ecuador	783	70.0	GDP*MILGDP+MILAID
71	EEU	Bulgaria	708	71.0	GDP*MILGDP+MILAID
72	EEU	Croatia	674	72.0	GDP*MILGDP+MILAID
73	MEA	Libya	665	73.0	GDP*MILGDP+MILAID
74	EEU	Serbia	641	74.0	GDP*MILGDP+MILAID
75	SAS	Sri Lanka	636	75.0	GDP*MILGDP+MILAID
76	EEU	Slovenia	634	76.0	GDP*MILGDP+MILAID
77	AFR	Nigeria	623	77.0	GDP*MILGDP+MILAID
78	USR	Belarus	567	78.0	GDP*MILGDP+MILAID
79	USR	Kazakhstan	544	79.0	GDP*MILGDP+MILAID
80	USR	Azerbaijan	523	80.0	GDP*MILGDP+MILAID
81	MEA	Bahrain	469	81.0	GDP*MILGDP+MILAID
82	MEA	Tunisia	438	82.0	GDP*MILGDP+MILAID
83	AFR	Kenya	352	83.0	GDP*MILGDP+MILAID
84	AFR	Ethiopia	337	84.0	GDP*MILGDP+MILAID
85	USR	Lithuania	321	85.0	GDP*MILGDP+MILAID
86	AFR	Botswana	312	86.0	GDP*MILGDP+MILAID
87	USR	Latvia	309	87.0	GDP*MILGDP+MILAID
88	MEA	West Bank	265	88.0	GDP*MILGDP+MILAID
89	DME	Luxembourg	263	89.0	GDP*MILGDP+MILAID
90	AFR	Ivory Coast	257	90.0	GDP*MILGDP+MILAID
91	AFR	Cameroon	253	91.0	GDP*MILGDP+MILAID
92	SEA	Brunei	251	92.0	GDP*MILGDP+MILAID
93	MEA	Cyprus	242	93.0	GDP*MILGDP+MILAID

TABLE 2.8 – MILITARY EXPENDITURES AT MARKET EXCHANGE RATES
PLUS FOREIGN MILITARY AID, MILLIONS OF DOLLARS, 2006

OBS	REGION	COUNTRY	MILEXP	RANK	SOURCE
94	LAM	El Salvador	235	94.0	GDP*MILGDP+MILAID
95	USR	Georgia	231	95.0	GDP*MILGDP+MILAID
96	USR	Estonia	226	96.0	GDP*MILGDP+MILAID
97	EEU	Bosnia	215	97.0	GDP*MILGDP+MILAID
98	AFR	Eritrea	214	98.0	GDP*MILGDP+MILAID
99	LAM	Uruguay	206	99.0	GDP*MILGDP+MILAID
100	AFR	Namibia	193	100.0	GDP*MILGDP+MILAID
101	AFR	Uganda	188	101.0	GDP*MILGDP+MILAID
102	CPA	Burma	172	102.0	GDP*MILGDP+MILAID
103	USR	Armenia	167	103.0	GDP*MILGDP+MILAID
104	AFR	Zambia	167	104.0	GDP*MILGDP+MILAID
105	LAM	Panama	166	105.0	GDP*MILGDP+MILAID
106	SAS	Nepal	166	106.0	GDP*MILGDP+MILAID
107	EEU	Albania	152	107.0	GDP*MILGDP+MILAID
108	AFR	Tanzania	150	108.0	GDP*MILGDP+MILAID
109	LAM	Bolivia	149	109.0	GDP*MILGDP+MILAID
110	AFR	Senegal	148	110.0	GDP*MILGDP+MILAID
111	AFR	Congo, Dem. Rep.	147	111.0	GDP*MILGDP+MILAID
112	LAM	Dominican Rep.	145	112.0	GDP*MILGDP+MILAID
113	MEA	Gaza Strip	142	113.0	GDP*MILGDP+MILAID
114	LAM	Guatemala	139	114.0	GDP*MILGDP+MILAID
115	EEU	Macedonia	132	115.0	GDP*MILGDP+MILAID
116	AFR	Mali	125	116.0	GDP*MILGDP+MILAID
117	USR	Uzbekistan	121	117.0	GDP*MILGDP+MILAID
118	CPA	Cambodia	118	118.0	GDP*MILGDP+MILAID
119	AFR	Somalia	93	119.0	GDP*MILGDP+MILAID
120	LAM	Costa Rica	88	120.0	GDP*MILGDP+MILAID
121	AFR	Burkina Faso	86	121.0	GDP*MILGDP+MILAID
122	AFR	Gabon	85	122.0	GDP*MILGDP+MILAID
123	USR	Kyrgyzstan	84	123.0	GDP*MILGDP+MILAID
124	AFR	Ghana	84	124.0	GDP*MILGDP+MILAID
125	AFR	Guinea	75	125.0	GDP*MILGDP+MILAID
126	LAM	Paraguay	69	126.0	GDP*MILGDP+MILAID
127	AFR	Rwanda	64	127.0	GDP*MILGDP+MILAID
128	USR	Turkmenistan	60	128.0	GDP*MILGDP+MILAID
129	CPA	Laos	60	129.0	GDP*MILGDP+MILAID
130	EEU	Montenegro	60	130.0	GDP*MILGDP+MILAID
131	AFR	Mauritania	57	131.0	GDP*MILGDP+MILAID
132	USR	Tajikistan	57	132.0	GDP*MILGDP+MILAID
133	AFR	Liberia	57	133.0	GDP*MILGDP+MILAID
134	SAS	Maldives	55	134.0	GDP*MILGDP+MILAID
135	LAM	Jamaica	55	135.0	GDP*MILGDP+MILAID
136	LAM	Honduras	54	136.0	GDP*MILGDP+MILAID
137	AFR	Swaziland	53	137.0	GDP*MILGDP+MILAID
138	AFR	Madagascar	53	138.0	GDP*MILGDP+MILAID
139	AFR	Mozambique	52	139.0	GDP*MILGDP+MILAID

TABLE 2.8 – MILITARY EXPENDITURES AT MARKET EXCHANGE RATES
PLUS FOREIGN MILITARY AID, MILLIONS OF DOLLARS, 2006

OBS	REGION	COUNTRY	MILEXP	RANK	SOURCE
140	LAM	Trinidad & Tobago	50	140.0	GDP*MILGDP+MILAID
141	AFR	Benin	47	141.0	GDP*MILGDP+MILAID
142	AFR	Lesotho	46	142.0	GDP*MILGDP+MILAID
143	DME	Iceland	45	143.0	GDP*MILGDP+MILAID
144	AFR	Zimbabwe	45	144.0	GDP*MILGDP+MILAID
145	AFR	Burundi	45	145.0	GDP*MILGDP+MILAID
146	AFR	Congo, Rep.	45	146.0	GDP*MILGDP+MILAID
147	AFR	Chad	43	147.0	GDP*MILGDP+MILAID
148	LAM	Haiti	42	148.0	GDP*MILGDP+MILAID
149	AFR	Djibouti	41	149.0	GDP*MILGDP+MILAID
150	AFR	Niger	41	150.0	GDP*MILGDP+MILAID
151	LAM	Bahamas	40	151.0	GDP*MILGDP+MILAID
152	DME	Malta	40	152.0	GDP*MILGDP+MILAID
153	CPA	Mongolia	37	153.0	GDP*MILGDP+MILAID
154	SEA	Fiji	37	154.0	GDP*MILGDP+MILAID
155	AFR	Togo	36	155.0	GDP*MILGDP+MILAID
156	LAM	Nicaragua	35	156.0	GDP*MILGDP+MILAID
157	SAS	Bhutan	31	157.0	GDP*MILGDP+MILAID
158	LAM	Barbados	25	158.0	GDP*MILGDP+MILAID
159	LAM	Suriname	25	159.0	GDP*MILGDP+MILAID
160	SEA	Papua New Guinea	24	160.0	GDP*MILGDP+MILAID
161	AFR	Malawi	17	161.0	GDP*MILGDP+MILAID
162	LAM	Belize	17	162.0	GDP*MILGDP+MILAID
163	AFR	CAR	17	163.0	GDP*MILGDP+MILAID
164	LAM	Guyana	16	164.0	GDP*MILGDP+MILAID
165	AFR	Mauritius	14	165.0	GDP*MILGDP+MILAID
166	AFR	Seychelles	14	166.0	GDP*MILGDP+MILAID
167	AFR	Sierra Leone	13	167.0	GDP*MILGDP+MILAID
168	USR	Moldova	13	168.0	GDP*MILGDP+MILAID
169	AFR	GuineaBissau	12	169.0	GDP*MILGDP+MILAID
170	SEA	East Timor	12	170.0	GDP*MILGDP+MILAID
171	AFR	Cape Verde	8	171.0	GDP*MILGDP+MILAID
172	LAM	Antigua & Barbuda	5	172.0	GDP*MILGDP+MILAID
173	AFR	Equatorial Guinea	4	173.0	GDP*MILGDP+MILAID
174	SEA	Tonga	3	174.0	GDP*MILGDP+MILAID
175	AFR	Gambia	2	175.0	GDP*MILGDP+MILAID
176	AFR	San Tome & Principe	1	176.0	GDP*MILGDP+MILAID
177	AFR	Comoros	1	177.0	GDP*MILGDP+MILAID
178	SEA	Solomon Islands	0	178.5	GDP*MILGDP+MILAID
179	SEA	Vanuatu	0	178.5	GDP*MILGDP+MILAID
180	DME	Andorra	0	205.5	GDP*MILGDP+MILAID
181	LAM	Anguilla	0	205.5	GDP*MILGDP+MILAID

TABLE 2.8 – MILITARY EXPENDITURES AT MARKET EXCHANGE RATES PLUS FOREIGN MILITARY AID, MILLIONS OF DOLLARS, 2006

OBS	REGION	COUNTRY	MILEXP	RANK	SOURCE
182	LAM	Aruba	0	205.5	GDP*MILGDP+MILAID
183	DME	Bermuda	0	205.5	GDP*MILGDP+MILAID
184	LAM	Cayman Islands	0	205.5	GDP*MILGDP+MILAID
185	SEA	Cook Islands	0	205.5	GDP*MILGDP+MILAID
186	LAM	Dominica	0	205.5	GDP*MILGDP+MILAID
187	DME	Faeroe Islands	0	205.5	GDP*MILGDP+MILAID
188	DME	Falkland Islands	0	205.5	GDP*MILGDP+MILAID
189	SEA	French Polynesia	0	205.5	GDP*MILGDP+MILAID
190	DME	Gibraltar	0	205.5	GDP*MILGDP+MILAID
191	DME	Greenland	0	205.5	GDP*MILGDP+MILAID
192	LAM	Grenada	0	205.5	GDP*MILGDP+MILAID
193	LAM	Guadeloupe	0	205.5	GDP*MILGDP+MILAID
194	SEA	Guam	0	205.5	GDP*MILGDP+MILAID
195	DME	Guernsey	0	205.5	GDP*MILGDP+MILAID
196	LAM	Guiana, French	0	205.5	GDP*MILGDP+MILAID
197	SEA	Hong Kong	0	205.5	GDP*MILGDP+MILAID
198	DME	Isle of Man	0	205.5	GDP*MILGDP+MILAID
199	DME	Jersey	0	205.5	GDP*MILGDP+MILAID
200	SEA	Kiribati	0	205.5	GDP*MILGDP+MILAID
201	DME	Liechtenstein	0	205.5	GDP*MILGDP+MILAID
202	SEA	Macao	0	205.5	GDP*MILGDP+MILAID
203	SEA	Marshall Islands	0	205.5	GDP*MILGDP+MILAID
204	LAM	Martinique	0	205.5	GDP*MILGDP+MILAID
205	AFR	Mayotte	0	205.5	GDP*MILGDP+MILAID
206	SEA	Micronesia	0	205.5	GDP*MILGDP+MILAID
207	DME	Monaco	0	205.5	GDP*MILGDP+MILAID
208	LAM	Montserrat	0	205.5	GDP*MILGDP+MILAID
209	SEA	Nauru	0	205.5	GDP*MILGDP+MILAID
210	LAM	Neth. Antilles	0	205.5	GDP*MILGDP+MILAID
211	SEA	New Caledonia	0	205.5	GDP*MILGDP+MILAID
212	SEA	Niue	0	205.5	GDP*MILGDP+MILAID
213	SEA	Northern Mariana Is.	0	205.5	GDP*MILGDP+MILAID
214	SEA	Palau	0	205.5	GDP*MILGDP+MILAID
215	LAM	Puerto Rico	0	205.5	GDP*MILGDP+MILAID
216	AFR	Reunion	0	205.5	GDP*MILGDP+MILAID
217	SEA	Samoa, American	0	205.5	GDP*MILGDP+MILAID
218	SEA	Samoa, Western	0	205.5	GDP*MILGDP+MILAID
219	DME	San Marino	0	205.5	GDP*MILGDP+MILAID
220	AFR	St. Helena	0	205.5	GDP*MILGDP+MILAID
221	LAM	St. Kitts & Nevis	0	205.5	GDP*MILGDP+MILAID
222	LAM	St. Lucia	0	205.5	GDP*MILGDP+MILAID
223	DME	St. Pierre & Miquelon	0	205.5	GDP*MILGDP+MILAID
224	LAM	St. Vincent	0	205.5	GDP*MILGDP+MILAID
225	SEA	Tokelau	0	205.5	GDP*MILGDP+MILAID

TABLE 2.8 – MILITARY EXPENDITURES AT MARKET EXCHANGE RATES PLUS FOREIGN MILITARY AID, MILLIONS OF DOLLARS, 2006					
OBS	REGION	COUNTRY	MILEXP	RANK	SOURCE
226	SEA	Turks & Caicos Is.	0	205.5	GDP*MILGDP+MILAID
227	SEA	Tuvalu	0	205.5	GDP*MILGDP+MILAID
228	LAM	Virgin Islands, Brit.	0	205.5	GDP*MILGDP+MILAID
229	LAM	Virgin Islands, US	0	205.5	GDP*MILGDP+MILAID
230	SEA	Wallis & Futuna	0	205.5	GDP*MILGDP+MILAID
231	AFR	Western Sahara	0	205.5	GDP*MILGDP+MILAID

NAME/ DESIGNATION	AKA	NUMBER OF SYSTEMS Active+Spares	YEAR FIRST DEPLOYED	WARHEAD TYPE	NUMBER OF WARHEADS x YIELD (kilotons)	RANGE (km)	TOTAL NUMBER AR-HEADS Active+Spares
TABLE 2.9 – OPERATIONAL NUCLEAR DELIVERY SYSTEMS, 2007-2008							
LAND BALLISTIC MISSILES							
UNITED STATES							
ICBM							
LGM-30G	Minuteman III					13,000	
	MK-12	138	1970	Single	1 x 170		214 + 20
	MK-12A	250	1979	MIRV, Single	1-3 x 335		450 + 20
	MK-21 SERV	100	2006 (1986)	Single	1 x 300		100 + 10
TOTAL 08(BULL)		488					764 + 50
SSM							
ATACMS Block I		Some	1991	Single	1 x 560kg payload	165	Some
ATACMS Block IA		Some	1998	Single	1 x 160kg payload	300	Some
ATACMS Block II		Some	2002	Single	1 x 270kg payload	140	Some
TOTAL 08(BULL)		Some					Some
RUSSIA							
ICBM							
SS-18	Satan	75	1979	MIRV	10 x 550-750	11,000-15,000	750
SS-19	Stiletto	100	1980	MIRV	6 x 550-750	10,000	600
SS-25	Sickle	201	1985	Single	1 x 550	10,500	201
SS-27	Topol-M (SILO)	48	1997	Single	1 x 550	10,500	48
SS-27	Topol-M (MOBILE)	6	2006	Single	1 x 550	10,500	6
SS-27	Topol-M (RS-24)	0	(2009)	MIRV	6 x 550	10,500	0
TOTAL 08(BULL)		430					1,605

TABLE 2.9 – OPERATIONAL NUCLEAR DELIVERY SYSTEMS, 2007-2008							
NAME/ DESIGNATION	*AKA*	*NUMBER OF SYSTEMS Active+Spares*	*YEAR FIRST DEPLOYED*	*WARHEAD TYPE*	*NUMBER OF WARHEADS x YIELD (kilotons)*	*RANGE (km)*	*TOTAL NUMBER AR-HEADS Active+Spares*
SSM							
SS-1c Mod 1	Scud-B	Some	1964	Single	1 x 1,000kg payload	300	Some
SS-1c Mod 2	Scud-B	Some	1964	Single	1 x 950kg payload	240	Some
SS-26	Iskander	Some	1995	Single	1 x 480kg payload	400	Some
	Iskander-E	Some	1999	Single	1 x 480kg payload	280	Some
TOTAL 08(BULL)		Some					Some
CHINA							
ICBM							
CSS-4	DF-5A	20	1981	Single	1 x 4,000-5,000	13,000	20
CSS-X-10	DF-31	0	(2007)			-7,250	
				Single	1 x 0.35-1,000		0
				MIRV	3 x 50-100		0
?	DF-31A	0	(2008-2010)			-11,270	
				Single	1 x 20-150		0
				MIRV	3-5 x 20-150		0
TOTAL 07(SIPRI)		20					20
IRBM							
CSS-2	DF-3A	16	1971	Single	1 x 3,300	3,300	16
CSS-3	DF-4	22	1980	Single	1 x 3,300	>5,500	22
CSS-5	DF-21, DF-21A	35	1991	Single	1 x 200-300	2,100	35
TOTAL 07(SIPRI)		73					73
SSM							

TABLE 2.9 – OPERATIONAL NUCLEAR DELIVERY SYSTEMS, 2007-2008							
NAME/ DESIGNATION	AKA	NUMBER OF SYSTEMS Active+Spares	YEAR FIRST DEPLOYED	WARHEAD TYPE	NUMBER OF WARHEADS x YIELD (kilotons)	RANGE (km)	TOTAL NUMBER AR-HEADS Active+Spares
CSS-6	DF-15/M-9	24	1989	Single	1 x 50-350	600	?
CSS-7	DF-11/M-11	32	1999	Single	1 x 0.5	300	?
CSS-8	DF-7	30	?	Single	1 x 500kg payload	150	?
TOTAL 04(IISS)		96					?
INDIA							
IRBM							
Agni II		Some	2004	Single	1 x 15-250	2,500-4,800	Some
Agni III		0	(2007)	Single	1 x 15-250	3,500-5,500	0
TOTAL 07(SIPRI)		Some					Some
SSM							
Agni I		Some	2004	Single	1 x 1,000kg payload	700-850	?
Prithvi I		<50	1994	Single	1 x 1,000kg payload	150	?
Prithvi II		Some	2004	Single	1 x 500kg payload	250	?
Prithvi III		30	2004	Single	1 x 10-20	350-600	?
TOTAL 07(SIPRI)		<80					25-30
PAKISTAN							
IRBM							
Ghauri-1	Haft 5	<50	2003	Single	1 x 700-1,000kg payload	1,500	?
Ghauri-2	Haft 5A	~100+	2003	Single	1 x 1,200kg payload	2,400	?

NAME/ DESIGNATION	AKA	NUMBER OF SYSTEMS Active+Spares	YEAR FIRST DEPLOYED	WARHEAD TYPE	NUMBER OF WARHEADS x YIELD (kilotons)	RANGE (km)	TOTAL NUMBER AR-HEADS Active+Spares
Shaheen-2	Haft 6	200+	2006	Single	1 x 1,000+ kg payload	2,000-2,500	?
TOTAL 07(SIPRI)		Some					-30
SSM							
Abdali	Haft 2	Some	2006	Single	1 x 250-450kg payload	180-200	?
Ghaznavi	Haft 3	<50	2004	Single	1 x 500kg payload	~400	?
Shaheen-1	Haft 4	<50	2003	Single	1 x 750kg payload	750	?
TOTAL 07(SIPRI)		Some					?
ISRAEL							
ICBM Jericho 3		Some	2005				Some
				Single	1 x 350kg payload	7,800	
				MIRV	2-3 x 350kg payload	4,800	
				Single	1 x 1,000-1,300kg payload	4,800	
TOTAL 08(WIKI)		Some					Some
IRBM							
Jericho 2		50	1985	Single	1 x 750-1,000kg payload	2,000	~40
TOTAL 07(SIPRI)		50					~40
SSM							
Jericho 1		0	1971	Single	1 x 450-650kg payload	500	0

TABLE 2.9 – OPERATIONAL NUCLEAR DELIVERY SYSTEMS, 2007-2008

NAME/ DESIGNATION	AKA	NUMBER OF SYSTEMS Active+Spares	YEAR FIRST DEPLOYED	WARHEAD TYPE	NUMBER OF WARHEADS x YIELD (kilotons)	RANGE (km)	TOTAL NUMBER AR-HEADS Active+Spares
TABLE 2.9 – OPERATIONAL NUCLEAR DELIVERY SYSTEMS, 2007-2008							
TOTAL 07(SIPRI)		0					0
NORTH KOREA							
IRBM							
No-Dong-1		Some	1997	Single	1 x 700-1,000kg payload	1,300	Some
TOTAL 07(SIPRI)		Some					Some
SSM							
Scud-B		Some	1979-1980	Single	1 x 1,000kg payload	300	?
Scud-C variant		Some	1989	Single	1 x 700kg payload	500	?
TOTAL 07(SIPRI)		Some					?
SLBM							
UNITED STATES							
UGM-133	Trident II D-5	288					
	MK-4		1992	MIRV	6 x 100	12,000	1,344+80
	MK-5		1990	MIRV	6 x 455	12,000	384+20
TOTAL 08(BULL)		288					1,728+100
UNITED KINGDOM							
UGM-135	Trident II D-5	48	1994	MIRV	1-3 x 100	12,000	-160
TOTAL 07(SIPRI)		48					-160
RUSSIA							
SS-N-18 M1	Stingray	5/80	1978	MIRV	3 x 200	6,500	240
SS-N-23	Skiff	4/64	1986	MIRV	4 x 100	9,000	256
SS-N-23 M1	Sineva	2/32	2007	MIRV	4 x 100	9,000	128
SS-NX-30	Bulava	0	(2008)	MIRV	6 x 100	8,000-10,000	0

TABLE 2.9 – OPERATIONAL NUCLEAR DELIVERY SYSTEMS, 2007-2008							
NAME/ DESIGNATION	*AKA*	*NUMBER OF SYSTEMS Active+Spares*	*YEAR FIRST DEPLOYED*	*WARHEAD TYPE*	*NUMBER OF WARHEADS x YIELD (kilotons)*	*RANGE (km)*	*TOTAL NUMBER AR-HEADS Active+Spares*
TOTAL 08(BULL)		11/176					624
FRANCE							
M-45		48	1996	MIRV	6 x 100	6,000	288
M-51		0	(2010-2015)	MIRV	6 x 100	8,000-10,000	0
TOTAL 07(SIPRI)		48					288
CHINA							
CSS-NX-3		12	1986				12
	JL-1			Single	1 x 200-300	1,000-1,700	
	JL-1			Single	1 x 25-50	2,150	
	JL-1A			Single	1 x 25-50	2,500	
CSS-NX-4	JL-2	0	(2008-2010)			>8,000	0
				Single	1 x 25-1,000		
				MIRV	3-4 x 90		
TOTAL 07(SIPRI)		12					12
INDIA							
Dhanush		Some	2006	Single	1 x 1,000kg payload	400	Some
TOTAL 07(SIPRI)		Some					Some
AIRCRAFT							
UNITED STATES STRATEGIC							
B-52H	Stratofortress	94+56	1961	ALCM ACM	5-150 5-150	16,000	528+25
B-2	Spirit	21+16	1994	Bombs B61-7, B83-1	ACM 5-150	11,000	555+25
TOTAL 08(BULL)		115+72					1,083+50
SUB-STRATEGIC							

TABLE 2.9 – OPERATIONAL NUCLEAR DELIVERY SYSTEMS, 2007-2008

NAME/ DESIGNATION	AKA	NUMBER OF SYSTEMS Active+Spares	YEAR FIRST DEPLOYED	WARHEAD TYPE	NUMBER OF WARHEADS x YIELD (kilotons)	RANGE (km)	TOTAL NUMBER AR-HEADS Active+Spares
F-15E	Strike Eagle	Some	1988	Bomb B61-3, B61-4	1 x 0.3-170, 1 x 0.3-45	2,500	Some
F-16A/B/ C/D	Fighting Falcon	Some	1976	Bomb B61-3, B61-4	1 x 0.3-170, 1 x 0.3-45	2,500	Some
F-117A	Nighthawk	Some	1983	Bomb B61-3, B61-4	1 x 0.3-170, 1 x 0.3-45	2,100	Some
TOTAL 08(BULL)		Some					400
RUSSIA STRATEGIC							
Tu-95 MS6	Bear H6	32	1984	ALCM	6 x ?	6,500-10,500	192
				Bombs	? x ?		
Tu-95 MS16	Bear H16	32	1984	ALCM	16 x ?	6,500-10,500	512
				Bombs	? x ?		
Tu-160	Blackjack	15	1987	ALCM	12 x ?	10,500-13,200	180
				SRAM	? x ?		
				Bombs	? x ?		
TOTAL 08(BULL)		79					884
SUB-STRATEGIC							
Tu-22M-3	Backfire	174 07(SIPRI)	1974	ASM	2 x ?	4,800-7,000	Some
				Bombs	? x ?		
Su-24	Fencer	429 07(SIPRI)	1974	Bombs	2 x ?	2,100-3,000	Some
TOTAL 08(BULL)		524					648
FRANCE STRATEGIC							
Mirage 2000N		60	1988	ASMP	1 x 300	2,750	50
TOTAL 07(SIPRI)		60					50

TABLE 2.9 – OPERATIONAL NUCLEAR DELIVERY SYSTEMS, 2007-2008							
NAME/ DESIGNATION	AKA	NUMBER OF SYSTEMS Active+Spares	YEAR FIRST DEPLOYED	WARHEAD TYPE	NUMBER OF WARHEADS x YIELD (kilotons)	RANGE (km)	TOTAL NUMBER AR-HEADS Active+Spares
SUB-STRATEGIC							
Super Etendard		24	1978	ASMP	1 x 300	650	10
TOTAL 07(SIPRI)		24					10
CHINA STRATEGIC							
H-6	Tu-16	20	1965	Bomb	1 x 3,000kg payload	3,100	~20
TOTAL 07(SIPRI)		20					~20
SUB-STRATEGIC							
Q-5	Mig-19	Some	1972-?	Bomb	1 x 1,000kg payload	400	~20
TOTAL 07(SIPRI)		Some					~20
ISRAEL SUB-STRATEGIC							
F-4E-2000	Kurnass	Some	1989	Bomb	1 x 8,480kg payload	2,200	Some
F-16A/B/ C/D	Fighting Falcon	Some	1980	Bomb	1 x 5,400kg payload	2,500	Some
F-15I	Thunder	Some	1997	Bomb	1 x 10,400kg payload	2,500	Some
TOTAL 07(BULL), 07(SIPRI)		205 07(SIPRI)					~40
INDIA SUB-STRATEGIC							
Jaguar S(I)	Shamsher	131 07(WIKI)	1979	Bomb	1 x 4,775kg payload	1,600	Some
MiG-27M	Bahadur	165 07(WIKI)	1982	Bomb	1 x 3,000kg payload	1,000	Some

TABLE 2.9 – OPERATIONAL NUCLEAR DELIVERY SYSTEMS, 2007-2008							
NAME/ DESIGNATION	*AKA*	*NUMBER OF SYSTEMS Active+Spares*	*YEAR FIRST DEPLOYED*	*WARHEAD TYPE*	*NUMBER OF WARHEADS x YIELD (kilotons)*	*RANGE (km)*	*TOTAL NUMBER AR-HEADS Active+Spares*
Mirage 2000H	Vajra	40 07(WIKI)	1998	Bomb	1 x 6,300kg payload	1,850-3,000	Some
TOTAL 07(SIPRI)		336 07(WIKI)					25-30
PAKISTAN							
SUB-STRATEGIC							
F-16A/B/ C/D	Fighting Falcon	34	1983	Bomb/ Babur LACM	1 x 4,500kg payload	2,500	Some
Mirage 2000-5		Some	2002	Bomb	1 x 6,300kg payload	1,200	Some
Q-5	MiG-19	Some	1980s	Bomb	1 x 1,000kg payload	1,200	Some
TOTAL 07(SIPRI)		>34					25-30
NORTH KOREA							
SUB-STRATEGIC							
H-5	Il-28	80	1950	Bomb	1 x 3,000kg payload	2,100	-6
TOTAL 07(SIPRI)		80					-6
SLCM							
UNITED STATES							
Tomahawk	TLAM-N	325	1984	Single	1 x 5-150	2,500	100
TOTAL 08(BULL)		325					100
RUSSIA							
SS-N-9	Siren	Some	1972	Single	1 x 200	110	Some
SS-N-12	Sandbox	Some	1959-1960	Single	1 x 350	550	Some
SS-N-19	Shipwreck	Some	1980	Single	1 x 500	550	Some
SS-N-21	Sampson	Some	1984	Single	1 x 200	2,400	Some
SS-N-22	Sunburn	Some	1980	Single	1 x 320kg payload	120	Some
TOTAL 07(SIPRI)		Some					698
ISRAEL							

TABLE 2.9 – OPERATIONAL NUCLEAR DELIVERY SYSTEMS, 2007-2008							
NAME/ DESIGNATION	*AKA*	*NUMBER OF SYSTEMS Active+Spares*	*YEAR FIRST DEPLOYED*	*WARHEAD TYPE*	*NUMBER OF WARHEADS x YIELD (kilotons)*	*RANGE (km)*	*TOTAL NUMBER AR-HEADS Active+Spares*
Turbo-Popeye 3		Some	2000	Single	1 x 200kg payload	1,500	10
TOTAL 04(IISS)		Some					10
ALCM							
UNITED STATES							
AGM-868		1,140	1982/1991	Single	1 x 900-1,400kg payload	2,500	Some
AGM-129		460	1990	Single	1 x 5-200	3,500	Some
TOTAL 08(BULL)		1,600					Some
RUSSIA							
AS-4	Kh-24 Kitchen	Some	1964	Single	1 x 1,000	310	Some
AS-15A	Kh-55 Kent	Some	1971	Single	1 x 200-250	2,500	Some
AS-15B	Kh-55SM Kent	Some	1986	Single	1 x 200-250	3,000	Some
AS-16	Kh-15 Kickback	Some	1980	Single	1 x 350	150	Some
TOTAL 07(SIPRI)		Some					Some
FRANCE							
ASMP		Some	1985	Single	1 x 300	250	Some
TOTAL 07(SIPRI)		Some					Some
PAKISTAN							
Babur	Haft-7	Some	2005	Single	1 x 500kg payload	-500-700	Some
TOTAL 07(SIPRI)		Some					Some
STRATEGIC DEFENSIVE SYSTEMS							
RUSSIA							
51T6	SH-11 Gorgon	32	1989	Single	1 x 1,000	350	32
53T6	SH-08 Gazelle	68	1986	Single	1 x 10	80	68

TABLE 2.9 – OPERATIONAL NUCLEAR DELIVERY SYSTEMS, 2007-2008							
NAME/ DESIGNATION	AKA	NUMBER OF SYSTEMS Active+Spares	YEAR FIRST DEPLOYED	WARHEAD TYPE	NUMBER OF WARHEADS x YIELD (kilotons)	RANGE (km)	TOTAL NUMBER AR-HEADS Active+Spares
SA-10	Grumble	633	1980	Single	1 x low yield	5-150	633
TOTAL 07(SIPRI)		733					733

ACM advanced cruise missile
AKA also known as
ALCM air-launched cruise missile
ASM air-to-surface missile
MIRV multiple independently targetable re-entry vehicles
ICBM intercontinental ballistic missile
IRBM intermediate-range ballistic missile
SLBM submarine-launched ballistic missile
SLCM submarine-launched cruise missile
SSM surface-to-surface missile
LACM land-attack cruise missile

SOURCES: 07(SIPRI), 07(BULL), 07(WIKI), 06(BULL), 04(BULL), 04(IISS)

OBS	COUNTRY	ICBM	IRBM	SLBM	ALCM/ BOMBS	TOTAL
			TABLE 2.10 – OPERATIONAL NUCLEAR WARHEADS, 2007-2008, STRATEGIC			
1	U.S.	814		1,828	1,113	3,755
2	Russia	1,605		624	884	3,113
3	France			288	60	348
4	U.K.			160		160
5	China	20	69	12	-40	151
6	Israel	Some				Some
7	India					
8	Pakistan					
9	N. Korea					

ALCM   air-launched cruise missile
ICBM   intercontinental ballistic missile
IRBM   intermediate-range ballistic missile
SLBM   submarine-launched ballistic missile

SOURCES: 08(BULL), 07(SIPRI)

OBS	COUNTRY	SSM	SLCM	AIR DEFENSE	AIRCAFT	TOTAL
		TABLE 2.11 – OPERATIONAL NUCLEAR WARHEADS, 2007-2008, SUB-STRATEGIC				
1	Russia		698	733	648	2,079
2	U.S.		100		400	500
3	Israel	-40	Some		-40	80
4	Pakistan	30+			30+	-60
5	India	25-30			25-30	50-60
6	N. Korea				-6	-6
7	China	?			?	?
8	France					0
9	U.K.					0

SLCM   sea-launched cruise missile
SSM   surface-to-surface missile

SOURCES: 08(BULL), 07(SIPRI)

	TABLE 2.12 – OPERATIONAL NUCLEAR WARHEADS, 2007-2008, TOTAL STRATEGIC AND SUB-STRATEGIC			
OBS	COUNTRY	STOCKPILE 08(BULL), 07(SIPRI)	DELIVERABLE 08(BULL), 07(SIPRI)	DELIVERABLE 08(IISS)
1	Russia	14,000	5,192	
2	U.S.	10,400	4,275	
3	France		348	
4	U.K.	-200	-160	
5	China		-145	
6	Israel		<=100	-200
7	Pakistan		-60	
8	India		-50	
9	N. Korea		-6	

SOURCES: 07(SIPRI), 07(EST), 00(BULL), 04(E), 07(CIA)

TABLE 2.13 – STATES POSSESSING, PURSUING OR CAPABLE OF ACQUIRING WEAPONS OF MASS DESTRUCTION, 2007

STATE	NUCLEAR ENERGY	URANIUM ENRICHMENT	PLUTONIUM PRODUCTION	NUCLEAR WEAPONS	CHEMICAL WEAPONS	BIOLOGICAL WEAPONS	MISSILE TECHNOLOGY
Algeria				Pursuing			
Argentina	Possessing		Possessing	Capable			Pursuing
Armenia	Possessing		Possessing				
Australia				Capable	Capable	Capable	Capable
Belarus				Capable			
Belgium	Possessing		Possessing				
Brazil	Possessing	Pursuing	Possessing	Capable		Capable	Possessing
Bulgaria	Possessing						
Burma					Pursuing		
Canada	Possessing		Possessing				
Chile					Capable	Capable	
China	Possessing	Possessing	Possessing	Possessing	Possessing	Possessing	Possessing
Cuba	Possessing		Possessing				
Czechia	Possessing		Possessing				
Ethiopia					Pursuing		
Egypt					Possessing	Capable	Pursuing
Finland	Possessing		Possessing				
France	Possessing	Possessing	Possessing	Possessing	Possessing	Capable	Possessing
Germany	Possessing	Possessing	Possessing	Capable	Capable	Capable	Capable
Hungary	Possessing		Possessing				
India	Possessing	Possessing	Possessing	Possessing	Possessing	Possessing	Possessing
Indonesia					Pursuing		
Iran	Pursuing	Pursuing			Possessing	Possessing	Possessing
Israel		Pursuing	Possessing	Possessing	Possessing	Possessing	Possessing

Country							
Japan	Possessing	Possessing	Possessing	Capable	Capable	Capable	Possessing
Kazakhstan				Capable			
Laos					Pursuing	Pursuing	Pursuing
Libya					Pursuing	Pursuing	
Lithuania	Possessing		Possessing				
Mexico	Possessing	Possessing	Possessing				
Netherlands	Possessing		Possessing				
North Korea	Possessing	Possessing	Possessing	Possessing	Possessing	Possessing	Possessing
Pakistan	Possessing	Possessing	Possessing	Possessing	Possessing	Possessing	Possessing
Romania	Possessing		Possessing				
Russia	Possessing	Possessing	Possessing	Possessing	Possessing	Possessing	Possessing
Saudi Arabia				Pursuing	Pursuing	Pursuing	Pursuing
Serbia				Pursuing	Capable		
Slovakia	Possessing		Possessing				
Slovenia	Possessing		Possessing				
South Africa	Possessing		Possessing	Capable	Capable	Capable	Capable
South Korea	Possessing		Possessing		Capable	Capable	Capable
Spain	Possessing		Possessing		Pursuing		
Sudan							
Sweden	Possessing		Possessing				
Switzerland	Possessing		Possessing	Capable			
Syria	Possessing	Possessing	Possessing		Pursuing	Pursuing	Pursuing
Taiwan	Possessing				Possessing	Possessing	Possessing
Thailand	Possessing				Pursuing		
Ukraine	Possessing		Possessing		Pursuing	Pursuing	
Vietnam							
United Kingdom	Possessing	Possessing	Possessing	Possessing	Capable	Capable	Possessing
United States	Possessing	Possessing	Possessing	Possessing	Possessing	Possessing	Possessing

3. DEVELOPED MARKET ECONOMIES

TABLE 3.1 – GNI PER CAPITA AT MARKET EXCHANGE RATES

TABLE 3.1.1 – GNI PER CAPITA AT MARKET EXCHANGE RATES, YEAR 1970			
OBS	COUNTRY	GPC70	RANK
1	United States whites	5,187	1
2	United States	5,000	2
3	Sweden	4,450	3
4	Canada	3,930	4
5	Switzerland	3,740	5
6	Australia	3,500	6
7	Norway	3,130	7
8	Denmark	3,110	8
9	France	3,010	9
10	Luxembourg	2,870	10
11	Germany	2,850	11
12	Belgium	2,780	12
13	Netherlands	2,760	13
14	Iceland	2,530	14
15	Finland	2,450	15
16	United Kingdom	2,210	16
17	New Zealand	2,180	17
18	Austria	2,060	18
19	Italy	2,020	19
20	Japan	1,920	20
21	Israel	1,750	21
22	Greece	1,700	22
23	Ireland	1,460	23
24	Spain	1,160	24
25	Cyprus	879	25
26	Portugal	860	26
27	Malta	760	27
28	South Korea	270	28

TABLE 3.1.2 – GNI PER CAPITA AT MARKET EXCHANGE RATES, YEAR 1980			
OBS	COUNTRY	GPC80	RANK
1	Switzerland	20,080	1
2	Sweden	16,250	2
3	Norway	15,520	3
4	Iceland	15,040	4
5	Denmark	15,000	5
6	Luxembourg	14,480	6
7	Belgium	13,760	7
8	United States whites	13,723	8
9	Netherlands	13,670	9
10	United States	12,980	10
11	France	12,920	11
12	Germany	12,600	12
13	Australia	12,190	13
14	Canada	11,320	14
15	Austria	11,210	15
16	Finland	11,120	16
17	Japan	10,310	17
18	United Kingdom	8,410	18
19	Italy	8,090	19
20	New Zealand	7,530	20
21	Greece	7,170	21
22	Ireland	6,130	22
23	Spain	6,060	23
24	Israel	5,350	24
25	Cyprus	4,280	25
26	Malta	3,380	26
27	Portugal	3,160	27
28	South Korea	1,810	28

TABLE 3.1.3 – GNI PER CAPITA AT MARKET EXCHANGE RATES, YEAR 1990			
OBS	COUNTRY	GPC90	RANK
1	Switzerland	34,230	1
2	Luxembourg	29,530	2
3	Japan	26,660	3
4	Sweden	26,070	4
5	Norway	25,810	5
6	Finland	25,280	6
7	United States whites	24,754	7
8	Iceland	24,150	8
9	Denmark	24,100	9
10	United States	23,330	10
11	Germany	20,630	11
12	France	20,240	12
13	Austria	20,180	13
14	Canada	20,150	14
15	Belgium	18,980	15
16	Netherlands	18,820	16
17	Australia	18,190	17
18	Italy	17,900	18
19	United Kingdom	16,210	19
20	New Zealand	12,910	20
21	Ireland	12,060	21
22	Spain	11,890	22
23	Israel	10,860	23
24	Greece	9,940	24
25	Cyprus	9,530	25
26	Portugal	6,790	26
27	Malta	6,780	27
28	South Korea	6,000	28

OBS	COUNTRY	GPC00	RANK
1	Luxembourg	43,490	1
2	Switzerland	40,110	2
3	United States whites	36,303	3
4	Norway	35,870	4
5	Japan	34,620	5
6	United States	34,400	6
7	Denmark	31,850	7
8	Iceland	30,750	8
9	Sweden	28,870	9
10	Netherlands	26,580	10
11	Austria	26,010	11
12	Germany	25,510	12
13	Finland	25,400	13
14	Belgium	25,360	14
15	United Kingdom	24,970	15
16	France	24,450	16
17	Ireland	23,160	17
18	Canada	22,130	18
19	Italy	20,900	19
20	Australia	20,720	20
21	Israel	17,890	21
22	Spain	15,420	22
23	Greece	14,430	23
24	New Zealand	13,760	24
25	Cyprus	13,440	25
26	Portugal	11,600	26
27	South Korea	9,800	27
28	Malta	9,670	28

TABLE 3.1.4 – GNI PER CAPITA AT MARKET EXCHANGE RATES, YEAR 2000

TABLE 3.1.5 – GNI PER CAPITA AT MARKET EXCHANGE RATES, YEAR 2006			
OBS	COUNTRY	GPC06	RANK
1	Luxembourg	71,240	1
2	Norway	68,440	2
3	Switzerland	58,050	3
4	Denmark	52,110	4
5	Iceland	49,960	5
6	United States whites	47,317	6
7	Ireland	44,830	7
8	United States	44,710	8
9	Sweden	43,530	9
10	Netherlands	43,050	10
11	Finland	41,360	11
12	United Kingdom	40,560	12
13	Austria	39,750	13
14	Japan	38,630	14
15	Belgium	38,460	15
16	Germany	36,810	16
17	Canada	36,650	17
18	France	36,560	18
19	Australia	35,860	19
20	Italy	31,990	20
21	Greece	27,390	21
22	Spain	27,340	22
23	New Zealand	26,750	23
24	Cyprus	23,270	24
25	Israel	20,170	25
26	Portugal	17,850	26
27	South Korea	17,690	27
28	Malta	15,310	28

TABLE 3.1.6 – GROWTH RATES OF GNI PER CAPITA AT MARKET EXCHANGE RATES, 1970-2006			
OBS	*COUNTRY*	*GRPCMER*	*RANK*
1	South Korea	12.32	1
2	Ireland	9.98	2
3	Cyprus	9.53	3
4	Luxembourg	9.33	4
5	Spain	9.17	5
6	Norway	8.95	6
7	Portugal	8.79	7
8	Malta	8.70	8
9	Japan	8.70	9
10	Iceland	8.64	10
11	Austria	8.57	11
12	United Kingdom	8.42	12
13	Finland	8.17	13
14	Denmark	8.14	14
15	Greece	8.03	15
16	Italy	7.98	16
17	Netherlands	7.93	17
18	Switzerland	7.91	18
19	Belgium	7.57	19
20	Germany	7.37	20
21	New Zealand	7.21	21
22	France	7.18	22
23	Israel	7.03	23
24	Australia	6.68	24
25	Sweden	6.54	25
26	Canada	6.40	26
27	United States whites	6.33	27
28	United States	6.27	28

TABLE 3.2 – GDP PER CAPITA AT PPP

TABLE 3.2.1 – GDP PER CAPITA AT PPP, YEAR 1970			
OBS	COUNTRY	GPCPPP70	RANK
1	United States whites	5,106	1
2	United States	4,922	2
3	Switzerland	4,840	3
4	Canada	3,969	4
5	Sweden	3,855	5
6	Luxembourg	3,714	6
7	Denmark	3,523	7
8	Netherlands	3,500	8
9	Australia	3,465	9
10	New Zealand	3,331	10
11	United Kingdom	3,273	11
12	Germany	3,227	12
13	France	3,215	13
14	Norway	3,113	14
15	Italy	3,045	15
16	Belgium	2,989	16
17	Iceland	2,980	17
18	Finland	2,902	18
19	Japan	2,811	19
20	Austria	2,757	20
21	Israel	2,667	21
22	Spain	2,179	22
23	Ireland	1,852	23
24	Greece	1,562	24
25	Portugal	1,454	25
26	Malta	1,276	26
27	Cyprus	1,032	27
28	South Korea	500	28

TABLE 3.2.2 – GDP PER CAPITA AT PPP, YEAR 1980			
OBS	COUNTRY	GPCPPP80	RANK
1	Switzerland	13,616	1
2	Luxembourg	13,577	2
3	United States whites	12,899	3
4	Norway	12,506	4
5	United States	12,186	5
6	Canada	11,022	6
7	Iceland	10,658	7
8	Netherlands	10,530	8
9	Austria	10,285	9
10	Australia	10,139	10
11	Denmark	10,054	11
12	Belgium	9,956	12
13	France	9,900	13
14	Sweden	9,838	14
15	Greece	9,670	15
16	Germany	9,596	16
17	Italy	8,979	17
18	Japan	8,929	18
19	United Kingdom	8,653	19
20	Finland	8,630	20
21	New Zealand	8,275	21
22	Spain	7,323	22
23	Israel	7,091	23
24	Ireland	6,055	24
25	Portugal	5,428	25
26	Cyprus	5,385	26
27	Malta	4,376	27
28	South Korea	2,479	28

TABLE 3.2.3 – GDP PER CAPITA AT PPP, YEAR 1990			
OBS	COUNTRY	GPCPPP90	RANK
1	Luxembourg	31,787	1
2	United States whites	24,569	2
3	Switzerland	24,097	3
4	Norway	23,371	4
5	United States	23,064	5
6	Canada	19,454	6
7	Austria	19,047	7
8	Iceland	18,887	8
9	Netherlands	18,832	9
10	Japan	18,776	10
11	Denmark	18,575	11
12	Belgium	18,138	12
13	France	18,016	13
14	Germany	17,996	14
15	Sweden	17,937	15
16	Australia	17,648	16
17	Italy	17,127	17
18	Finland	16,843	18
19	United Kingdom	16,566	19
20	Greece	14,852	20
21	Spain	14,227	21
22	New Zealand	13,602	22
23	Cyprus	13,167	23
24	Israel	12,738	24
25	Ireland	12,670	25
26	Portugal	11,149	26
27	Malta	9,802	27
28	South Korea	7,692	28

TABLE 3.2.4 – GDP PER CAPITA AT PPP, YEAR 2000			
OBS	COUNTRY	GPCPPP00	RANK
1	Luxembourg	55,512	1
2	Norway	38,917	2
3	United States whites	35,849	3
4	United States	34,600	4
5	Switzerland	30,618	5
6	Netherlands	29,591	6
7	Austria	28,901	7
8	Canada	28,711	8
9	Ireland	28,505	9
10	Denmark	28,325	10
11	Australia	27,404	11
12	Iceland	27,007	12
13	Belgium	26,725	13
14	Germany	26,237	14
15	France	25,867	15
16	Sweden	25,721	16
17	Japan	25,367	17
18	United Kingdom	24,848	18
19	Italy	24,471	19
20	Finland	24,158	20
21	Spain	22,161	21
22	Greece	21,351	22
23	Cyprus	20,275	23
24	Israel	20,046	24
25	New Zealand	19,704	25
26	Malta	18,047	26
27	Portugal	17,577	27
28	South Korea	15,511	28

TABLE 3.2.5 – GDP PER CAPITA AT PPP, YEAR 2006			
OBS	COUNTRY	GPCPPP06	RANK
1	Luxembourg	75,611	1
2	Norway	50,078	2
3	United States whites	46,532	3
4	United States	43,968	4
5	Ireland	40,268	5
6	Switzerland	37,194	6
7	Iceland	36,923	7
8	Canada	36,713	8
9	Netherlands	36,560	9
10	Austria	36,049	10
11	Denmark	35,692	11
12	Australia	35,547	12
13	Sweden	34,193	13
14	Belgium	33,543	14
15	United Kingdom	33,087	15
16	Finland	33,022	16
17	Germany	32,322	17
18	France	31,992	18
19	Japan	31,947	19
20	Greece	31,382	20
21	Italy	29,053	21
22	Spain	28,649	22
23	Cyprus	25,882	23
24	New Zealand	25,517	24
25	Israel	24,097	25
26	South Korea	22,988	26
27	Malta	21,720	27
28	Portugal	20,784	28

TABLE 3.2.6 – GROWTH RATES OF GDP PER CAPITA AT PPP, 1970-2006			
OBS	COUNTRY	GRPCPPP	RANK
1	South Korea	11.22	1
2	Cyprus	9.36	2
3	Ireland	8.93	3
4	Luxembourg	8.73	4
5	Greece	8.69	5
6	Malta	8.19	6
7	Norway	8.02	7
8	Portugal	7.67	8
9	Spain	7.42	9
10	Austria	7.40	10
11	Iceland	7.24	11
12	Finland	6.99	12
13	Japan	6.98	13
14	Belgium	6.95	14
15	Netherlands	6.73	15
16	Australia	6.68	16
17	Denmark	6.64	17
18	United Kingdom	6.64	18
19	Germany	6.61	19
20	France	6.59	20
21	Italy	6.47	21
22	Canada	6.37	22
23	United States whites	6.33	23
24	Israel	6.31	24
25	United States	6.27	25
26	Sweden	6.25	26
27	Switzerland	5.83	27
28	New Zealand	5.82	28

TABLE 3.3 – INFANT MORTALITY

TABLE 3.3.1 – INFANT MORTALITY, YEAR 1960			
OBS	COUNTRY	INFMRT60	RANK
1	Sweden	16.6	1
2	Netherlands	16.8	2
3	Iceland	17.2	3
4	Norway	17.6	4
5	Australia	20.2	5
6	Finland	21.0	6
7	Switzerland	21.1	7
8	Denmark	21.5	8
9	United Kingdom	22.2	9
10	New Zealand	22.6	10
11	United States whites	23.1	11
12	United States	26.0	12
13	Canada	27.3	13
14	France	27.4	14
15	Ireland	29.3	15
16	Cyprus	29.8	16
17	Japan	30.4	17
18	Belgium	31.2	18
19	Luxembourg	31.5	19
20	Israel	32.4	20
21	Germany	35.0	21
22	Malta	37.2	22
23	Austria	37.5	23
24	Italy	43.9	24
25	Spain	45.4	25
26	Greece	53.2	26
27	Portugal	81.3	27
28	South Korea	90.0	28

TABLE 3.3.2 – INFANT MORTALITY, YEAR 1970			
OBS	COUNTRY	INFMRT70	RANK
1	Sweden	11.0	1.0
2	Netherlands	12.0	2.5
3	Norway	12.0	2.5
4	Iceland	12.5	4.0
5	Japan	13.1	5.0
6	Finland	13.4	6.0
7	Denmark	14.2	7.0
8	Switzerland	15.4	8.0
9	New Zealand	16.7	9.0
10	United States whites	17.8	10.0
11	Australia	17.9	11.0
12	United Kingdom	18.0	12.0
13	France	18.2	13.0
14	Canada	18.8	14.0
15	Ireland	19.5	15.0
16	United States	20.0	16.0
17	Belgium	21.1	17.0
18	Germany	22.5	18.0
19	Israel	24.2	19.0
20	Luxembourg	24.9	20.0
21	Malta	25.0	21.0
22	Austria	25.9	22.0
23	Spain	28.1	23.0
24	Cyprus	28.9	24.0
25	Italy	29.6	25.0
26	Greece	38.3	26.0
27	South Korea	43.0	27.0
28	Portugal	52.6	28.0

TABLE 3.3.3 – INFANT MORTALITY, YEAR 1980			
OBS	COUNTRY	INFMRT80	RANK
1	Sweden	6.9	1.0
2	Iceland	7.5	2.5
3	Japan	7.5	2.5
4	Finland	7.6	4.5
5	Norway	7.6	4.5
6	Denmark	8.4	6.0
7	Netherlands	8.7	7.0
8	Switzerland	9.1	8.0
9	Canada	10.4	9.5
10	France	10.4	9.5
11	Australia	10.7	11.0
12	United States whites	10.9	12.0
13	Ireland	11.1	13.0
14	Luxembourg	11.5	14.0
15	Spain	11.8	15.0
16	Belgium	12.1	16.0
17	United Kingdom	12.3	17.0
18	Germany	12.4	18.0
19	United States	12.6	19.0
20	New Zealand	12.8	20.0
21	Malta	14.2	21.0
22	Austria	14.3	22.0
23	Italy	14.6	23.0
24	South Korea	16.0	24.0
25	Israel	16.1	25.0
26	Cyprus	18.1	26.0
27	Greece	20.2	27.0
28	Portugal	25.3	28.0

TABLE 3.3.4 – INFANT MORTALITY, YEAR 1990			
OBS	COUNTRY	INFMRT90	RANK
1	Japan	4.60	1.0
2	Iceland	5.43	2.0
3	Finland	5.70	3.0
4	Sweden	6.00	4.0
5	Canada	6.80	5.5
6	Switzerland	6.80	5.5
7	Germany	7.00	7.0
8	Netherlands	7.20	8.0
9	Luxembourg	7.30	9.5
10	Norway	7.30	9.5
11	France	7.40	11.0
12	Denmark	7.50	12.0
13	Spain	7.60	13.5
14	United States whites	7.60	13.5
15	Austria	7.80	15.0
16	Belgium	7.90	16.0
17	Australia	8.00	18.0
18	South Korea	8.00	18.0
19	United Kingdom	8.00	18.0
20	Ireland	8.20	20.5
21	Italy	8.20	20.5
22	New Zealand	8.30	22.0
23	United States	9.40	23.0
24	Greece	9.46	24.0
25	Malta	9.81	25.0
26	Israel	10.02	26.0
27	Cyprus	10.78	27.0
28	Portugal	11.31	28.0

TABLE 3.3.5 – INFANT MORTALITY, YEAR 2000			
OBS	COUNTRY	INFMRT00	RANK
1	Iceland	2.68	1.0
2	Japan	3.20	2.5
3	Sweden	3.20	2.5
4	Finland	3.70	4.0
5	Norway	3.80	5.0
6	France	4.40	6.5
7	Germany	4.40	6.5
8	Spain	4.50	8.0
9	Italy	4.60	9.5
10	Netherlands	4.60	9.5
11	Austria	4.80	11.5
12	Belgium	4.80	11.5
13	Australia	4.90	13.5
14	Switzerland	4.90	13.5
15	Luxembourg	5.00	15.5
16	South Korea	5.00	15.5
17	Canada	5.20	17.0
18	Denmark	5.30	18.0
19	Cyprus	5.31	19.0
20	Israel	5.56	20.0
21	United Kingdom	5.60	21.0
22	United States whites	5.70	22.0
23	Malta	5.82	23.0
24	New Zealand	5.89	24.0
25	Ireland	5.90	25.0
26	Portugal	5.92	26.0
27	Greece	5.93	27.0
28	United States	6.90	28.0

TABLE 3.3.6 – INFANT MORTALITY, YEAR 2006			
OBS	*COUNTRY*	*INFMRT06*	*RANK*
1	Iceland	2.22	1.0
2	Japan	2.62	2.0
3	Finland	2.89	3.0
4	Sweden	2.94	4.0
5	Norway	3.02	5.0
6	Cyprus	3.32	6.0
7	Portugal	3.39	7.0
8	Italy	3.52	8.0
9	Belgium	3.55	9.0
10	France	3.58	10.0
11	Greece	3.62	11.0
12	Luxembourg	3.63	12.5
13	Spain	3.63	12.5
14	Germany	3.73	14.0
15	Austria	3.90	15.0
16	Denmark	3.99	16.0
17	Switzerland	4.14	17.0
18	Israel	4.17	18.0
19	Netherlands	4.24	19.0
20	Ireland	4.29	20.0
21	South Korea	4.52	21.0
22	Australia	4.72	22.0
23	Canada	4.87	23.5
24	United Kingdom	4.87	23.5
25	Malta	5.10	25.0
26	New Zealand	5.18	26.0
27	United States whites	5.40	27.0
28	United States	6.45	28.0

TABLE 3.3.7 – DECREASE IN RATES OF INFANT MORTALITY, 1960-2006			
OBS	COUNTRY	DRIM	RANK
1	Portugal	7.15	1
2	South Korea	6.72	2
3	Greece	6.02	3
4	Spain	5.65	4
5	Italy	5.64	5
6	Japan	5.47	6
7	Austria	5.04	7
8	Germany	4.99	8
9	Cyprus	4.89	9
10	Belgium	4.84	10
11	Luxembourg	4.81	11
12	Israel	4.56	12
13	Iceland	4.55	13
14	France	4.52	14
15	Malta	4.41	15
16	Finland	4.41	16
17	Ireland	4.27	17
18	Norway	3.91	18
19	Sweden	3.83	19
20	Canada	3.82	20
21	Denmark	3.73	21
22	Switzerland	3.60	22
23	United Kingdom	3.35	23
24	New Zealand	3.25	24
25	Australia	3.21	25
26	United States whites	3.21	26
27	United States	3.08	27
28	Netherlands	3.04	28

TABLE 3.4 LIFE EXPECTANCY

TABLE 3.4.1 – LIFE EXPECTANCY, YEAR 1960			
OBS	COUNTRY	LIFEXP60	RANK
1	Norway	73.550	1
2	Netherlands	73.393	2
3	Iceland	73.249	3
4	Sweden	73.006	4
5	Denmark	72.177	5
6	Israel	71.684	6
7	Switzerland	71.313	7
8	New Zealand	71.237	8
9	Canada	71.133	9
10	United Kingdom	71.127	10
11	Australia	70.773	11
12	United States whites	70.700	12
13	Belgium	70.368	13
14	France	70.240	14
15	United States	69.771	15
16	Ireland	69.745	16
17	Germany	69.543	17
18	Italy	69.124	18
19	Spain	69.109	19
20	Luxembourg	68.929	20
21	Greece	68.850	21
22	Finland	68.820	22
23	Cyprus	68.765	23
24	Austria	68.586	24
25	Malta	68.554	25
26	Japan	67.666	26
27	Portugal	63.442	27
28	South Korea	54.151	28

TABLE 3.4.2 – LIFE EXPECTANCY, YEAR 1970			
OBS	COUNTRY	LIFEXP70	RANK
1	Sweden	74.649	1
2	Norway	74.088	2
3	Iceland	73.969	3
4	Netherlands	73.586	4
5	Denmark	73.343	5
6	Switzerland	73.020	6
7	Canada	72.700	7
8	Spain	72.027	8
9	France	72.009	9
10	United Kingdom	71.973	10
11	Japan	71.950	11
12	Greece	71.842	12
13	United States whites	71.700	13
14	Italy	71.559	14
15	New Zealand	71.273	15
16	Israel	71.213	16
17	Belgium	71.211	17
18	Ireland	71.161	18
19	Australia	71.019	19
20	Cyprus	70.973	20
21	United States	70.807	21
22	Germany	70.459	22
23	Luxembourg	70.338	23
24	Finland	70.180	24
25	Malta	70.120	25
26	Austria	69.891	26
27	Portugal	67.420	27
28	South Korea	61.247	28

TABLE 3.4.3 – LIFE EXPECTANCY, YEAR 1980			
OBS	COUNTRY	LIFEXP80	RANK
1	Japan	76.092	1.0
2	Sweden	75.741	2.0
3	Netherlands	75.714	3.0
4	Norway	75.672	4.0
5	Switzerland	75.459	5.0
6	Spain	75.349	6.0
7	Canada	75.078	7.0
8	Cyprus	74.600	8.0
9	United States whites	74.400	9.0
10	Greece	74.359	10.0
11	Australia	74.334	11.0
12	France	74.180	12.0
13	Denmark	74.102	13.0
14	Italy	73.943	14.0
15	Iceland	73.876	15.5
16	Israel	73.876	15.5
17	United Kingdom	73.676	17.0
18	United States	73.659	18.0
19	Finland	73.440	19.0
20	Belgium	73.247	20.0
21	Malta	72.936	21.0
22	New Zealand	72.829	22.0
23	Luxembourg	72.704	23.0
24	Ireland	72.665	24.0
25	Germany	72.626	25.0
26	Austria	72.424	26.0
27	Portugal	71.392	27.0
28	South Korea	65.802	28.0

TABLE 3.4.4 – LIFE EXPECTANCY, YEAR 1990			
OBS	COUNTRY	LIFEXP90	RANK
1	Japan	78.837	1.0
2	Sweden	77.537	2.0
3	Canada	77.377	3.0
4	Switzerland	77.242	4.0
5	Australia	76.995	5.0
6	Greece	76.939	6.0
7	Netherlands	76.878	7.0
8	Italy	76.859	8.0
9	Spain	76.838	9.0
10	France	76.745	10.0
11	Iceland	76.607	11.5
12	Israel	76.607	11.5
13	Norway	76.537	13.0
14	Cyprus	76.295	14.0
15	United States whites	76.100	15.0
16	Belgium	75.968	16.0
17	United Kingdom	75.880	17.0
18	Austria	75.530	18.0
19	Malta	75.498	19.0
20	New Zealand	75.378	20.0
21	United States	75.215	21.0
22	Germany	75.207	22.0
23	Finland	74.813	23.0
24	Denmark	74.805	24.0
25	Luxembourg	74.671	25.0
26	Ireland	74.583	26.0
27	Portugal	73.663	27.0
28	South Korea	71.295	28.0

TABLE 3.4.5 – LIFE EXPECTANCY, YEAR 2000			
OBS	COUNTRY	LIFEXP00	RANK
1	Japan	81.076	1.0
2	Switzerland	79.681	2.0
3	Sweden	79.648	3.0
4	Australia	79.634	4.0
5	Italy	79.522	5.0
6	Canada	79.185	6.0
7	Spain	78.966	7.0
8	Iceland	78.954	8.5
9	Israel	78.954	8.5
10	France	78.910	10.0
11	New Zealand	78.637	11.0
12	Norway	78.604	12.0
13	Malta	78.200	13.0
14	Cyprus	78.139	14.0
15	Austria	78.042	15.0
16	Greece	77.988	16.5
17	Netherlands	77.988	16.5
18	Germany	77.927	18.0
19	Luxembourg	77.873	19.0
20	United Kingdom	77.741	20.0
21	Belgium	77.624	21.0
22	United States whites	77.600	22.0
23	Finland	77.501	23.0
24	United States	77.034	24.0
25	Denmark	76.754	25.0
26	Portugal	76.517	26.0
27	Ireland	76.437	27.0
28	South Korea	75.855	28.0

TABLE 3.4.6 – LIFE EXPECTANCY, YEAR 2006			
OBS	COUNTRY	LIFEXP06	RANK
1	Japan	82.322	1
2	Switzerland	81.515	2
3	Iceland	81.171	3
4	Italy	81.081	4
5	Australia	80.999	5
6	Spain	80.801	6
7	Sweden	80.768	7
8	France	80.555	8
9	Canada	80.356	9
10	Norway	80.335	10
11	Israel	80.021	11
12	New Zealand	79.930	12
13	Austria	79.837	13
14	Netherlands	79.698	14
15	Belgium	79.480	15
16	Greece	79.415	16
17	Ireland	79.393	17
18	Cyprus	79.293	18
19	Finland	79.229	19
20	Luxembourg	79.176	20
21	United Kingdom	79.137	21
22	Germany	79.132	22
23	Malta	78.549	23
24	South Korea	78.499	24
25	Portugal	78.385	25
26	United States whites	78.300	26
27	Denmark	78.100	27
28	United States	77.849	28

TABLE 3.4.7 – GROWTH RATES OF LIFE EXPECTANCY, 1960-2006			
OBS	COUNTRY	GRLE	RANK
1	South Korea	0.81	1
2	Portugal	0.46	2
3	Japan	0.43	3
4	Italy	0.35	4
5	Spain	0.34	5
6	Austria	0.33	6
7	Greece	0.31	7
8	Cyprus	0.31	8
9	Finland	0.31	9
10	Luxembourg	0.30	10
11	France	0.30	11
12	Malta	0.30	12
13	Australia	0.29	13
14	Switzerland	0.29	14
15	Ireland	0.28	15
16	Germany	0.28	16
17	Canada	0.27	17
18	Belgium	0.27	18
19	New Zealand	0.25	19
20	Israel	0.24	20
21	United States	0.24	21
22	United Kingdom	0.23	22
23	Iceland	0.22	23
24	United States whites	0.22	24
25	Sweden	0.22	25
26	Norway	0.19	26
27	Netherlands	0.18	27
28	Denmark	0.17	28

TABLE 3.5 – HEALTH EXPENDITURES, YEAR 2005

TABLE 3.5.1 – TOTAL HEALTH EXPENDITURES AS PERCENT OF GDP			
OBS	COUNTRY	HLTGDP	RANK
1	United States	15.9	1.0
2	Switzerland	11.4	2.0
3	France	11.1	3.0
4	Germany	10.7	4.0
5	Austria	10.2	5.5
6	Portugal	10.2	5.5
7	Greece	10.1	7.0
8	Canada	9.7	8.0
9	Belgium	9.6	9.0
10	Iceland	9.5	10.0
11	Netherlands	9.2	11.0
12	Denmark	9.1	12.0
13	Norway	9.0	13.0
14	Italy	8.9	15.0
15	New Zealand	8.9	15.0
16	Sweden	8.9	15.0
17	Australia	8.8	17.0
18	Malta	8.4	18.0
19	Ireland	8.2	20.5
20	Japan	8.2	20.5
21	Spain	8.2	20.5
22	United Kingdom	8.2	20.5
23	Israel	7.9	23.0
24	Luxembourg	7.7	24.0
25	Finland	7.5	25.0
26	Cyprus	6.0	26.0
27	South Korea	5.9	27.0

TABLE 3.5.2 – PUBLIC HEALTH EXPENDITURES AS PERCENT OF TOTAL HEALTH EXPENDITURES			
OBS	*COUNTRY*	*PUBHLT*	*RANK*
1	Luxembourg	90.7	1.0
2	United Kingdom	87.1	2.0
3	Sweden	84.6	3.0
4	Denmark	84.1	4.0
5	Norway	83.6	5.0
6	Iceland	82.5	6.0
7	Japan	82.2	7.0
8	France	79.8	8.0
9	Ireland	79.5	9.0
10	Finland	77.8	10.0
11	Malta	77.4	11.5
12	New Zealand	77.4	11.5
13	Germany	76.9	13.0
14	Italy	76.6	14.0
15	Austria	75.7	15.0
16	Portugal	72.3	16.0
17	Belgium	71.4	17.5
18	Spain	71.4	17.5
19	Canada	70.3	19.0
20	Australia	67.0	20.0
21	Netherlands	64.9	21.0
22	Israel	61.3	22.0
23	Switzerland	59.7	23.0
24	South Korea	53.0	24.0
25	United States	45.4	25.0
26	Greece	42.8	26.0
27	Cyprus	42.3	27.0

TABLE 3.6 – TAXES AS SHARE OF GDP

TABLE 3.6.1 – TAXES AS SHARE OF GDP, YEAR 1970			
OBS	COUNTRY	TAXGDP70	RANK
1	Sweden	43.4	1.0
2	Denmark	40.4	2.0
3	Austria	38.5	3.0
4	Belgium	38.3	4.0
5	Israel	38.2	5.0
6	Netherlands	37.7	6.0
7	France	37.4	7.0
8	Norway	37.3	8.0
9	Germany	37.2	9.0
10	United Kingdom	35.6	10.0
11	Finland	33.0	11.0
12	Canada	31.3	12.0
13	Luxembourg	30.8	13.0
14	Ireland	30.7	14.0
15	United States	28.9	15.0
16	Iceland	28.1	16.0
17	Italy	27.9	17.0
18	New Zealand	26.6	18.0
19	Australia	25.4	19.0
20	Switzerland	23.8	20.0
21	Greece	21.6	21.0
22	Portugal	20.9	22.5
23	Spain	20.9	22.5
24	Malta	20.0	24.0
25	Japan	19.7	25.0
26	Cyprus	18.5	26.0
27	South Korea	17.5	27.0

TABLE 3.6.2 – TAXES AS SHARE OF GDP, YEAR 1980			
OBS	*COUNTRY*	*TAXGDP80*	*RANK*
1	Sweden	50.6	1.0
2	Denmark	48.1	2.0
3	Belgium	47.4	3.0
4	Netherlands	45.9	4.0
5	Norway	45.8	5.0
6	Austria	44.5	6.0
7	Germany	43.9	7.0
8	France	43.6	8.0
9	Finland	38.4	9.0
10	Israel	37.4	10.0
11	Luxembourg	36.2	11.0
12	United Kingdom	35.1	12.0
13	Ireland	33.1	13.5
14	New Zealand	33.1	13.5
15	Italy	32.4	15.0
16	Iceland	31.8	16.0
17	Switzerland	30.8	17.0
18	Canada	30.3	18.0
19	United States	30.0	19.0
20	Spain	29.1	20.0
21	Portugal	27.9	21.0
22	Australia	27.7	22.0
23	Japan	25.6	23.0
24	Greece	25.1	24.0
25	Cyprus	22.4	25.0
26	Malta	21.6	26.0
27	South Korea	18.7	27.0

TABLE 3.6.3 – TAXES AS SHARE OF GDP, YEAR 1990			
OBS	COUNTRY	TAXGDP90	RANK
1	Sweden	64.7	1
2	Norway	56.2	2
3	Denmark	54.6	3
4	Finland	53.4	4
5	Austria	48.9	5
6	New Zealand	48.7	6
7	Netherlands	47.8	7
8	France	47.1	8
9	Belgium	45.5	9
10	Canada	43.0	10
11	Germany	41.7	11
12	Italy	41.5	12
13	United Kingdom	40.6	13
14	Ireland	40.3	14
15	Spain	38.7	15
16	Iceland	38.3	16
17	Israel	37.4	17
18	Luxembourg	35.7	18
19	Portugal	34.0	19
20	Japan	33.9	20
21	Greece	33.8	21
22	Australia	33.6	22
23	United States	32.8	23
24	Switzerland	31.5	24
25	Malta	28.0	25
26	Cyprus	27.5	26
27	South Korea	23.1	27

TABLE 3.6.4 – TAXES AS SHARE OF GDP, YEAR 2000			
OBS	*COUNTRY*	*TAXGDP00*	*RANK*
1	Sweden	61.8	1
2	Norway	58.2	2
3	Denmark	56.2	3
4	Finland	55.2	4
5	France	50.1	5
6	Austria	49.7	6
7	Belgium	49.1	7
8	Greece	47.1	8
9	Germany	46.4	9
10	Netherlands	46.0	10
11	Italy	45.3	11
12	Iceland	44.5	12
13	Canada	44.1	13
14	United Kingdom	41.5	14
15	New Zealand	41.2	15
16	Portugal	40.2	16
17	Israel	40.1	17
18	Luxembourg	39.1	18
19	Spain	38.1	19
20	Switzerland	37.6	20
21	Ireland	36.2	21
22	United States	35.8	22
23	Australia	35.7	23
24	Malta	33.4	24
25	Cyprus	32.5	25
26	Japan	31.5	26
27	South Korea	29.3	27

TABLE 3.6.5 – TAXES AS SHARE OF GDP, YEAR 2006			
OBS	COUNTRY	TAXGDP06	RANK
1	Norway	61.1	1
2	Sweden	58.8	2
3	Denmark	55.2	3
4	Finland	51.4	4
5	France	51.1	5
6	Belgium	49.0	6
7	Austria	47.8	7
8	Iceland	47.5	8
9	Netherlands	46.3	9
10	Italy	44.9	10
11	Germany	43.5	11
12	New Zealand	43.4	12
13	Greece	42.9	13
14	Portugal	42.8	14
15	United Kingdom	42.3	15
16	Canada	40.5	16
17	Luxembourg	39.9	17
18	Spain	39.4	18
19	Israel	38.9	19
20	Malta	37.7	20
21	Cyprus	37.1	21
22	Australia	36.5	22
23	Switzerland	36.2	23
24	Ireland	35.6	24
25	United States	34.2	25
26	South Korea	31.9	26
27	Japan	31.7	27

TABLE 3.6.6 – GROWTH RATES OF TAXES AS SHARE OF GDP, 1970-2006			
OBS	COUNTRY	GRTX	RANK
1	Portugal	2.93	1
2	Greece	2.83	2
3	Norway	2.73	3
4	Cyprus	2.69	4
5	Spain	2.53	5
6	Malta	2.49	6
7	Iceland	2.36	7
8	South Korea	2.23	8
9	Finland	2.15	9
10	New Zealand	2.10	10
11	Italy	2.09	11
12	Japan	1.79	12
13	Sweden	1.74	13
14	Denmark	1.67	14
15	Switzerland	1.67	15
16	France	1.57	16
17	Australia	1.47	17
18	Belgium	1.22	18
19	Canada	1.12	19
20	Luxembourg	1.12	20
21	Austria	1.06	21
22	Netherlands	0.99	22
23	United Kingdom	0.79	23
24	Germany	0.73	24
25	United States	0.69	25
26	Ireland	0.62	26
27	Israel	0.08	27

Appendix: Methodology and Definitions

Selection of Indicators

These parameters were first assembled to illustrate the comparative position of the countries of the world. The aim was to select indicators that were:

- few in number;
- important;
- available for the maximum number of countries;
- statistically reliable;
- independent of the technological and industrial level of the countries.

Missing data was projected with the help of regressions.

Definition of Principal Component 1

I have used "Principal Component 1" for the definition of several indexes.

Principal component analysis is a multidimensional technique for studying the interrelationship between several quantitative variables. For a given set of data with p numerical variables, p principal components can be computed. Each principal component is a linear combination of the initial variables with coefficients equal to the eigenvector of the correlational or covariational matrix. The eigenvectors are typically selected to have a length of one. The principal components are sorted in descending order of characteristic values, which are equal to the variation of the components. Principal components have a number of useful properties; among them are:

- The first principal component accounts for the greatest variation of any linear combination of observed variables of the unit length.
- In geometrical terms, a j-dimensional linear subspace of the first j principal components provides the best possible arrangement of data points measured as the sum of squares of the perpendicular distances from each point to the subspace.[1]

---

1. Mathematics: SAS Institute, Inc. (1988), Kiyosi (2000), Kotz (1985).

DEFINITION OF THE ECONOMIC QUALITY-OF-LIFE INDEX

I computed an Economic Quality-of-Life Index as Principal Component 1 of the four economic indicators of the quality of life given in this yearbook:

$log(GPC)$	logarithm of GNI per capita at market exchange rates;
$log(GPCPPP)$	logarithm of GDP per capita at purchasing power parities;
$log(INFMRT)$	logarithm of infant mortality;
$log(max(LIFEXP) - LIFEXP)$	logarithm of the difference between maximum life expectancy and life expectancy in the country in question (in 2006, the maximum life expectancy was that of women of Andorra at 86.61 years).

DEFINITION OF THE HUMAN RIGHTS INDEX

In an attempt to give an estimate of the level of human rights, I computed a human rights index as Principal Component 1 of four indicators of the political quality of life:

$SCINTX$	the index of societal integration;
CPR	the index of civil and political rights;
HDX	the human development index;
$GINI$	GINI coefficient of income inequality.

DEFINITION OF THE ECONOMICO-POLITICAL QUALITY-OF-LIFE INDEX

I computed an Economico-Political Quality-of-Life Index as Principal Component 1 using the four economic and the four political (human rights) indicators of the quality of life described above.

DEFINITION OF GROSS NATIONAL INCOME AT MARKET EXCHANGE RATES

The Gross Domestic Product is the most frequently used indicator of national productivity. It represents the total value of products and services produced.

GNI (or gross national product in the terminology of the 1968 United Nations System of National Accounts) measures the total domestic and foreign value added claimed by residents. GNI comprises GDP plus net receipts of primary income (compensation of employees and property income) from nonresident sources.[2]

The GDP or GNI, which is recorded in terms of the national currency, has to be translated into a single currency to enable international comparison. GNI per capita at market exchange rates provides GNI data translated into U.S. dollars on the basis of the market exchange rate. In addition to the actual ratios among the buying powers of different currencies, the market rate is based on a number of other factors. From the point of view of actual buying power, the market typically overestimates the discrepancies in the income earned in different countries. (See also, GDP at purchasing power parities.)

In instances where there was a choice between sources, priority was given to data from the World Bank, since it uses a more advanced procedure for computing the exchange rate, smoothing fluctuations in the market exchange rate.

---

2 *Economics*: Finfacts.

In cases where values were missing, the following regression was used:

$$\log(GPC) = REG(\log(GPCPPP))$$

where

log(GPC)	logarithm of GNI per capita at market exchange rates
log(GPCPPP)	logarithm of GDP per capita at purchasing power parities

Number of observations	212
Correlation coefficient	0.97

DEFINITION OF INFANT MORTALITY

The indicator of infant mortality is computed from the number of deaths during the first year of life per 1000 live births. This is one of the most important indicators used, since it indirectly measures the state of health care, transportation, communications, and level of culture of the given country (this list can be extended indefinitely).

In cases where values were missing, the following regression was used:

$$\log(INFMRT) = REG(\log(GPC))$$

where

log(INFMRT)	Logarithm of infant mortality
log(GPC)	Logarithm of GNI per capita at market exchange rates

Number of observations	230
Correlation coefficient	0.87

DEFINITION OF LIFE EXPECTANCY

Life expectancy is probably the most accurate single indicator of the quality of life in a given country. It sums up in one number all the natural and social stresses that affect an individual.

In cases where the data are taken from the *Encyclopedia Britannica*, I used the arithmetic mean of the life expectancies of men and women.

In cases where values were missing, the following regression was used:

$$\log(\max(LIFEXP) - LIFEXP) = REG(GPC, \log(INFMRT))$$

where

log(max(LIFEXP) – LIFEXP)	Logarithm of the difference between maximum life expectancy and life expectancy of this country
GPC	GNI per capita at market exchange rates
log(INFMRT)	Logarithm of infant mortality

Number of observations	230
Correlation coefficient	0.93

DEFINITION OF GROSS DOMESTIC PRODUCT AT PURCHASING POWER PARITIES

Typically GDP is translated into U.S. dollars. The market foreign currency exchange rate, however, does not necessarily reflect differences in actual purchasing power in different countries. The use of purchasing power parities is designed to eliminate this distortion. Purchasing power parities indicate how many currency units are needed in one country to buy the amount of goods and services that can be purchased for a currency unit in another country.

In cases where values were missing, the following regression was used:

$$\log(GPCPPP) = REG(\log(GPC))$$

where

log(GPCPPP)	Logarithm of GDP per capita at purchasing power parities
log(GPC)	Logarithm of GNI per capita at market exchange rates

Number of observations	224
Correlation coefficient	0.97

DEFINITION OF THE SOCIETAL INTEGRATION INDEX

The index of societal integration is an indicator of the intensity of open political life. It is computed as a coefficient of heterogeneity of a parliament (legislature) of a country, under the condition that party seats in the parliament (legislature) are obtained as a result of competitive elections. This indicator can have values between 0 and 1; zero means that all seats in the parliament (legislature) belong to one party or that there are no competitive elections; it approaches 1 if every person in the parliament (legislature) is his own party.

The concept of integration was introduced by Emile Durkheim in his work *Suicide*.[3] Durkheim interpreted integration as a function of the intensity of social communication. I have interpreted this conception on the societal level, defining societal integration as the intensity of non-trivial exchanges of information at the highest level of society. I provide a purely structural definition of exchange of information, defining it as a number between 0 and 1, equal to the probability of interparty (i.e., political party) dialogue in society. As a measure of interparty exchange of information, I took the probability of interparty communication in parliament (the legislative body):

where

$$SCINTX = \sum_{i=1}^{X} P_i \left(1 - P_i\right)$$

P(i) is the proportion of members of party number (i) in parliament (the legislative body),

X is the total number of political parties in parliament (the legislative body).

---

3 Sociology: Durkheim (1993).

Data on the distribution of seats among parties is taken from an open CIA publication. This indicator can be considered objective because no ruling party would give seats in the parliament (legislature) to the opposition willingly. The introduction of this indicator into the formula for computing the human rights index is based on the concept that the condition of political institutions (and the degree to which they can be called democratic) is closely related to human rights.

DEFINITION OF THE CIVIL AND POLITICAL RIGHTS INDEX

The index of civil and political rights is subjective. As such, I used the index of freedom of the press published by Freedom House, based in New York. For the sake of objectivity it should be noted that Freedom House in the view of many observers is biased in favor of the United States, especially taking into account the drastic change of the political climate in America since the attacks of September 11, 2001. And in the cases of certain foreign countries, it gives absurdly high or absurdly low ratings. The advantage of this indicator is that it is available for all countries in question and is computed annually.

In cases where values were missing, the following regression was used:

$$CPRX = REG(\log(GPC), SCINTX)$$

where

CPRX	the index of civil and political rights
log(GPC)	Logarithm of GNI per capita at market exchange rates
SCINTX	the index of societal integration
Number of observations	199
Correlation coefficient	0.68

DEFINITION OF THE HUMAN DEVELOPMENT INDEX

The human development index is an objective indicator. It is the average of the level of income per capita in purchasing power parities, level of education, and level of health care. It is computed annually by a well-respected UN program. The introduction of this indicator into the formula for computing the human rights index is based on the idea that socio-economic rights are part of human rights. Some right-wing lawyers in the U.S. consider the socio-economic rights a bad concept for a well-developed law-abiding state, because it is allegedly difficult to conduct the judicial process if socio-economic rights are recognized as full-blown rights. Even if we agree that there is some truth in this assertion and that there are difficulties for a strict judicial process that would take socio-economic rights as real rights, nevertheless, outside the U.S. socio-economic rights are commonly recognized as a lawful component of human rights. This can be seen, for example, from the Universal Declaration of Human Rights adopted by the UN in 1948.

In cases where values were missing, the following regression was used:

$$HDX = REG(\log(GPCPPP), \log(INFMRT))$$

where

HDX	The human development index
Log(GPCPPP)	Logarithm of GDP per capita at purchasing power parities
Log(INFMRT)	Logarithm of infant mortality
Number of observations	178
Correlation coefficient	0.96

DEFINITION OF THE GINI COEFFICIENT OF INCOME INEQUALITY

The fourth component of the human rights index is the Gini coefficient of income inequality. This indicator is computed as an integral of distance between equal distribution and the observed distribution of income in a given country. Its values range between 0 and 100; 0 signifies that observed distribution of income is equal, and 100 signifies that all income of the country belongs to one person. The idea of including the Gini coefficient is based on an observation that formal judicial rights are only a potential that can be realized in a specific social context, and that the greater the inequality, the more difficult it is for an average person of a given society to insist on his or her formal judicial rights. Thus in countries with developed market economies, the price of good lawyers is dictated by the material possibilities of the top stratum of the society. For example, in the social context of the U.S., an average person often simply cannot afford a good lawyer. Because of this, it is possible to say that in order to realize the judicial rights that are formally proclaimed, a person must possess a certain material potential. The less inequality there is in a country, the more formal judicial rights are realized.

In cases where values were missing, the following regression was used:

$$GINI = REG(GPC, \log(GPCPPP), \log(INFMRT), CPRX)$$

where

GINI	Gini coefficient of income inequality
GPC	GNI per capita at market exchange rates
log(GPCPPP)	Logarithm of GDP per capita at purchasing power parities
log(INFMRT)	Logarithm of infant mortality
CPRX	Civil and political rights index
Number of observations	136
Correlation coefficient	0.56

DEFINITION OF POPULATION

The population of a country includes all residents regardless of legal status or citizenship — except for refugees not permanently settled in the country of asylum, who are generally considered part of the population of their country of origin. The values shown are midyear estimates.[4]

DEFINITION OF ARMED FORCES PERSONNEL

Armed forces personnel are active duty military personnel, including paramilitary forces if the training, organization, equipment, and control suggest they may be used to support or replace regular military forces.[5]

DEFINITION OF MILITARY EXPENDITURES

Military expenditures data are primarily based on World Bank data. They are taken from Stockholm International Peace Research Institute (SIPRI) and are derived from the NATO definition, which includes all current and capital expenditures on the armed forces, including peacekeeping forces; defense ministries and other government agencies engaged in defense projects; paramilitary forces, if these are judged to be trained and equipped for military operations; and military space activities. Such expenditures include military and civil personnel and social services for personnel; operation and maintenance; procurement; military aid (in the military expenditures of the donor country). Excluded are civil defense and current expenditures for previous military activities, such as veterans' benefits, demobilization, conversion, and destruction of weapons.[6]

DEFINITION OF OPERATIONAL OFFENSIVE NUCLEAR DELIVERY SYSTEMS

I follow the definition of the International Institute for Strategic Studies and the *Bulletin of the Atomic Scientists.*

DEFINITION OF OPERATIONAL NUCLEAR WARHEADS

Here, I include strategic and sub-strategic operational warheads aligned to an in-service delivery system, excluding artillery shells and mini-nukes.[7]

DEFINITION OF STATES POSSESSING, PURSUING OR CAPABLE OF ACQUIRING WEAPONS OF MASS DESTRUCTION

The main part of this data is taken from the *Bulletin of the Atomic Scientists*[8] for 2000. The *Bulletin* data originally included information about WMD programs in Iraq. This information is now thoroughly discredited and therefore is not included here. It is worth noting that anybody looking at military budgets by countries in the beginning of the 2000s would notice that the military expenditures of Iraq were less than the military expenditures of most countries in the Middle East. Such a person would have grave doubts that Iraq was economically capable of sustaining WMD programs. Similarly, the same table from *The Bulletin of the Atomic Scientists* lists poor countries like Ethiopia, Laos

---

4 *Economics*: The World Bank (1).
5 *Economics*: The World Bank (1).
6 *Economics*: The World Bank (1).
7 Military: International Institute for Strategic Studies.
8 Military: Bulletin of the Atomic Scientists.

and Sudan as pursuing WMD programs. It is highly doubtful that these impoverished countries are in a socio-economical position to succeed in the weaponizing of dangerous biological and chemical substances.

Conversely, I have concluded that all countries which have nuclear power plants, should be considered to some degree capable of acquiring nuclear weapons. The list of such countries is available from Encyclopedia Britannica[9] for 2002 and the CIA[10] for 2006.

I also decided that such highly developed economic powers as the United Kingdom, France, Japan, and Germany, should be capable of acquiring the whole range of WMD. In the case of Japan and Germany, which have nuclear power plants, it is reasonable to believe that they also have the capability for biological, chemical, and missile technology. In the case of the United Kingdom and France, which are acknowledged by the *Bulletin of the Atomic Scientists* as nuclear, chemical and missile powers, I think they are also capable of biological weapons. Finally, based on information about satellite launches by Japan and Brazil, I consider these two countries as actually possessing missile technology.

Definition of Developed Market Economies

In section 3, I used data for the period since 1960/1970 for 23 original member countries of the Organization for Economic Cooperation and Development (excluding Turkey, which is too poor to be compared to the other OECD countries) plus other countries which also have high per capita GDP and are democracies and for which there exists relevant historical data for the period since 1960/1970 (Cyprus, Israel, Malta, and South Korea qualify).

Definition of the Scope of Data for Developed Market Economies

In the tables presented in section 3, I have attempted to provide measurable facts against which one may test certain theories that are promoted in the U.S. (and possibly also in the former centrally-planned economies of Central and Eastern Europe). I considered, for example, the debates about health care reform in the United States.

Some of the arguments used against health care reform in the U.S. are:

1) The U.S. has fewer social support programs than other countries and this gives it an advantage in economic competition.

2) The U.S. health care system is the best in the world, so why disrupt it?

3) The U.S. has the most economically effective system of health care and social efforts to improve it may only destroy it, creating an ineffective bureaucracy (a variant of the preceding thesis).

4) The current American model of economy with lower taxes and lesser social programs provides for faster economic growth and a better quality of life.

5) Even if health care reform can give better social/economic results, it presents a risk (in the form of the putative socialist order) to freedom in the U.S. It would be better to remain the freest country in the world.

For item number 5, I refer the reader to the political quality-of-life indicators presented in section 1. For items 1 through 4, the relevant statistics for the developed market economies are presented in section 3.

---

9 *Economics*: Encyclopedia Britannica.
10 *Economics*: Central Intelligence Agency.

DEFINITION OF TOTAL HEALTH EXPENDITURES

Total health expenditure is the sum of public and private health expenditure. It covers the provision of health services (preventive and curative), family planning activities, nutrition activities, and emergency aid designated for health but does not include provision of water and sanitation.[11]

DEFINITION OF PUBLIC HEALTH EXPENDITURES

Public health expenditure consists of recurrent and capital spending from government (central and local) budgets, external borrowing and grants (including donations from international agencies and nongovernmental organizations), and social (or compulsory) health insurance funds.[12]

DEFINITION OF TAXES AS SHARE OF GDP

Taxes refer to general government sector, which is a consolidation of accounts for the central, state, and local governments plus social security.[13]

DEFINITION OF GROWTH RATES OF TAXES AS SHARE OF GDP

Growth rates of taxes as share of GDP are defined as such relative growth rates, which cause the observed changes of taxes as share of GDP. The corresponding formula for computation is

$$GRTX = (((100 / (100 - TAXGDP_1)$$
$$* (TAXGDP_1 / TAXGDP_0)$$
$$- (TAXGDP_1 / 100))$$
$$** (1 / N) - 1) * 100$$

where

GRTX	growth rates of taxes as share of GDP
TAXGDP_0	taxes as share of GDP at the beginning of the period
TAXGDP_1	taxes as share of GDP at the end of the period
N	number of years in the period

---

11 *Economics*: The World Bank (1).
12 *Economics*: The World Bank (1).
13 *Economics*: U.S. Bureau of Census (1).

References

Reference

Encyclopedia Britannica (1983) *The New Encyclopedia Britannica*, 15th edition, in 30 Volumes, Chicago

Law

Freedom House, *Freedom of the Press: A Global Survey of Media Independence*, Rowman & Littlefield Publishers, Inc., New York, annual

Sociology

Durkheim, Emile (1993) *Suicide: A Study in Sociology* (Translated by John A. Spaulding and George Simpson), Routledge, London

Military

Bulletin of the Atomic Scientists
International Institute for Strategic Studies, *The Military Balance*, Oxford University Press, annual
Stockholm International Peace Research Institute, *SIPRI Yearbook: Armaments, Disarmament and International Security*, Oxford University Press, annual
Union of Concerned Scientists

Economics

Central Intelligence Agency, *The World Factbook*, annual
Encyclopedia Britannica, *Book of the Year*, annual
Eurostat Press Office, *Tax Burden and Structure of Taxes*, annual
Finfacts, http://www.finfacts.com/biz10/globalworldincomepercapita.htm

Israel Finance Ministry, Press Releases

OECD, *Revenue Statistics*, Paris, annual

The World Bank (1989-1994) *World Tables*, annual, The John Hopkins University Press

_____ (1995) *World Data 1995*. World Bank Indicators on CD-ROM

_____ (2008) *World Development Indicators Online*

U.S. Agency for International Development, *U.S. Overseas Loans and Grants [Greenbook]*, http://qesdb.cdie.org/gbk/index.html

U.S. Bureau of the Census (1) *Statistical Abstract of the United States*, annual

_____ (1975) *Historical Statistics of the United States, Colonial Times to 1970*, Vols 1 and 2, Washington, D.C.

United Nations Development Programme, *Human Development Report*, annual, Oxford University Press, New York

MATHEMATICS

Itô, Kiyosi, Ed. (2000) *Encyclopedic Dictionary of Mathematics*, by the Mathematical Society of Japan, The MIT Press, Cambridge, Massachusetts

Kotz, Samuel, Norman L. Johnson, Eds. (1985) *Encyclopedia of Statistical Sciences, Vols. 1-9*, John Wiley & Sons, New York

SAS Institute Inc. (1988) *SAS/STAT User's Guide, Release 6.03 Edition*, Cary, North Carolina